A SPECIAL INTEREST

A Special Interest

The Atomic Energy Commission,
Argonne National Laboratory,
and the Midwestern Universities

Leonard Greenbaum

Ann Arbor
The University of Michigan Press

"I think on this we probably pushed the Commission and they regarded us as people who were, after all, largely professors and university presidents and we were pleading a special interest. We did plead a special interest, but we believed it to be in the national interest too."

—J. Robert Oppenheimer

Foreword

This book is a study of the relationships between the Argonne National Laboratory and the universities of the Midwest from 1945 to 1968, a period encompassing the first two decades of the existence of the Argonne National Laboratory at its present site in Du Page County, Illinois. The Argonne National Laboratory is a great national asset, one of the family of research and development laboratories built and operated by the United States Atomic Energy Commission (AEC). In addition to its well-known accomplishments in the development of fission reactors for electric power and propulsion, the Argonne National Laboratory has established itself as a leading scientific institution, including a vital role in high energy physics in the Midwest.

There are four AEC laboratories which have the word "national" in their names—Argonne, Brookhaven, Oak Ridge, and the new National Accelerator Laboratory at Batavia, Illinois. For each of these, a definite mechanism exists for maintaining its relationship with the educational community. Other AEC laboratories also maintain working relationships with the world of education—some are located on the campuses of university operators, while others are operated by universities at locations off campus. These major laboratories of the AEC are operated under contract with industrial firms, with single universities, with associations of universities, and with a not-for-profit research corporation. After a quarter century, no one of these forms of management contracting has emerged as the one that provides the best environment for a research and development institution. From 1946 to 1966, the University of Chicago provided policy guidance for and operated the Argonne National Laboratory for the AEC. Since 1966, the University of Chicago has continued the operation under policy guidance from the Argonne Universities Association (AUA), a consortium of thirty universities, largely of the Midwest.

The preparation of a history of the relations between the Argonne National Laboratory and the universities of the Midwest was suggested in 1968 by Professor Warren F. Stubbins, then a member of the Board of Directors of the Associated Midwest Universities (AMU), a consortium of thirty-three universities, chiefly of the Midwest, which was involved with educational interaction with the Argonne National Laboratory, and which was in the process of being merged with the AUA, with which AMU had an almost common membership. The Board of Directors of AMU set aside a fund to finance the preparation and publication of this history, which was to be scholarly, interesting, and useful as a record of science. An Advisory Committee on the History of AMU was set up, with Professors William Kerr and Armon F. Yanders and the undersigned as members, Dr. John H. Roberson, Executive Director of the former AMU, as Secretary, and following the merger with AUA, the President of AUA, Professor Philip N. Powers, as an ex officio member.

Dr. Leonard Greenbaum of The University of Michigan was chosen to write the history. What started out to be a story of the ten years of existence of AMU and its relations with the Argonne National Laboratory quickly became a history of the relations between the Argonne National Laboratory and the universities of the Midwest over a twenty-year period. Our Committee approved Dr. Greenbaum's approach and gave him free rein in the conduct of the work.

Following completion of the first draft, the manuscript was reviewed by the members of our Committee and then by about twenty-five or more selected outside readers representing different points of view based on actual experience and knowledge of, and working with, the Argonne National Laboratory. These reviewers included persons from the University of Chicago and other universities of the Midwest, from the Argonne National Laboratory, from the AEC, and from the former AMU and the present AUA.

The opinions contained in this history, and the conclusions drawn in it, are those of the author. Neither our Committee nor the Argonne Universities Association assumes responsibility for them. Similarly, it should be recognized that the scientific and technical accomplishments of the Argonne National Laboratory serve only as background in this study and deserve a separate story, which we hope will be written some day as a companion history.*

*Argonne's technical achievements are summarized in a speech by Glenn T. Seaborg, Chairman of the Atomic Energy Commission, delivered on June 19, 1971, on the occasion of the laboratory's twenty-fifth anniversary. Published in *The Argonne News*, special issue.

We are convinced that *A Special Interest* is an important instrument in clarifying and understanding the relationships of the Argonne National Laboratory and the universities of the Midwest during the twenty-year period covered. This book will be most useful in providing important background for all those having responsibility for the future progress of federal laboratories and their cooperative relationships within the scientific and educational communities of America.

> FREDERICK D. ROSSINI, Chairman
> Advisory Committee on the
> History of the Associated Midwest Universities
> Argonne Universities Association

Acknowledgments

In writing this book, I have been greatly dependent on the keepers of records, those people who file and order and save the minutes of meetings, the carbons of letters, and even the memos that administrators often write to themselves. The bulk of this book is drawn from three such collections: the files of Associated Midwest Universities, the historical files of Argonne National Laboratory, and the files of the Policy Advisory Board of Argonne National Laboratory. In addition, the files of the Williams Committee, the Harlan Hatcher Papers in the University of Michigan Historical Collections, and the Arthur Holly Compton Papers in Washington University's Archives were made available to me.

It is, therefore, with sincere thanks that I acknowledge the openness and the bibliographical skills and the cooperation of John Roberson, the Executive Director of AMU, and Kay Chellew, who was Secretary of that organization throughout its active existence. Similarly, E. Newman Pettitt, Classification Officer at Argonne National Laboratory, and C. C. McSwain, Assistant Manager for Administration, Chicago Operations Office of the Atomic Energy Commission, were indispensable in making unclassified segments of the Argonne files available to me. This was particularly useful in those sections concerned with high energy accelerators. Vice President Emeritus William B. Harrell and Vice President William B. Cannon of the University of Chicago were responsible for opening the files of the Policy Advisory Board. Mr. Harrell, in addition, was kind enough to answer questions and supply documents from the University of Chicago files that detailed contractual arrangements between that school and the AEC involving the universities of the Midwest. Richard Adams and Mauritz Gahlon of the Directors Office at Argonne were also helpful in providing files and checking data. The photographs were provided through the courtesy of

Daniel Giroux and Sophie Stephens of the Photography Department.

I was assisted in examining the archival collection at the University of Michigan by Professor Robert Warner, Curator, and Mary Pugh, Assistant Curator. The Arthur Holly Compton Papers were made available by William A. Deiss of the University Archives and Research Collection, Olin Library, Washington University Archives. Edwin L. Goldwasser was thoughtful enough to offer the files of the Williams Committee, which were in his possession.

It should also be noted that any work on the Atomic Energy Commission that covers the period from 1945 to 1952 is beholden to the two volumes of the official history of the AEC, *The New World* by Richard Hewlett and Oscar Anderson, Jr., and *Atomic Shield* by Richard Hewlett and Francis Duncan. In addition, Harold Orlan's book *Contracting for Atoms* is an indispensable guide to the AEC's research structure, while *Government of the Atom*, by Harold Green and Alan Rosenthal, is a valuable study of the Joint Committee on Atomic Energy. Another source valuable for its discussion of MURA has been Daniel Greenberg's *The Politics of Pure Science*. Two journals, the *Bulletin of the Atomic Scientists* and *Science*, have also been of continuing help.

The facility with which this work was pursued would not have been possible without the presence of the Phoenix Library one floor below my office in the Phoenix Memorial Laboratory. Besides being an AEC Depository Library, it has a broad collection of books on nuclear energy that is not easily duplicated. To the Chief Librarian, Margaret Underwood, and her assistants, Elizabeth Barrett and M. Elizabeth Brandt, I am indebted for searches and loan courtesies that were exceptional.

The secretaries of the Michigan Memorial-Phoenix Project, Dorothy Kiehl and Pat Buck, were helpful in typing and bibliographical work. Helen Lum, who did the bulk of the typing and retyping, can, I am certain, recite whole chapters footnote by footnote. I am also grateful to her for the consistency of her copy editing. The secretaries at the AUA office at Argonne, Kay Chellew again, and Theresa Kelly, were most helpful in assembling data and making the arrangements that enabled me to use the collections housed at Argonne. In this regard, the hospitality and social amenities of the Argonne Laboratory staff are highly recommended.

A number of people have read the book in manuscript. Rudolf Schmerl and Bradford Perkins provided close editorial criticism. In addition, Joseph Boyce, William Cannon, Edwin L. Goldwasser, Newell Gingrich, Norman Hackerman, P. G. Kruger, Farrington

Daniels, Richard G. Hewlett, William Harrell, Robert Duffield, Laurence Lunden, George Beadle, Lawrence Kimpton, Kenneth Dunbar, C. C. McSwain, A. G. Norman, and Kent Terwilliger have read the manuscript and responded, some with suggestions, some with criticism, some simply with courtesy. I have greatly appreciated the willingness of each of them to respond. In acknowledging my appreciation, I wish to stress that this in no way indicates their concurrence with the interpretations of this account.

I would also like to thank Vice President A. Geoffrey Norman of the University of Michigan and William Kerr, Director of the Michigan Memorial-Phoenix Project, for enabling me to work on this history on released time.

Finally, I wish to mention the members of the AUA Advisory Committee on History, William Kerr, Frederick Rossini (Chairman), Armon Yanders, and Philip Powers (ex officio). They have been constructively critical and at the same time encouraging.

Though the responsibility for this history is mine, obviously it represents the cooperative efforts of numerous people, those mentioned here and others not mentioned, with whom I conversed during my research. I thank them all and hope they find the final product worth the assistance they offered.

L. GREENBAUM

Ann Arbor, Michigan
January, 1971

Prologue

Argonne National Laboratory is big—thirty-seven hundred acres; large clusters of large buildings styled in eclectic federal architecture; five thousand-plus employees, seven hundred of whom are Ph.D's; facilities valued at $400 million; an annual operating budget of $90 million; and all of it twenty-five miles southwest of the city of Chicago, where an organization called Argonne Universities Association has its offices on North Michigan Avenue. A visitor can go to Argonne and never see Chicago. The Laboratory sits out in Du Page County, within Downers Grove Township, a place founded by a New Yorker named Pierce Downer who came west in 1832. It lies in the middle of what used to be rolling Illinois farm land and today is changing from rural estates to suburban developments, the kind of countryside that is a pleasant change from the city but not exactly prime scenic viewing.

The way most university visitors get to Argonne is to fly into O'Hare Field and wait for a Laboratory driver in a gray government-property car. The ride is south on the Tri-State Tollway to the Stevenson Expressway, which is also Interstate Highway 55, a divided four-lane, and sometimes six-lane, track resting on the old transcontinental Route 66 that in its own time had been built on top of a Potawatomi Indian trail. What the visitor sees on the drive down the tollway are contemporary warehouses and office buildings and factories of brick and glass or poured concrete and some large, expensive, single-family frame houses built on top of one another as if ten miles down the road there wasn't really going to be any more open space. Off Interstate 55, the driver turns left on Cass Avenue, passes a stand of pines about twenty-five years old, an abandoned NIKE missile base, and then a picnic grounds called Argonne Park —and that's it. Cass Avenue is on the site.

To the right, behind a chain link fence, is the Laboratory proper —the central heating plant and steam pipes; clumps of gray Quonset huts and square cinderblock buildings. Here the administration is housed, together with the non-technical support services—the fire department, the post office, the employees' credit union, the university relations offices. The scientific pieces of the Laboratory—the accelerator, looking like the stone crushers at a gravel pit, the reactors with a touch of domed modern styling, the laboratories, chemistry, mathematics, biology, all institutional red brick—are on higher land, beyond a service railroad track and an older stand of oak trees. And there are white deer, the contented members of a multiplying herd that lives the ideal cervine life, with plenty of room and food and no enemies, animal or human. The deer, who are always there, don't make Argonne seem idyllic, but rather enigmatic. What are they doing hanging around a proton accelerator?

Argonne is a hard place to characterize. The Atomic Energy Commission, which owns Argonne, calls it a "multi-program laboratory," a designation first used in 1960 and still part of the cataloguing system in the 1970's. The term is assigned to seven laboratories that engage "in a wide range of research and development activities both as to the fields of science and technology involved and the type of work conducted—basic research, applied research, and general development, etc." The AEC considers these laboratories "integrated institutions" with an internal "balance" between and within disciplines that shifts to "keep pace" or to "meet requirements." The "etc." has always been intended to cover any ground that didn't seem included.[1]

That Argonne has many programs is made apparent simply by the existence of eleven research and development divisions—Applied Mathematics, Applied Physics, Biological and Medical Research, Chemistry, Physics, High Energy Physics, Reactor Analysis and Safety, Radiological Physics, Chemical Engineering, Materials Science, Solid State Science—and the Experimental Breeder Reactor II Project. In addition, Argonne operates four reactors at the National Reactor Testing Station in Idaho. The range of research is broad, producing papers like "The Three Dimensional Structure of Immuno-Proteins," or "K-Meson Diffraction in Deuterium," or "Corrosion Problems with Liquid Nitrogen," that speak clearly to people within disciplines and hardly at all to those outside.

A significant fact about three of the AEC's multi-program laboratories—the ones that have the word "National" in the middle of their names (Brookhaven, Oak Ridge, and Argonne)—is that each has a different contractual arrangement that places the management responsibilities in a different type of organization. Oak Ridge is managed by an industrial firm, Union Carbide Corporation, Nuclear Division. Brookhaven is managed by a non-profit organization, Associated Universities, Inc., formed by nine private northeastern schools.[2] Argonne is more complicated. Originally operated by a single university, the University of Chicago, it is now operated under a tripartite contract between the AEC, the University of Chicago, and Argonne Universities Association, a non-profit group formed by thirty schools. AUA is responsible for formulating policies and programs, what is usually meant by "management," while the University of Chicago is responsible for the actual operation within the policies and programs of AUA.

The other four "multi-program" laboratories—Ames in Iowa, the Lawrence Radiation Laboratory at two locations, Berkeley and Livermore, and the Los Alamos Scientific Laboratory—are operated by single universities, as Argonne formerly was.

These variations in management are sometimes attributed to the AEC's flexibility, its willingness to function through a variety of systems, and sometimes to the AEC's uncertainty as to the best way of managing the peculiar blend of science it needs to support. The uncertainty grows where there is an interface between complementary but competing systems. Originally, the federal laboratories were begun and staffed by university people. The common "mission" was clear—to build bombs, to design propulsion reactors, to design electric power-producing reactors. Over time, as the missions were accomplished and the laboratories moved into less programmatic and more basic research, they also assumed some educational functions normally associated with universities. Conversely, as the federal government broadened its contractual support of science, universities assumed some functions normally associated with development laboratories. The annual research budgets of the larger universities began to approach and sometimes surpass the operating budgets of the large federal laboratories.[3]

The primary source of research funds for both types of institutions is the federal government, the tangible result of the general recognition that the support of science is "a primary national purpose." Federal expenditures for science and technology total about $16 billion a year, with eighty per cent going to the "non-federal" institutions, a category that includes Argonne because of the contractual arrangement under which it is managed.[4] As federal support has grown, from the negligible pre-World War II activities to the present immensity, the symbiotic relationship between science and public policy has also grown, but without the nature of that relationship clearly understood, even by the direct participants.

Attendant problems—how to determine priorities between different areas of research, whether to shape scientific development to meet recognizable national needs, whether finite funds should be allocated along regional as well as scientific criteria, whether raising the levels of "underdeveloped" schools is preferable to supporting existing "centers of excellence"—are all intertwined and then compounded by the constant competition between development research and basic research. The former is sometimes called applied, programmatic, mission-oriented; while the latter, basic research, to expand a definition, is the pursuit of "abstract and theoretical knowledge, which is by its nature free of human purposes and passion," but about which scientists get very passionate indeed.

Within these problems, the concept of the scientific community as a unified, categorical group is tested and found wanting. It is not the rivalries between individuals that are so important, but rather the rivalries between the different structures under which science is pursued—the relatively undisciplined pattern that dominates universities, where teaching departments and tenured faculty enjoy both permanency and independence so long as they can find funding, versus its relatively disciplined opposite, the hierarchical order of the research laboratory that is dependent on a single budgetary source.

This rivalry is a major reason for the contractual arrangements by which universities, singly or in groups, are asked (and seek) to manage national and regional laboratories. It is as if, unable to decide with confidence how to resolve the conflict, the government ties the two contending forces together with the expectation that what will emerge from the shared confinement will be the best possible peace. The surface issues over which the forces contend are often questions of siting, of determining who uses what accelerator or what reactor at what time, of distinguishing between major universities that need to be taken into account and minor universities that can be ignored (and some schools that don't even have to be ignored). The underlying issues are less tangible—questions of the relative status of laboratory scientists and university faculty, of differences in self-esteem, of overt insensitivity, of illusions about the quality of other people's grass. Put together, the open issues and the hidden ones add up to one question—Who's in charge?

This book is intended to illuminate some of the problems that have arisen in the attempt to answer that question for Argonne National Laboratory. It is the story of how one administrative arrangement, the tripartite contract for Argonne, came into existence, how the desires and interests of four different groups—the Laboratory, a single major university, a community of universities, and the Atomic Energy Commission—have been played out over more than twenty years in a continuing attempt to arrive at the best arrangement that would meet the special interests of each group and still include all four. This history transects three organizational arrangements that preceded the tripartite contract:

The Board of Governors of Argonne National
Laboratory 1946–1950
The Executive Board of the Council of
Participating Institutions 1950–1958
The Board of Directors of Associated
Midwest Universities 1958–1968

The current Argonne Universities Association grew out of these three, overlapped with the last, and absorbed it.

The Argonne episode is part of a larger story that goes beyond the regional interests of the Midwest or the agency interests of the Atomic Energy Commission. It exemplifies what has long been obvious, that creating productive university-laboratory relations is a difficult art. It also suggests a conclusion that many scientists and science administrators may not wish to support—that science, both basic and developmental, is not managed so much as it occurs. It is a series of happenings, some dramatic but most pedestrian, within the environments provided by the organizations that sponsor, house, and fund research. Even this implies more control than exists. In real time, defining the best environment and attempting to achieve it is a quixotic adventure that is even yet occurring for the people and the institutions this book is about.

Contents

PART ONE

The Board of Governors
of
Argonne National Laboratory
1946–1950

The Board of Governors
Argonne National Laboratory
May 1, 1946, to May, 1950

Name	Institution	Years Served
A. H. Compton	Washington U.	1946–1947
Farrington Daniels	Wisconsin	1946–1949 Chairman 46, 47
Ovid W. Eshbach	Northwestern	1946–1947
R. G. Gustavson	Chicago	1946–1949
F. Wheeler Loomis	Illinois	1946–1948
F. H. Spedding	Iowa State	1946–1948
John T. Tate	Minnesota	1946–1949 Chairman 48
Paul Klopsteg	Northwestern	1947–1950 Chairman 49, 50
Louis A. Turner	Iowa	1947–1950
Andrew C. Ivy	Illinois	1948–1950
Warren C. Johnson	Chicago	1948–1950
Edward Creutz	Carnegie	1949–1950
Ernest F. Barker	Michigan	1949–1950
Allan C. G. Mitchell	Indiana	1949–1950

Secretary: Norman Hilberry, Argonne, 1946–1950

CHAPTER 1

The Met Lab Backdrop

In the year that followed the destruction of Hiroshima and Nagasaki, the scientists who had designed and built the nuclear reactors, the diffusion plants, the separation plants, and the atomic bombs concentrated on two political problems: the domestic struggle to decide whether the development of atomic energy in the United States would be under military or civilian control; and the international negotiations to determine if agreements could be reached and supranational agencies created that would prevent an atomic arms race and eliminate the threat of nuclear war. Though international control was a wisp of idealism, polluted in conferences and blown away by weapons tests, civilian control at home was established by action of Congress. On August 1, 1946, a month after Operation Crossroads had demonstrated the destructive impact of nuclear weapons on a fleet of World War II naval vessels anchored near Bikini Atoll, President Truman signed the McMahon Bill that created a civilian Atomic Energy Commission. He appointed the five-man Commission on October 28, and on December 31, signed an executive order formally transferring from the War Department to the Commission the raw materials, the bombs, the plants, and the laboratories of the Manhattan Engineer District. General Leslie Groves lost a four-year-old command. David Lilienthal took charge, though he was three months away from being confirmed by Congress as the first Chairman of the new Atomic Energy Commission. Among the least of the physical assets transferred from the Army to the Commission at midnight, January 1, 1947, was the Argonne National Laboratory.

The Argonne, as it was called familiarly, had come into existence through the transmutation of the Metallurgical Laboratory during the preceding year, an interim period when it was not clear that military control was entirely going out or that a civilian commission was coming in. The Met Lab, as it was familiarly called, was a division of the Metallurgical Project, the code name for the pursuit of plutonium with which to build atomic bombs that had gotten under way in 1942. It was at the Met Lab that the romance of nuclear energy began. There Arthur Holly Compton gathered what were to be the famous nuclear names from universities throughout the country—Fermi and Szilard from Columbia, Smyth and Wigner from Princeton, Seaborg and Oppenheimer from California, Teller from George Washington University, Franck and Allison from Chicago.

It was at the Met Lab, in the incongruous setting of a squash court under the sumac-covered stands of an abandoned football field that Fermi transformed a pile of graphite bricks and uranium lumps into the first nuclear reactor. "On December 2, 1942," the oft-photographed plaque reads, "man achieved here the first self-sustaining chain reaction and thereby initiated the controlled release of nuclear energy." The site is designated a National Historic Landmark, but it too has since been transmuted. Alonzo Stagg Field is gone. The Joseph Regenstein Library rises in its place. The plaque, moved to the sidewalk, is bolted to a platform that supports a Henry Moore sculpture conveniently called "Nuclear Energy."*

The Met Lab is full of nuclear nostalgia. Another plaque from the National Historic Landmark Commission identifies Room 405 of Jones Hall, one of the medieval-looking stone buildings that make up the central campus of the University of Chicago, as the place where Glenn Seaborg first weighed plutonium, a balancing act that made it possible for him to devise the chemical processes that would recover plutonium from production reactors. And it was at the Met Lab that James Franck, Eugene Rabinowitch, and Leo Szilard, among others, founded the Atomic Scientists of Chicago, the first political organization of scientists that published, lectured, and lobbied to influence national and international policy.**

The Met Lab, as it existed physically in 1945, still under the command of General Groves, was scattered bits and pieces: chemistry and physics laboratories in Jones, Ryerson, and Eckhart Halls on the central campus of the University of Chicago, off the Midway; the administration lodged in the Museum of Science and Industry

---

*The title of the sculpture was originally "Atom Piece." According to Moore, he changed it because he felt some people might think "piece" was meant to be "peace."

**The first and temporary executive committee included, in addition to Rabinowitch and Szilard, J. J. Nickson, J. Simpson, A. M. Brues, D. Hill, and G. Seaborg.

in Jackson Park, near Lake Michigan; metallurgy, biology, and machine shops in a former bottling plant on University Avenue, referred to as the Brewery, code name Site B (it might just as well have been called Site S for the former stables that were also used); and the nuclear reactors at Site A, twenty acres in the Argonne Forest, part of the Cook County Forest Preserve, eighteen miles southwest of the University, between the town of Palos Park and the Des Plaines River.

It was to Site A, in March, 1943, that Fermi's graphite-moderated reactor, the Chicago Pile 1, abbreviated CP-1, was moved from Stagg Field, rebuilt and renamed CP-2. And it was here that the first reactor moderated by heavy water, CP-3, designed by Eugene Wigner and built by Walter Zinn, was operated in 1944. Site A was a modest place—cinderblock and corrugated iron buildings, a water tower and a gasoline pump. Photographs make it look like any small manufacturing complex that tourists chance upon in hill country, lathing wood or distilling liquor. Though Site A housed only fifty people, the uniqueness of its reactor and its staff had elevated it administratively, in 1944, to the status of a separate laboratory, called Argonne Laboratory, with Enrico Fermi as Director. The other nine sites in the Chicago area continued to be called the Metallurgical Laboratory. Administrative definitions notwithstanding, the terms Met Lab and Argonne were often used loosely, so at times they meant separate physical places and at other times were interchangeable and meant all of the Chicago area laboratory complex and even some future physical plant that could be extensive or diminutive, depending on the scope of a man's imagination.

With the war still to be won, the future of government laboratories was a relatively unimportant question. Still, the consideration of a postwar policy began in 1943, as soon as the immediacy of the work at the Met Lab waned. When the focal point of the Manhattan District shifted to the production sites at Hanford (Site W) and Oak Ridge (Site X), and to the weapons development center at Los Alamos (Site Y), the Met Lab staff turned from what were known as pile-engineering problems to more basic research on the fission process. This "basic" or "fundamental" research was distinguished by calling it "third priority" as opposed to "first and second priority work," "long term research and development" as opposed to "essential services," or sometimes simply "research" as opposed to "war services." General Groves and the Military Policy Committee gave first priority to winning the war and felt that postwar considerations were not within their authorized function. Compton, on the other hand, believed that the nation's long-term welfare depended on establishing scientific leadership in nuclear energy by doing a maximum amount of basic research as soon as possible. His idea of an appropriate division was indicated in the budget he submitted for fiscal 1945–1946: eight and one-half million dollars for war services, six million for research.[1]

Planning the postwar nuclear future was an important concern of most of the Chicago-based staff and brought them into continual conflict with General Groves. The differences between the military sense of proper security and the scientists' sense of personal responsibility have been well reported in Alice K. Smith's history, *A Peril and a Hope*. One anecdote from the Met Lab files can illustrate the continual dichotomy. In June 1945, the Laboratory staff held an evening meeting in Eckhart Hall to discuss "The Political and Social Implications of Nuclear Energy." Groves, upon learning of the meeting, requested a list of all who attended and ordered Compton not to hold "group discussions of problems associated with the use of your product." Compton complied. He sent Groves a list, compiled from the sign-in sheet at the security guard station plus a few names added by observation, that was a list of almost every senior scientist at the Laboratory—Franck, Daniels, Szilard, Wigner, Dempster, Stearns, and on down the roll. Compton also agreed to cancel the next scheduled meeting, but noted not only that he disagreed with Groves's policy "as not in the best interests of all concerned," but also that the subject would continue to be examined by discussions between individuals and by a small committee that he would appoint.[2]

This concern with social, political, and military ramifications was paralleled by the less intensive concern for postwar scientific needs. Compton had first expressed the importance of planning ahead in March 1943, at a time when the only reactor that had existed was CP-1, and even it was momentarily dismantled and in the process of being rebuilt in Argonne Forest. Compton felt that one postwar objective of the "49 Project"* was to maintain the scientific lead in nuclear research that it was establishing. The most efficient place for the necessary fundamental research, he said, would be at "a university in or adjacent to a city." Later that same year, in what Compton termed his "State of the Nation" report to the Met Lab staff, he regretted that there had been little opportunity for "fundamental research" and hoped that they could expand such work in the immediate future. His hopes were not supported by his su-

*The code number for plutonium was formed by combining the last figures in its atomic number and its atomic mass: $94 - 239 = 49$.

periors. In June 1944, the Army refused to allow him to hire new personnel for "third priority work" and authorized only that work which would utilize the stand-by staff. Groves placed a quantitative limit on allowable basic research—"not to exceed ten per cent of the total"—and even this he referred to euphemistically as research toward power production.[3]

As the Met Lab and Argonne Lab diminished, primarily because staff members were reassigned to Hanford and Los Alamos, Compton tried to make definite plans for the continuity of reactor research both at Argonne and at the University of Chicago. In July 1944, as Dean of Physical Sciences, Compton offered Fermi a professorship in physics at the University, an offer that was seen as self-aggrandizement on behalf of Chicago. Isidor I. Rabi of the Columbia faculty protested to Vannevar Bush who, as Director of the Office of Scientific Research and Development, was the single most powerful scientist in the government. Bush, in turn, phoned Compton and proposed to move Argonne to another site, stating that he could not "be party to leaving the Argonne Laboratory in any sense under the control of the University of Chicago." Compton immediately proposed to have the University return the Laboratory to the government and reiterated his offer to Fermi, granting him the further authority to select a group of five physicists whom he could bring with him to the University. Compton, trying to separate Chicago's interest in Fermi from any interest it might have in Argonne, proposed that the University create its own Institute for Nuclear Studies.

There was much pique in the exchanges over the offer to Fermi. Letters were drafted by Compton suggesting that Argonne be turned over to another institution or agency and that the Met Lab be absorbed into the University by June 1945. What eventually emerged as the University's official position was a strong objection to Bush's inference that Chicago had used its contractual activities to its own advantage and an invitation that he investigate the conduct of the University in administering the contract for the Metallurgical Project. The immediacy of this dispute quickly passed, the need to make judgments was put aside, but in the process Compton stated a principle that he was to reiterate later when he was no longer Dean at Chicago but the Chancellor of Washington University—"that laboratories such as the Argonne are national assets and should be made equally available to all scientific men." Whether the laboratory was operated by the government, a university, or a cooperative organization was not as important, he wrote, as establishing the means for "open use."[4]

In stating this position, Compton referred to a proposal for regional laboratories that had been made by H. D. Smyth in January 1944 as part of a preliminary report on peacetime plans for the Metallurgical Project. Smyth's argument followed five steps: reactors were expensive to build and dangerous to operate; research on reactors was best done by university scientists rather than by government or industry scientists; Argonne was not on University of Chicago property; Argonne could be a research center for the entire region, serving schools such as Illinois, Wisconsin, Michigan, and Northwestern; similar laboratories could be established elsewhere, for example, in the New York-Philadelphia area.[5]

Later that year, in the fall of 1944, two committee reports were issued on postwar organization. "Prospectus on Nucleonics" was prepared by the Jeffries Committee, a Met Lab group appointed by Compton upon the suggestion of his Advisory Council.[*] The report called for cooperation on research between government and universities and the creation of government-supported nucleonics laboratories at universities for both basic and applied research. The use of the terminology "with special facilities" implied campus-based research reactors. A more prestigious group, the Committee on Post War Policy,[**] appointed by General Groves, recommended that fundamental nuclear energy research be carried on in government laboratories, some military, some civilian, with the civilian laboratories under a new government agency responsible for developing peaceful uses of nuclear energy. As for universities, the Committee only recommended the general strengthening of existing departments of physics and chemistry.[6]

As these studies were being digested, the Laboratory diminished even more. In December 1944, Compton reported that the latest shift of physicists to Los Alamos to support the bomb work had left the Metallurgical Project with three tasks—certain war assignments, the preparation of final technical reports, and the preparation of

[*]The Jeffries Committee consisted of Zay Jeffries (chairman), R. S. Mulliken (secretary), Enrico Fermi, James Franck, T. R. Hogness, R. S. Stone, and C. A. Thomas. It submitted its report on November 18, 1944. The Advisory Council, which had no official status in General Groves's mind, had a floating membership. It was primarily composed of many of the same people who were on the Jeffries Committee and, in addition, included Colonel Nichols and Colonel Peterson of Groves's staff.

[**]The Committee on Post War Policy was often called the Tolman Committee after its chairman, Richard C. Tolman, who had been one of Groves's personal scientific advisors. Other members were: W. K. Lewis, Rear Admiral E. W. Mills, and H. D. Smyth.

recommendations on future work essential to the national safety. By January 1945, the Met Lab, which had once employed twelve hundred scientists and technicians, employed four hundred, with an additional thirty at the Argonne Lab. The Chicago complex had become a small part of an atomic energy establishment that had thirty-eight thousand employees spread throughout the country. In March, Compton received orders to reduce the Chicago staff to one-fifth of its already reduced size and assign most of those left to the Argonne site. He relayed the order to his directors along with his personal thanks to those people who had given their services to the Project. The Clinton Laboratory, which Chicago was also managing, was transferred to Monsanto Chemical Company on July 1, 1945. Compton, in what had become a habitual reaction, requested authorization to close the Project by January 1946.[7]

Colonel K. D. Nichols, Groves's assistant, assured Compton that the Manhattan District was going to keep the Metallurgical Project going as well as could be and tried to persuade him to keep it functioning. Compton's response was to set conditions—that research be determined by the scientific staff and that free discussion be allowed within security conditions agreed on between the government and the scientists. By this time, Compton was not as interested in perpetuating the Metallurgical Project *per se* as he was in establishing regional laboratories at Berkeley, Chicago, Washington, and Cambridge that would be operated in the interest of universities.[8]

There were subsequent variations in proposals and reactions, most of them originating in the Chicago area. In early 1945, Compton wanted the vestiges of the Met Lab, including Argonne, to be transferred to the University, which was prepared to absorb the staff. Groves rejected an informal request to this effect. The scientists of the Met Lab—including Walter Zinn, Szilard, and Norman Hilberry—proposed an opposite solution in a report to the Interim Committee, the policy group that was a predecessor to the Atomic Energy Commission. Under the staff's proposal, Argonne would be managed by a Board of Control, comprised of representatives from the twenty-odd institutions in the region that had an interest in the continued operation of the Laboratory. This would be part of a broad plan to establish "regional cooperative laboratories" to undertake projects too large for single institutions. The regional laboratories were to be financed by the government, but they would not necessarily be government laboratories. More specific than either of these proposals was the formal establishment in July 1945, of an Institute for Basic Research at the University of Chicago. The principal division was an Institute for Nuclear Studies, with Enrico Fermi as one of its founders.[9]

The Chicago action apparently brought generally negative reactions. Chancellor Hutchins of Chicago felt obligated to write General Groves in October 1945, refuting the "unwarranted" and "damaging" reports circulating about the University of Chicago: that the university had "sought and received undue publicity" for its role in the development of nuclear energy; that the university was "seeking a monopoly in nucleonics"; and that it was "seeking to capitalize on the Argonne Laboratory."

"It seems to be assumed," Hutchins wrote, "that the University expects the Argonne Laboratory to fall into its lap and that it is fostering this impression in order to attract men to its faculty who want to work in the Argonne Laboratory. This assumption is false. The University here and now formally repudiates any desire to own, to control or to operate the Argonne Laboratory. The University formally proposes that the Argonne Laboratory be made available to the scientists of the country on equal terms under such form of organization as may be approved by the responsible authorities."[10]

The war was over and the optimum time for planning was rapidly passing. Not until several months later, however, was the specific question of how to run Argonne, a modest reality but a potentially large abstraction, posed by the Army to two different university groups.

CHAPTER 2

Forming a National Laboratory

The first group the Army approached was a committee intended to represent the colleges and universities of the Midwest. It was chaired by Compton, who had recently become Chancellor of Washington University in St. Louis. F. H. Spedding, the Director of the Ames Laboratory, a subdivision of the Metallurgical Project at Iowa State College, represented his academic base. Farrington Daniels, Director of the Met Lab in its last year, represented the University of Wisconsin, where he was Professor of Chemistry. The other schools represented were Northwestern University and the Universities of Illinois, Minnesota, and Chicago.*

The committee met on December 2, 1945, significantly the third anniversary of Fermi's controlled chain reaction. The charge, put to them by Colonel K. D. Nichols, was:

> To recommend a plan for continued operation of the Argonne facilities on a cooperative basis between the government and various universities, with the objectives of: a) continuing current research and development programs and initiating programs essential to the Atomic Energy Project; b) undertaking programs designed to facilitate the training of scientific personnel; c) making the facilities available on a widespread basis to qualified groups interested in pursuing related research programs.[1]

Two months later the Army, again through Nichols, now promoted to Brigadier General, turned to a second group, the Uni-

*Dean O. W. Eshbach (Northwestern), F. W. Loomis (Illinois), John T. Tate (Minnesota), and R. A. Gustavson (Vice President of Chicago) completed the committee. Norman Hilberry acted as secretary, and Major E. J. Bloch of the Manhattan District sat in as an observer.

14 A Special Interest

versity of Chicago administration.** In a series of meetings during February 1946, the University of Chicago was asked ". . . to consider a proposal that effective July 1, 1946, the university undertake the operation of a laboratory at Argonne for cooperative research in nucleonics. . . ."[2]

There were obvious reasons for the Army to single out the University of Chicago. In 1941, at Compton's instigation, the University had signed a no-fee contract with the Office of Scientific Research and Development, the first official government contract for work on what was at the time only a remotely possible atomic weapon. Under this contract, the Metallurgical Project was organized on the Chicago campus, the Stagg Field reactor was built, and the Argonne Forest site developed as a reactor research laboratory. When the Manhattan Engineer District was formed in 1942, the OSRD contract was replaced by a War Department contract under which the University operated all divisions of the Metallurgical Project, not only the Chicago-based laboratories, but also the Clinton Laboratory at Oak Ridge, the Ames Laboratory in Iowa, and nine smaller research projects on campuses throughout the country. In late 1945, when the search for a postwar policy for the atomic energy laboratories had yet to reach even interim conclusions, Chicago was still the contracting agent for all but the Clinton Laboratory.

Against a background of multiple recommendations from previous committees, of a diminishing staff, of individual actions that seemed to favor the University of Chicago over other schools, the multiuniversity committee appointed by Colonel Nichols and charged with formulating a plan for cooperative operation of Argonne met on December 2, 1945. Its report, stamped "Restricted" and later "Confidential" and eventually "For Official Use Only," made six majority recommendations.

The first was that "The Argonne Laboratory should be continued as a regional laboratory designed primarily to serve institutions in the north central United States."

Second, that research should be both of the "pure" and the "process" variety and "should be designed to supplement the programs of associated research institutions." Research which could be done at associated institutions should not be programmed, except in minor "incidental" ways.

**The principal administrators involved were William B. Harrell, Business Manager; R. A. Gustavson, Vice President and Dean of Faculties; and Walter Bartky, the new Dean of Physical Sciences.

Third, that the "immediate operation" should continue under the University of Chicago, with the addition of a regional advisory council which would be composed of representatives from twenty-two schools and two research institutes. And then, as part of the third recommendation, there followed a key principle:

However, the ultimate objective should be the formation of a government corporation created and financed by the permanent federal agency established to supervise development in the atomic energy field. The members of this corporation should consist of representatives from leading research institutions in the region.

The fourth recommendation listed the schools and institutions the committee had in mind. They stretched from Carnegie Institute of Technology in Pittsburgh to the University of Missouri in Columbia and north to the University of Minnesota in Minneapolis.*

The fifth recommendation was to have the regional advisory council elect an executive board that would "act as advisor to the government in programming and administering the activities of the Argonne Laboratory" and that would, when "the ultimate organization was established. . . . act as a board of directors."

The final recommendation was that the work at Argonne should include both classified and unclassified research, and that participation should be subject to the "proper security."

The report to Nichols was brief, the language unambiguous. It said that Argonne should be a regional laboratory that should be run eventually by the universities and colleges of the north central United States to serve their research and teaching needs.[3]

In February 1946, the question put by Nichols to the University of Chicago reflected the Compton Committee's recommendation in a marginal way. Chicago was asked to consider a proposal to operate Argonne for "cooperative research," a term that was not defined. Chicago gave its definition in a letter signed by Business

*The full list consisted of: The University of Minnesota, The Mayo Foundation, The University of Wisconsin, The University of Michigan, Michigan State University, Battelle Memorial Institute, Ohio State University, The University of Cincinnati, The Case School of Applied Science, Western Reserve University, Indiana University, Purdue University, The University of Notre Dame, The University of Illinois, The University of Chicago, Northwestern University, The Illinois Institute of Technology, Iowa State College, University of Iowa, Washington University, The University of Missouri, St. Louis University, The Carnegie Institute of Technology, and The University of Pittsburgh.

Manager William Harrell that limited the role of other universities and maximized the authority of the University of Chicago.

Harrell proposed that the Laboratory have a dual research program: one part originating in the Laboratory staff; and the other part to be proposed by people from the cooperating institutions and subject to approval by the representatives of both the institutions and the government. Such approval would not be required of Laboratory-initiated research. The proportion of Laboratory research versus university research was not indicated. The only criterion was that scientists from one participating institution would not be treated more favorably than scientists from another, the implication being that a Chicago faculty member would have no more prerogatives than a professor from Ohio State University.

In return, Chicago would appoint the Director, who would have to be acceptable to the cooperating institutions. Together with all Laboratory personnel, he would be directly responsible to the University. As for administrative rules and regulations, Chicago agreed to consult representatives of the government and the cooperating institutions, but wished to retain the authority to determine what the rules would be. The final sentences of Harrell's letter stated:

> The problem of retaining present personnel and of recruiting additional staff is acute. The University will be in a much better position to deal with the problem of personnel effectively if a decision to proceed is reached at the earliest possible moment. In any event, the basic terms of the operating contract should be agreed upon not later than April 1.

The letter was dated March 9.[4] The Army contract with Chicago to operate the Metallurgical Project was to expire June 30.

At the same time that the University of Chicago was stating its terms, General Groves was receiving advice from yet another committee that he had appointed, the Advisory Committee on Research and Development, which presented him with a two-page document entitled "Broad Policy on National Laboratories."* This Committee, on which Compton sat, recommended that the work at national laboratories be primarily basic unclassified research of the type that required equipment too costly for a university or a private laboratory to build and operate. Specifically, the Committee recommended

---

*Members were: Robert F. Bacher, A. H. Compton, Warren K. Lewis, John R. Ruhoff, Charles A. Thomas, Richard C. Tolman, and John A. Wheeler.

one national laboratory at Argonne and another in the "Northeastern United States." Each should be administered by "a financially responsible agency," but "the responsibility for proposing the programs should rest with the board of directors," which would be chosen from the participating institutions, and its Chairman, who would serve as director of the laboratory. "The permanent senior staff of the laboratory," the report concluded, "should be supplied from the participating institutions on a rotating basis."[5]

Even more substantial was the Committee's recommendation that in Fiscal Year 1947 Argonne receive $5 million for construction and approximately the same for operations. This recommendation eventually formed the basis for the Military Appropriations Act of 1946, under which Argonne would be operated until some form of an Atomic Energy Commission had been established. The site on the hill in the Cook County Forest Preserve might have been a modest place in 1946, but it obviously would not be in the future.[6]

At the end of March 1946, Colonel A. V. Peterson relayed to General Nichols the answers of the University of Chicago to questions Nichols had raised. Nichols had asked that representatives of the participating institutions appoint the Laboratory Director subject to approval by Chicago, rather than the reverse procedure. Harrell, answering for the University, responded that Chicago would not operate Argonne unless it appointed the Director, and proposed offering the job to the Met Lab's current Director, Farrington Daniels. Nichols had asked if the work proposed by the University of Chicago would be given special preference. Harrell said work proposed by Chicago staff would be treated in accordance with procedures established by the participating institutions and the government. Nichols had proposed that all research programs, including those developed by the Laboratory staff, be subject to approval by the representatives of the cooperating institutions. Harrell's response to this proposal was that the University would proceed only if "the University would have responsibility for the operation of the Argonne Laboratory." The General's final question was, if the University of Chicago did not operate Argonne, would the University make available, by contract, the on-campus facilities such as New Chem, Site B, and the machine shops. The answer was "No."

In addition, Colonel Peterson was convinced that a delay of more than two weeks in contracting for an operating agency would result in the departure from the Met Lab of a large number of qualified personnel who felt threatened by the ambiguities of the situation. This, in turn, he believed, would cause a delay of at least a year in establishing a working laboratory. Colonel Peterson recommended that the contract be awarded on the terms Harrell proposed, and that the plan be explained to the representatives of the participating institutions who had been invited to meet in Chicago a week later "for the purpose of determining how [the Chicago area] facilities could be used as a national laboratory."[7]

The representatives of twenty-two schools and two research institutes, Battelle Memorial Institute and the Mayo Foundation, met on April 5, 1946, in a group that was called the "Advisory Council." They heard about the achievements of the Met Lab, were shown the proposed budget for the coming year, and were told of the possibility of consolidation of the Laboratory in the Argonne Forest or some other suitable place. After touring Site A, the group reviewed the recommendations about organizing the new Laboratory that had been made by the December 2 Committee and by Groves's Advisory Committee on Research and Development. They then elected a seven-man Argonne Regional Committee to draft proposals for future policy and operations. The expectation, as stated by Farrington Daniels, was that the universities would provide the nucleus of the Laboratory's professional staff and that faculty would use Argonne under guest status. Firm plans were expected by June. The elected Regional Committee, whose name was immediately changed to Advisory Board, had the identical composition as the December 2 Committee. It met the next morning with General Nichols and Harrell. Compton was elected temporary Chairman. The first order of business was Harrell's letter of March 9, in which he had stated the University's terms for operating a laboratory.

The Committee's discussion led to its own interpretation of its power and the purpose of the Laboratory—namely, that the Laboratory would be made into "a scientific tool for the regional universities;" that the universities would recommend policies, but that "the advisory and committee boards" would determine policy; that the contractor, for the "ensuing fiscal year," the University of Chicago, would be responsible for carrying out "the program of the Board;" that the Advisory Board, together with the contractor and the government, would have veto power in appointing a Director, and that the Board could dismiss him at any time. To show that the Committee meant what it said, the job of Director was offered to Daniels on the spot, and when he refused, subcommittees were set up to find both a Director and an Associate Director.

The Committee, as its last item of business, renamed itself "Board of Governors, Argonne National Laboratory" and renamed the Advisory Council the "Council of Participating Institutions." It was a classic example of a committee hoisting itself up by its own bootstraps and achieving momentary levitation.[8]

On Monday, April 8, two days after the Committee had turned itself into a "Board of Governors," the Manhattan Engineer District sent the University of Chicago a letter contract "to undertake the establishment, management, and operation of the Argonne National Laboratory . . . for the purpose of conducting research in the field of atomic energy on a cooperative basis with other institutions, in accordance with the proposal by the University of Chicago. . . ." The letter reiterated the points in Harrell's letter of March 9, limiting the role of the representatives of the cooperating institutions to approving research proposed by staff from the institutions. In everything else, Chicago had the "authority commensurate with the responsibility." The University accepted the contract with some minor changes, the most important making clear that the University was entitled to charge overhead costs against the contract.[9]

The Board of Governors met again on May 6. The search for a Director had resulted in an offer to Walter Zinn, who had been Acting Director of the Argonne Laboratory ever since Fermi's departure to Los Alamos. Zinn, who reportedly had offers from the Canadian government's Chalk River Laboratory and from the yet-to-be-established Brookhaven National Laboratory, appeared before the Board to request assurance on two points—that there would be funds to build new reactors and a high-voltage particle accelerator. The Board only gave him assurance of its support, and did so in a qualified way, saying that it would have to look at each specific request against the perspective of national needs and in terms of available manpower. With this rather indecisive response, Zinn agreed to accept the directorship.

A discussion of proposed By-Laws* revealed some self-doubts. Should they call themselves Governors or Advisors? Were they writing By-Laws or something else not quite defined? No decisions were reached, though the Board did conclude that it had a "primary responsibility . . . to advise the government on matters of general research policy for the laboratory in terms of the over-all research needs of the area," and "to advise with the Contractor or if necessary with the government on the actual laboratory operations." The ambivalence of the Board was prophetic. On the one hand, there

*The official title was "Proposed By-Laws for the Operation of the Argonne National Laboratory for the Interim Period under the Supervision of the Manhattan District, U.S.E.D."

was hesitant self-definition. On the other, it hired Zinn as Director and, as a final item of business, approved $75,000 to construct a Van de Graaff electro-static generator.

The army had similar doubts. At the June meeting of the Board of Governors, General Nichols rejected the idea of a three-party agreement between the Army, the University of Chicago and the Participating Institutions. "It would lead," he said, "to misunderstanding." Moreover, the "government's relationships with the Contractor were more concrete than those with the Participating Institutions could possibly be." Nichols saw the By-Laws as "the proposed basis of cooperation," though he carefully said that the section which had the government delegating the responsibility for research was beyond his power to approve.[10]

The By-Laws, renamed "Argonne National Laboratory Plan of Organization and Statement of Operating Policy," were intended to resolve the problem of identity. Unfortunately, the document that was finally approved contained three different interpretations of the lines of authority. Section II, "Responsibility of the Participating Institutions," made all research, regardless of its origin, even research originating in the government, subject to the approval of the Board of Governors. However, Section III, "Responsibility of Contractor," limited the Board's right of approval to that research originating in the participating institutions and only if the government authorized the research. Section IV, titled "Director of Laboratory," was even less generous and granted the Board of Governors only the right of "review and recommendation." The Board's role in choosing the Laboratory Director was equally ambiguous. In Section III, the Contractor's choice of a Director had to be acceptable to the Board," while in Section IV, the Director was to be appointed by the Contractor "with the advice of the Board."

Despite these built-in conundrums, the Plan was adopted by forty-five representatives from the schools and institutes of the Midwest, meeting as the Council of Participating Institutions on June 6. General Groves, on August 21, 1946, signed a note saying ". . . [it] is hereby approved."[11]

Even the General's approval meant very little. On November 22, 1946, the War Department issued a Prime Contract, effective through December 1947, to the University of Chicago that replaced the Letter Contract of April 8. Article II, "Description of Work," distinguished between research developed by the Laboratory staff or the staff of Participating Institutions and research "of interest to the Atomic Energy Project." The former was subject to approval by the representatives of the Participating Institutions. The latter was

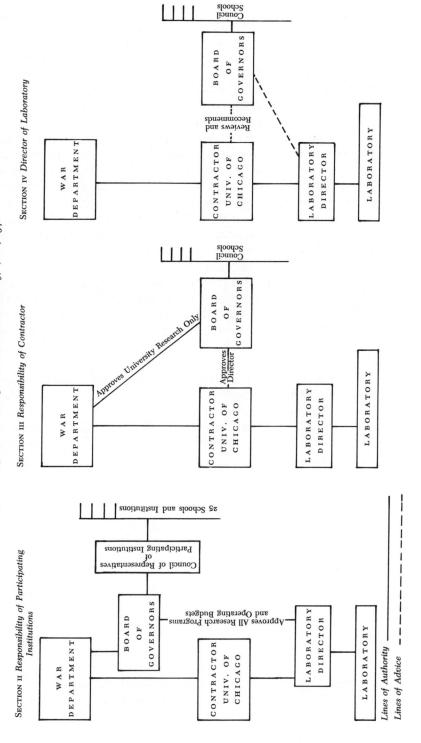

Three Interpretations of the Authority of the Board of Governors According to "Plan of Organization and Statement of Operating Procedure, Argonne National Laboratory," June, 1946

SECTION IV *Director of Laboratory*

Council Schools

BOARD OF GOVERNORS

Reviews and Recommends

WAR DEPARTMENT

CONTRACTOR UNIV. OF CHICAGO

LABORATORY DIRECTOR

LABORATORY

SECTION III *Responsibility of Contractor*

Council Schools

BOARD OF GOVERNORS

Approves University Research Only

Approves Director

WAR DEPARTMENT

CONTRACTOR UNIV. OF CHICAGO

LABORATORY DIRECTOR

LABORATORY

SECTION II *Responsibility of Participating Institutions*

25 Schools and Institutions

Council of Representatives of Participating Institutions

BOARD OF GOVERNORS

Approves All Research Programs and Operating Budgets

WAR DEPARTMENT

CONTRACTOR UNIV. OF CHICAGO

LABORATORY DIRECTOR

LABORATORY

Lines of Authority ————
Lines of Advice – – – – –

not. In addition, the contractor was to appoint a Laboratory Director, acceptable to the government, who was sympathetic toward the plan of participating with other institutions. Scientists from the Participating Institutions would use the facilities "to the extent consistent with the proper functioning of such laboratory and the obligations of the Contractor hereunder."[12]

Accompanied by these contradictory and ambiguous definitions, Argonne National Laboratory officially came into existence on July 1, 1946. The press release from the War Department, dated July 3, stated that the Manhattan Project's Metallurgical Laboratory at the University of Chicago had become the Argonne National Laboratory, "with the same functions and operations to be carried out under the new organization." The *Chicago Tribune* headlined its story, tucked away on page 5, "Continue University of Chicago Atomic Lab for Biology Study."[13]

While every public statement was full of amiable promise, when the parties involved got down to work, their different expectations eventually led to frustration and conflict. Compounding it all were rapid transitions imposed from outside. The McMahon Bill was to be signed on August 1, an Atomic Energy Commission would be appointed in October, and a new cast of characters would enter from stage center.* The day before the Army issued the Prime Contract for Argonne National Laboratory, the newly appointed but not-yet-confirmed Commissioners visited Chicago and began their stewardship by indicating a preference for building the permanent laboratory in the Argonne Forest. The Board of Governors had another site in mind.

---

*The first Commissioners were: David E. Lilienthal (Chairman), Robert F. Bacher, Sumner T. Pike, William W. Waymack, and Lewis L. Strauss.

CHAPTER 3

The First Decisions

The choice of a permanent site was the first important problem
that faced the new national laboratory when it came into existence
in July 1946. Everyone agreed, for local and regional reasons, that
the site should be in the Chicago area, defined as somewhere within
an hour's commuting time of the city. Such a location would not
require the present staff to move and, because Chicago was a trans-
portation center, would be relatively accessible to faculty from the
participating institutions. The prime candidate was 245 acres near
Site A in the Argonne Forest. Two reactors were already there, and
the Cook County Preserve was relatively isolated; but the primary
reason was one of those interpretive generalizations that attribute
actions to some external authority. General Nichols had reported
that the House Appropriations Committee preferred that the Manhattan District place new laboratories on existing government property. The nuclear research center for the northeast, what was to
become Brookhaven, was to be either at Fort Hancock in New Jer-
sey or Camp Upton, an old army base on Long Island. While the
Argonne Forest was not federal land, Groves felt that its acquisition
was more in keeping with the desires of Congress than the purchase
of private property. All that was required was the agreement of the
Cook County Board of Supervisors, and barring that, condemnation
proceedings. Walter Zinn, the Laboratory Director, also preferred
Site A. The Board of Governors, however, did not. They opposed
condemnation as impolitic, and urged an alternate site five miles
from Argonne Forest—3,700 acres of farm land in Downers Grove
Township, in Du Page County, on the western side of the Des
Plaines River. It was composed of one hundred and forty-eight
separately owned parcels of land ranging from less than an acre to
over two hundred acres in size. General Groves visited the Du Page
site, changed his mind, and, reportedly, sought the approval of the
Secretary of War to purchase it. However, as soon as President Tru-

23

man appointed the Atomic Energy Commission in October 1946, General Groves deferred the site question to his successors. Lilienthal's initial attitude was that the Army had not adequately considered sites already owned by the federal government; but the Commission, while barnstorming around the nation to look at its future property, stopped at Chicago, visited Zinn, and decided it too preferred the Argonne site.

The Board of Governors continued to advocate the Du Page site, and the Commission finally agreed to it as a second choice if negotiations failed to convince the Cook County Supervisors that it was in the national interest to give up their picnic grounds and riding trails. The Board, in turn, agreed to participate in the negotiations. The Cook County Supervisors remained unconvinced, and at the end of January 1947, the Commission decided to buy the Du Page site. In a letter officially informing Farrington Daniels, as Chairman of the Board of Governors, of the site decision, Lilienthal made an ambiguous policy statement. "It is the intention of the Commission to assist the Board of Directors [sic] to organize the research program along lines which will allow for a full measure of regional responsibility consistent with the national program for the development of atomic energy." While this appears to say that the research program at Argonne would be the responsibility of the Board of Governors, it did distinguish between research and national development, with the latter as the determinant.

The official AEC press release on the site acquisition had the announcement coming from Daniels as Chairman of the Board of Governors and quoted Zinn to the effect that Argonne was to be a center for research and development in the Midwest. The regional value may have been emphasized as a means of making the acquisitions, some of which would be through condemnation proceedings, more palatable, and also because the Commissioners, though already making decisions, had yet to be confirmed by Congress. Such reasons aside, the Board of Governors had played an important role in determining the location of the future Argonne Laboratory.[1]

There were other signs by which the Board appeared to be what it was called. In September 1946, the Chicago-based *Bulletin of the Atomic Scientists*, which was the primary source of topical information on nuclear energy, published an article on the new Laboratory that attributed to the Board of Governors "the authority to approve all research programs." Though the article distinguished fundamental research from process or development research, it did not say that the authority of the Board of Governors was limited to the former. Similarly, the Commission, in its semiannual reports to

Congress, continued to emphasize the university-related aspect of Argonne. The January 1947 report stated that the Board of Governors was composed of representatives of twenty-five Midwestern universities and research institutions. The July report said, "In several . . . laboratories research activities are not carried on exclusively by the resident staffs. There are already twenty-nine universities participating in the work at the Argonne National Laboratory."[2]

The realities of participation were somewhat less than implied. The Council of Participating Institutions met twice a year to hear reports and learn what it could about the Laboratory's operations. In December 1946, a special meeting was held, the purpose of which in Daniels' mind was to make the universities feel a part of the program. The day was the hoary Second of December. The Board of Governors tried to get a Commissioner to speak, but got a telegram from Lilienthal instead. Groves came and talked about international control of nuclear energy, which was much on both his and the public's mind. The group toured the Argonne Forest site and heard Zinn talk on reactor development. They then returned to their respective campuses until May, when they would meet again, for essentially the same fare.[3]

The Board of Governors did a little better. It met every three months, and in between Daniels exchanged letters with Zinn. The illusionary high point in the Board's governance was its December 1947 meeting. Zinn did not attend the morning session, preferring instead to conduct a press tour of the Argonne Forest site, the first time that reporters without security clearance were allowed to see reactors in operation. At the morning session, the Board was shown development plans for the Du Page site, now called Site D. They had been prepared by the consulting engineering firm and incorporated the requests of the Laboratory staff. Until permanent buildings could be finished, a matter of several years, "temporary" buildings, Quonset huts on cinderblock walls that are still used in the 1970's, were being erected. The Board approved of all that it heard. In the afternoon session, the Associate Laboratory Director, Norman Hilberry, reported on the Participating Institutions Program. Afterwards, the Board approved a Laboratory budget of $11,750,000 for Fiscal 1948-1949 and an expansion of the scientific staff from 330 to 442 people. At this point, Zinn joined the meeting for a discussion of industrial cooperation and the problems caused by the continued necessity of security clearance for people working at the Laboratory.

On the surface, the meeting appeared significant. The realities, however, were not. The plans for development of the new site did not include facilities for university research. There had been no specific planning to discover what those needs might be. The budget for the next year had been formulated without reference to the universities, and the approval by the Board was really a formality. The budget had already been reviewed in Washington. Most revealing is the report on the Participating Institutions Program. Though twenty-two of the twenty-five institutions were listed for the six-month period as having been involved with Argonne, the participation was marginal for almost all of them; requests for permission to visit the Laboratory, requests for information on radiation protection, instances in which university people had joined the Laboratory staff as permanent or temporary members, requests for exhibits or speakers. In two instances, materials were irradiated, but most of the substantive requests were listed as pending or referred to some other source. The notable exception was the University of Chicago, which had nine active programs which related Laboratory and university people in research. Illinois Institute of Technology was second with two projects.[4]

In an article in the *Bulletin of the Atomic Scientists*, published in June 1948, Farrington Daniels offered two reasons for the modest amount of participation. One was limited space—the Argonne site and the Chicago laboratories were saturated. The Laboratory staff agreed with Daniels. Each request from a university to use the facilities was seen by the Laboratory as an encroachment. In rejecting four requests for joint research projects, the head of the Chemistry Division wrote, "We do not see how further space can be made available for future requests without actually reducing our present research program." Daniels' second reason was the relative lack of university capabilities in nuclear energy. "It is anticipated," he wrote, "that the benefit which the twenty-nine participating institutions derive from the Argonne Laboratory will increase rapidly as these institutions learn more about nuclear physics and chemistry, and the engineering and biological problems connected with atomic energy."[5]

The Board of Governors was not really governing, but there was no sense of urgency that it do so. Facilities were being built on the new site. A staff member was to be added to the central administration of the Laboratory whose job would be to coordinate research between the Participating Institutions and the Laboratory. The lack of any startling cooperation was only in keeping with the national development of nuclear energy. The year 1947, according to the official AEC history, *Atomic Shield,* was a year in which the new Commission searched, without success, for a research policy and a plan for laboratory development. The equivocation that occurred in Washington and the failure to resolve a management crisis at the Clinton Laboratory had a far more powerful impact on the Argonne National Laboratory than anything that the Laboratory staff or the Board of Governors did. But that was the final act of 1947 and did not become known until January 1 of the new year.

The events of 1947 began inauspiciously. The Commission, particularly Lilienthal, had trouble getting confirmed by Congress and spent the first three months jockeying with the Joint Committee on Atomic Energy. The General Advisory Committee, the scientific board that advised the Commissioners and was chaired by J. Robert Oppenheimer, was highly critical of the lack of nuclear development. Essentially, the GAC felt that during the seventeen months since the end of the war nothing much had happened. No new reactors had been built, no reactor development program had been organized. The scientists were also unhappy, as was President Truman when they told him, that there were no nuclear weapons available for immediate use. The GAC recommended three solutions: 1) the revitalization of Los Alamos for weapons research, particularly thermonuclear weapons; 2) improvement of the plutonium production plants at Hanford; 3) the development of two new reactors, a power-breeder, which would produce more fissionable material than it consumed at the same time that it provided heat for producing electricity, and a high-flux test reactor that could be used for experiments on the effects of radiation on materials. The GAC favored the creation of a central laboratory for reactor development and felt it should be the new Argonne Laboratory that was to be built at site D (for Du Page). It was the GAC's thought that the facilities in the Argonne Forest could be kept as the regional center for the schools of the Midwest.

This concept of a single national reactor laboratory was juggled all year. Sometimes the GAC was for it, sometimes the Commission was against it. Compounding the issue was the management problem at the Clinton Laboratories, located at Oak Ridge, Tennessee. During the war, Clinton had been part of the Metallurgical Project under the direct management of Compton and, through him, of the University of Chicago. This arrangement ended in July 1945, one of the side effects of Compton's departure from the University of Chicago for the chancellorship at Washington University. Monsanto Chemical Company took over, but in the spring of 1947 indicated that it wished to withdraw by the end of the year because of a number of differences with the AEC that ranged from labor-management relationships to the location of the high-flux reactor. The solution proposed by the AEC's Director of Research was to return Clinton to the University of Chicago management, a move that would solve an additional problem, that the research staff at Clinton preferred to work under the aegis of a university, even a distant one, rather than an industrial firm. The GAC split on this solution, primarily because some members viewed it as defeating the concept of a central reactor laboratory. Another contender for the management position was the Oak Ridge Institute for Nuclear Studies, an association of fourteen Southern universities. The choice went to Chicago, because ORINS, the AEC decided, "was not yet prepared to undertake so great a burden as operation of Clinton involved." A four-year contract was proposed, at the termination of which the question of management would be raised again. The public announcement was made at the end of September, and from that point on the arrangements went downhill.

The official version, given by Lilienthal, is that the University was unable to find a director and generally was slow in bringing in staff to coordinate a changeover. In reality, the directorship was offered to one man who turned it down. A second person, proposed by the AEC, was unacceptable to the laboratory staff. A third, proposed by the laboratory, was unacceptable to the AEC. Warren Johnson, Director of Clinton's Chemistry Division and a faculty member at Chicago, was about to become the interim director, when the University was asked to withdraw. In its place came Carbide and Carbon Chemical Corporation, now known as Union Carbide, which was already operating the other Oak Ridge facility, the gaseous diffusion plant used in bomb production. Carbide was having union problems, which it believed were aggravated by the fact that there were two different management groups and two different unions at Oak Ridge: Monsanto and the American Federation of Labor for Clinton Laboratory; Carbide and the Congress of Industrial Organizations for the diffusion plants. Carbide viewed sole management with only one union as a way to alleviate difficulties and responded more than favorably to a suggestion from Lilienthal that it consider taking over Clinton. Carbide even suggested to the AEC that it would consider withdrawing totally if the dual management arrangement continued.

The final decision to transfer Clinton to Carbide was made on the day after Christmas at a special Commission meeting held at Lilienthal's home. Chicago was informed on the next day, and the staff at Oak Ridge on the day before New Year's. The decision, however, was not just to shift management; it was to concentrate reactor development at Argonne. This was assumed to mean that the high-flux reactor proposed by the GAC would be built at Argonne, that the development of a new submarine reactor program would take place there, and, since Zinn was the major advocate of the breeder reactor, that it would also go to Argonne. Naturally, there would be a transfer of personnel, an increase in budget, and a change in the function of the Laboratory.

The net effect was to make the Oak Ridge Laboratory seem to have no future, while Argonne had all its future in reactor development. The University of Chicago, though losing a management job a thousand miles from home, was continuing a much enlarged job just down Highway 66.[6]

The Board of Governors learned of the decision in the newspapers of January 1. *The New York Times* did not take notice, but the *Chicago Tribune* did. On page 22, with an Oak Ridge dateline and under a headline

SHIFT ATOM
RESEARCH TO
ARGONNE LAB

it said, "The atomic energy commission tonight announced the bulk of its research activities will be centralized at Argonne National Laboratory near Chicago, where a new 'high-flux reactor several times more powerful than the existing Oak Ridge pile' will be built." The Commission also said the University of Chicago would direct, at Argonne, the "expanded program on uranium change [breeder] reactors."

In the same issue of the *Tribune*, on page 2, there was a story announcing the elevation of Alfonso Tammaro from Acting Manager to Manager of the AEC's Chicago Operations Office. This story said, "He will be in charge of administering commission research contracts for the operation of the Argonne National Laboratory which centralizes the research and development work of 29 midwestern industrial and academic organizations."

While the two stories offered rather different versions of what was going on at Argonne, the members of the Board of Governors could be certain of one thing—despite their approval of budgets, plans, and personnel expansion, there was no longer any pretense that they were governing Argonne. The question on everyone's mind was whether Argonne could be both a regional laboratory and the national reactor development center. Whatever else that Christmas decision did, it created the first crisis between the universities, the Laboratory, and the AEC.

CHAPTER 4

Illusions and Realities

A special meeting of the Board of Governors was called on January 4, 1948. First William Harrell and then Walter Zinn reviewed the decision of the previous week and the events that had led to it. Zinn reported that he had opposed the decision—arguing that it would mean a loss of Clinton staff and a disruption of Argonne hierarchies. Zinn also said that he could not accept the added responsibilities until the matter had been discussed with the Board. He was not saying it had to be approved by the Board, but rather that the Board had a right to know before the shift became reality. Because of conflicts in personal schedules, it had not been possible to meet prior to a premature news release to the Oak Ridge paper by the understandably upset Clinton staff.

The reaction by the Board of Governors was to question its own authority. Farrington Daniels wondered if a precedent had been set for using the Board as a rubber stamp. Louis A. Turner (Iowa) remarked that it appeared the Board was "just a group of stooges," and F. Wheeler Loomis (Illinois) suggested that the Board resign if it was not functioning as a Board of Governors, which it obviously was not.

Having expressed its frustration, the Board turned to consideration of reactions less drastic than resigning. The proposed centralization of reactor development obviously threatened to diminish that research which might be termed "fundamental" or "basic" at the Laboratory, which in turn would further limit the opportunity for university-Laboratory cooperation. According to Zinn, the amount of such research had been determined by the Laboratory staff, but continuation of this power no longer seemed possible. The contractual distinctions between work originating in the Laboratory staff and work originating in the schools had not really mattered in operation, and, it appeared, would matter even less under the new reactor development program.

The Board adopted a motion which Zinn was asked to send to the AEC, accepting the Commission's decision, expressing concern for the possible effects on fundamental research at the Laboratory, and asking for assurance that its fears were not only groundless but that the opposite would occur, ". . . that enlargement of the basic program will, in fact, be initiated and carried forward vigorously. . . ."[1]

Such assurance came several months later in time for the Board's March 13 meeting. Zinn had not sent the Board's motion to Alfonso Tammaro, Manager of the AEC's Chicago Operations Office, until February 25. Tammaro, who had received a copy of the resolution directly from Daniels in early January, sent it on to the Director of Research in Washington on February 26. Carroll Wilson, the General Manager of the Atomic Energy Commission, responded to Tammaro on March 5, saying all the appropriate things—that the Commission did not intend the new responsibilities to hinder fundamental research, that the expansion was expected to make Argonne more useful to neighboring institutions, and that Zinn was about to hire that liaison man, first discussed a year earlier, who would facilitate cooperation between the Laboratory and the schools.

A different perspective was provided by the Third Semi-Annual Report of the Commission. The Board of Governors was no longer mentioned, while much was made of Argonne's new role as the center for reactor development. The impact on the Laboratory was quickly reflected in a change in budget from approximately $12,000,000 to $19,000,000, and an increase in scientific staff from 442 to about 650. The total staff was expected to jump from 1,500 to 2,500. Though only Quonset huts would be built in 1948, the cost of permanent buildings planned for the new site was now estimated at $57 million.[2]

Despite the Board of Governors' internal disappointment, it presented a picture of an understanding and harmonious relationship to the general public and to the schools in the Council of Participating Institutions. Daniels, in his article in the *Bulletin of the Atomic Scientists*, gave a brief history of Argonne and described the administrative structure so as to give the impression that the Board of Governors actually governed.

"The government," he wrote, "with the advice of the Board of Governors, selects a contractor to operate the Laboratory. . . . The Board of Governors meets every three months, and oftener as occasion demands, to review matters of general policy and make necessary recommendations to the contractor and the government.

The Board reviews the research programs and operating budgets presented by the Director and must approve them before they are submitted by the contractor to the government."

So his article went. After recounting some of the history of the transmutation from the Met Lab to ANL, and the reasons why the new site was chosen, Daniels came to the decision to concentrate reactor research at Argonne. "Fearing the possible effects of this decision on the Argonne Laboratory," he reported, "the Board of Governors made clear to the Atomic Energy Commission that the change in policy must not interfere with the Laboratory's program of fundamental research nor with the cooperation of the participating universities."[3]

While the words are not inaccurate, the implication that it mattered at all what the Board "made clear" is misleading. A possible reason for this public masking of private inadequacy lies in a comment F. W. Loomis made at the January 4 meeting, when the Board was so distressed at having been ignored in the decision to centralize reactor work. Loomis, who had earlier argued for a mass resignation, opposed a suggestion that the Board try to formalize its authority, by pointing out that if the Board continued to function "it would have the assumed power."[4] For physical scientists, who normally dealt with elements and particles, they were placing a great deal of faith in the concept that if they said something was so, it was so.

Occasionally, people tried to tell them differently. At a May 1948 meeting of the Council, the larger group of representatives from the Participating Institutions, there was a discussion of requests to use Argonne from several schools who were not members of the Council. When Loomis asked what the distinction was between participating and non-participating schools, Norman Hilberry, the Associate Director of ANL, answered, "It is mostly a matter of prestige."[5]

During 1948, the Board of Governors led a relatively placid existence. A Liaison Director, H. K. Stephenson, had been hired by the Laboratory and became the Secretary of the Board and its official correspondent. He was also assigned to coordinate an AEC public information program which the Participating Institutions were expected to sponsor in their home communities. In May, at the urging of Zinn, the Board passed a resolution calling for on-site housing for temporary staff. The Board also moved to formalize two cooperative programs—one was the loan of equipment by the Laboratory to the schools, the other was the exchange of staff for periods of six months to a year, with Laboratory people going to universities and assuming teaching responsibilities while university faculty and students would come to the Laboratory and perform research. The letter from Stephenson to Tammaro that accompanied the two Board-approved memoranda that explained these programs said, "The proposals are submitted for the approval of the Atomic Energy Commission as to the propriety of the Argonne Laboratory carrying out these activities." This submission, in October of 1948, represented the authority and initiative that the universities had after more than two years of "participation."[6]

Apparently, the world that the Board of Governors was trying to counteract was too somber for charades to replace reality. In 1948, the AEC was busy developing and testing new concepts in nuclear weapons. The Navy had begun to push for a nuclear propulsion system, and the Commission had decided this should be Zinn's highest priority. Primarily, though, the reactor development program remained unclarified, and this was the most disturbing fact of all. Though the announcements of the Christmas decision and all subsequently offered statements said that a high-flux reactor was to be built at Argonne, Zinn, according to the official history of the AEC, was not acquisitive enough to take it or the decision-making authority implicit in the centralized laboratory concept. To the contrary, he declined to preside over the reactor development plans of Clinton, and agreed with Alvin Weinberg, Director of Clinton's Physics Division, on a plan that would place high-flux reactors both at Oak Ridge and Argonne. The net result was little progress. In the spring of 1948, the General Advisory Committee, headed by Oppenheimer, told the Commission bluntly that it had failed. "We despair of progress in the reactor program," the GAC said. The solution it proposed was to restructure the operation of the Commission, create four directors, one for research, one for weapons, one for reactors, and one for production, each with line responsibility. The significant difference between this proposal and the previous organization was that reactor development, formerly under the Division of Research, would be elevated to a status parallel to weapons development. The new Director of Reactor Development would have authority over Argonne.

The reorganization was announced in August 1948, after the terms of the Commissioners themselves had been extended for two years to avoid a political struggle with Congress. It was decided to acquire a reactor testing ground distant from any large population, where the new reactor prototypes could be built. By the end of the year, the only progress was the establishment of priorities for building four reactors—the high-flux reactor, now called the

Materials Testing Reactor; a fast breeder reactor; an intermediate breeder reactor; and a submarine propulsion reactor. All but the intermediate breeder would be built at the yet-to-be-acquired testing site, which was to be linked with Argonne. What was still lacking at the end of 1948 was a Director of Reactor Development. This position went to Lawrence Hafstad in January 1949.

Hafstad, a practicing physicist before the war, had been co-author of the first paper on delayed neutrons, an important factor in the feasibility of controlled chain reactions. He had been Director of Research at the Applied Physics Laboratory at Johns Hopkins and had worked on proximity fuses, guided missiles, and weapons development. After the war he had been Executive Secretary of the Joint Research and Development Board, which considered strategic applications of science and coordinated the research and development of Army, Navy, and Air Force groups. He came to the job with a bias toward the development of reactors for military uses and for weapons production. The pursuit of nuclear-generated electric power, Hafstad thought, belonged in the private sector of the economy. Given his views, his responsibilities, and more significantly, considering the consistent negative appraisal of the Commission's reactor program, it should not have been hard to predict that Hafstad and the Board of Governors would come into conflict.[7]

The different expectations of too many groups were applied simultaneously in 1949. Principally, there was the pressure to produce a reactor program, which meant that any desires that could detract from the priorities established in 1948 were not going to get positive responses in Washington. Then there was the essential absence of interest in basic research or academic participation on the part of the Commission. Lilienthal regarded basic research as the "scientist's pet" and, in his own words, he was "getting a bit fed up with the terriffic appetite for funds of this side of the business." Ironically, these two factors combined to place the Laboratory staff in a position relative to the Commission that was similar to the position of the university people relative to the Laboratory. The Laboratory people wanted to do basic research, to eliminate the constant security fence that had been erected around nuclear energy, but when they voiced these concerns to the Commission they received pat answers. As a result, they came to view what basic research they had as an enclave that had to be preserved against programmatic demands of the Commission on the one hand and university requests to share facilities on the other.

The consistently negative attitudes toward requests to have professors or graduate students come to Argonne were not just a matter of competing for tightly used space, for the finite amount of service dollars available. These attitudes were encouraged by the continued university irritation of a problem that is more qualitative than quantitative, the relative scientific status of the respective staffs. The universities wanted their younger professors and their graduate students to go to Argonne to work for six months or a year in order to gain experience. Argonne wanted the senior faculty to come, the ones whom it saw as capable of making original contributions, of giving rather than receiving. Conversely, the Laboratory wished its senior people to have the opportunity to join the faculties of the Participating Institutions, to gain teaching experience and the attendant academic status. The universities' response to this was along traditional lines of departmental prerogatives in inviting and choosing faculty—which meant that the universities were willing to have Laboratory staff come for graduate work or one-day seminars. Many were doing just that, but it wasn't entirely what the Laboratory had in mind.[8]

From the Laboratory point of view, reflected in Zinn's behavior, the Board of Governors' primary value lay in its public relations image and its political potential as a pressure point that could be applied on Washington. This had been a traditional role, first played in the site acquisition, where the Board of Governors acted as advocates on behalf of the Commission, seeking to persuade the Cook County Commissioners to give up Argonne Forest. Later, in May 1948, it played the role again, in response to a request from Zinn that it ask the Commission for on-site housing for temporary staff. In March 1949, Zinn again approached the Board, this time to help him obtain a new research reactor for Argonne. Argonne was developing, together with Westinghouse, a reactor for the Navy. It was designing, with Oak Ridge, the Materials Testing Reactor, which would be built in Idaho at the about-to-be-acquired test grounds. This left for the ANL staff the old CP-3 in the Argonne Forest Preserve, that had been built in 1943. A reactor being constructed at Brookhaven National Laboratory, which would go critical in August 1950, would soon be the most intense source of neutrons for research in the United States. Zinn brought to the Board the year-old letter of reassurance from the AEC's General Manager, citing the Laboratory's commitment to basic research with the universities as a prime reason to build a new reactor. The irony was double-edged. A year earlier, Zinn was ostensibly going to have the

major responsibility for national reactor development; now, he
candidly admitted, he was in the position of having to be a politi-
cian, competing for his share of the non-programmatic reactor development budget. What Zinn wanted was a reactor that had a
high enough neutron flux to make it versatile for neutron diffraction
studies, radiation damage studies, and isotope production. Since
such a reactor would be necessary if a cooperative program ever
got underway, the Board, as it had in the past, gave the requested
support in the form of the appropriate motions and the appropriate
letters to Washington.*⁹

The willingness of the Board of Governors to continue its
equivocal existence was drawing to a close. In April 1949, the
Board Chairman, John Tate (Minnesota), wrote to Zinn asking him
to schedule an executive session at the next Board meeting, without
representatives from either the Laboratory or the University of
Chicago being present. While Tate said he had no particular issue
in mind, he did see this arrangement as "a safety valve." On May 2,
1949, the Board, meeting with Zinn and Harrell, had a session in
which blunt opinions crossed the table. The Board questioned its
real responsibility for operating the Laboratory. There were minor
complaints that the Laboratory had not been as cooperative as
possible with the schools, that the Participating Institutions Program was not successful, that Argonne was a developmental laboratory, and that, in comparison with Brookhaven, it was not considered a laboratory that engaged in research of interest to universities.
What the Board was asking in just so many words was what it would
mean if the Board went out of existence. The implication of the
comments was "nothing."

Zinn's response was equally direct. He denied that the Laboratory had not cooperated with the schools and asked for specific
instances. More significantly, he insisted on specifying the contractual realities of their relationship. The AEC, he told them, had
never approved the Statement of Operating Policy that had established the Board and from which it drew its own concept of its
authority. General Groves had approved, but not the Commission.

*Planning money was appropriated none too soon. The vessel of
the CP-3 proved to be corroding and, though it was overhauled, its
natural uranium fuel replaced with enriched uranium, and rechristened
CP-3′, its demise was predictable. Fortunately, the CP-5 went critical in
February 1954, and the CP-3′ was shut down and subsequently dramati-
cally buried by digging an enormous hole alongside it and then neatly
toppling the old unwanted reactor with a well-placed charge of dynamite.

The Board, in his opinion, was purely advisory to the contractor, which was the University of Chicago, and to the AEC. Zinn saw himself in the middle. There was no AEC policy statement on just what a national laboratory should be. He had money problems and space problems. There were indications of budgetary cutbacks. As far as he was concerned, the Board should have sought clarification of its status much earlier. He would have done so, he told the members of the Board, had he been in their position. Harrell supported Zinn's interpretation of the contractual relationship. He told the Board of Governors bluntly that its name was an obvious misnomer, that it did not govern.

The direct responses to this confrontation were either to resign or to seek official recognition from the AEC. A subcommittee was appointed to review the Plan of Organization and the Statement of Operating Policy and have them formally accepted as legal documents binding all parties, even possibly having the Board of Governors part of the operating contract between the AEC and the University of Chicago. L. A. Turner was appointed chairman; Farrington Daniels and W. C. Johnson of Chicago completed the subcommittee.

The next day at a meeting of the Council, the Board's new recognition of reality was explained to the representatives of the schools. The Board, Tate told them, was only an agent of the Council. The representatives got their own example of the true nature of the relationship between the schools when several of them said that they wanted more of their faculty to work at the Laboratory for short periods and proposed a fixed item in the Laboratory budget that would guarantee the Laboratory's availability to university people. Zinn explained to the Council what he had previously explained to the Board, that the tight budget, the lack of space, determined the amount of cooperation possible, but principally that the Laboratory wanted a two-way exchange—the schools' best people coming to the Laboratory and the Laboratory's best people going to the schools. The meeting ended inconclusively. The Laboratory and the schools had reached an impasse.[10]

CHAPTER 5

The Demise of the Board
of Governors

Two immediate results of the acknowledgment of the true nature of
the Board of Governors were the establishment of the Turner Committee and the hiring by Walter Zinn of a special consultant on university relations, Joseph Boyce, Chairman of the Physics Department at New York University. A summary report, submitted by
Boyce in August 1949, attributed the "misunderstandings" to the
creation of the Board of Governors in the pre-Commission days, the
assignment of reactor development to Argonne, and the close supervision of the Laboratory budget by the AEC. Boyce thought the
number of temporary staff, which he equated with university participation, comprised effective cooperation. This approached ten
per cent of the non-programmatic (as distinguished from reactor
development) work, which, in turn, was estimated at about forty
per cent of the total Laboratory effort. To put it another way, four
per cent of the staff were university people on temporary appointments. A distinction that was missing was whether these visiting
staff were working on projects of their own design, or on projects
that were part of the Laboratory's work. In his report, Boyce recommended that the Board of Governors be renamed the Executive
Committee of the Council of Participating Institutions. He submitted a set of By-Laws that would restrict the Executive Committee
to acting for the Council and advising only on matters that per-
tained to the relationship between the Laboratory and the schools.[1]

The Turner Committee rejected Boyce's draft as too limiting.
The members were willing to abandon any pretense of supervision of
the reactor development program at Argonne, but wished to formally
establish what the Board of Governors had always pretended it had,
the authority to approve "fundamental" research. To accomplish
this, they favored a transformation of the Board of Governors to a
Board of Trustees. However, they were unwilling to make any specific recommendations until they knew what the AEC's attitude was

38

toward the national laboratories in general and Argonne in particular.[2] This they learned shortly at a special meeting of the Board of Governors to which the Director of Reactor Development, Lawrence Hafstad, came.

Hafstad made his personal position on a Board of Trustees quite clear. The days of General Groves, he said, were over. He was "surprised to find out the Laboratory [was] still operating under a plan adopted in Groves's days." The reactor development business was constantly changing, the objectives shifting; new decisions were continually needed. ". . . It is impossible that any elected group," he told the Board, "elected by outsiders, should be inserted in line of command between myself, Zinn, and Hilberry." Whatever arrangements had previously existed between the AEC, the contractor, and the Participating Institutions were irrelevant. The understanding that Louis Turner took from the meeting was that the Board of Governors had been "operating in a vacuum and had to start over from scratch," within the limitations Hafstad had asserted.

Zinn took a more moderate position. He acknowledged the need for direct-line responsibilities of the University of Chicago as contractor, but feared that the Laboratory, without ties to the scientific community of the Midwest, would sink to a level of mediocrity. He wanted to maintain a relationship with the schools similar to what already existed but not one that placed the schools in a decision-making role. He used Hafstad's terminology—they had to be outside "the line of command."

Hafstad proposed that a board be created to advise Zinn, but not one elected by the Participating Institutions. The Board of Governors' response was pessimistic. "Maybe this is the last time we will meet," one member said.[3]

It was not, of course. The Board met the next month to consider, as a way of living within the relationship, a proposal from Hafstad that there be two boards advising the administration of Argonne. The first would be chosen by the Participating Institutions and would advise only on those matters concerning the cooperative programs between the Laboratory and the schools. The second board would be more prestigious, a body of senior advisors, "a stable high calibre advisory body capable both of critical analysis and of positive advice and assistance in the solution of the Laboratory's technical, administrative, and policy problems."[4]

This structure was the crux of a proposed set of By-Laws governing the relationship between the schools and the Laboratory that had already begun to circulate within the AEC, the Laboratory staff, and the University of Chicago. It defined a three-way partnership for determining operating policy at Argonne between the Director of the Laboratory, the AEC Manager of Chicago Operations, and the divisions of the AEC in Washington, primarily the Reactor Development Division, but also, where applicable, the Division of Biology and Medicine. Under this document, the new version of the Board of Governors would be advisory to a newly created "Associate Director in Charge of Programs and University Relations." The general advisory group which would be advisory to the Director of Argonne would be appointed by Zinn.

This document, which originated in Hafstad's office in October, was revised by Hilberry, presented to the directors of the Laboratory's several divisions, approved by both Zinn and William Harrell, and by the General Counsel of the AEC. Despite the various inputs, it remained Hafstad's document—establishing his line of command—and, in its original form, was mailed to the Board of Governors in time for its March 6, 1950, meeting.

The Board declined to take action on the proposed "Operating Policy of the Argonne National Laboratory." Some members felt that since the document relegated them to an inconsequential role, there was no point in even responding. Others objected on procedural grounds, that this was the first look at the proposed By-Laws they had been given, in a sense a repetition of their experience with the reactor development decision, and that the Board was waiting for a report of its own subcommittee, headed by Turner, on this precise problem.

Tammaro, the Manager of the AEC's Chicago Operations Office, pleaded with the Board not to object to Hafstad's document:

> It is all right for the Board to comment to the AEC on Hafstad's statement, but please don't protest it. I had been told by my staff that this statement was acceptable to the laboratory and the contractor and at the last meeting with Hafstad and Pitzer everyone was in agreement. I had no idea it had not been seen by the Board . . . so please don't protest it.

To which Warren Johnson of Chicago replied, "I think it is a question of cooperation not one of protest."[5]

Johnson, who was a Professor of Chemistry at the University of Chicago and a member of Turner's Committee, was in the middle. That afternoon Hilberry arranged to have Johnson drive into Chicago with Harrell and Zinn—"to go over the whole matter" with him. As a result, Hilberry wrote Hafstad, he thought Johnson "now has a clear picture of the major problems," and believed that the Turner Committee "will come up with a report which will supplement your draft." "I am sorry," he concluded, "that this business seems to be taking so long, but I believe that the end is really now in sight."[6]

Hilberry's prediction was correct. On March 30, the Board of Governors received the report of the Turner Committee, which was a revised version of Hafstad's draft. It differed in only one major respect, that two members of what had been the Board of Governors, but in the future would be the Executive Board of the Council of Participating Institutions, were to be seated on the Argonne Advisory Committee without requiring the approval of the Laboratory Director. The Argonne Advisory Committee was to have a total of seven members, meet at least six times a year, and "exercise a continuing review of the research and development programs in which it will render assistance and advice." Moreover, the Turner Committee recommended "that problems involving major changes in policy of importance to the programs of the Laboratory and of the Participating Institutions will be brought to the attention of the Argonne Advisory Committee and the Council Executive Committee for comment and advice."

The Turner Committee had also added to the Hafstad draft three sections describing the Participating Institutions, the Council of the Participating Institutions, and the Council Executive Board. The Board of Governors separated the sections on the Council and the Executive Board, re-labeled them By-Laws of the Council of Participating Institutions, and placed them in an appendix.[7]

The full report of the Turner Committee never got beyond the Board of Governors. A meeting of the Council had been called for May 2, and when Hilberry sent the representatives their pre-meeting packages he included only the appendix, now retitled "Proposed By-Laws of the Council of Participating Institutions of Argonne National Laboratory." He also sent them a brief history of the lack of a fixed relationship between the schools and Argonne and told them that "the Laboratory has recently received operating instructions in the form of a 'charter' from the AEC in Washington . . . [which] spells out the Laboratory's responsibilities to the AEC." He was, of course, referring to Hafstad's "Operating Policy" or, as it was sometimes called, "Hafstad's Charter."[8]

It was made clear at the last official meeting of the Board of Governors on May 1 and the Council meeting of the next day that there was a sharp division between what the AEC saw as the schools' proper sphere of interest and what the schools saw as their proper sphere. For reasons not made explicit in the minutes, the Board concurred in the procedure that had been insisted upon by

Hafstad. The next day, when the Council met, the representatives from the twenty-nine schools and two research institutes were told that there was no alternative but acceptance. Zinn played Hafstad's role to the Council, repeating the line that there was no way to have an elected group between the Laboratory and the Commission. Turner, speaking for the Board, said that they had been told any suggestions for revision of the Hafstad document would be considered at some indefinite future time when the document was up for revision. The Council representatives, essentially strangers to all the internal hassling, did as they were told; they approved their new By-Laws. The Board of Governors ceased to exist. In its place was a Council Executive Board.[9]

On June 1, 1950, at Meeting 416, the Atomic Energy Commission approved the Hafstad Charter exactly as it had been presented to the Board of Governors in March. The Turner Committee, the Board's own actions, had been irrelevant. Even the section on an advisory group remained as it had originally been written by Hafstad, with the power of appointment lying with the Laboratory director and no mention of required members from the Council Executive Board.

The Participating Institutions, under this document, were separated from both the Laboratory and the AEC. They were relegated to Section V.3, which began, "A mechanism to assure greater interaction between ANL and neighboring institutions will be established." The section, without being explicit, relegated the Board of Governors' successor to the role of advising an "Associate Director in Charge of Educational Programs and University Relations."

The Commission did not even accept the Council's own By-Laws. On June 9, Warren Johnson, now President of the Council, received a new version which was tied, via footnotes, to the Hafstad Charter.[10] In the proposed draft, the Commission was prepared to acquiesce to having two Council Executive Board members on the Argonne Advisory Committee, by stating that "The Argonne National Laboratory, with the concurrence of the Commission, agreed" to do so. By placing the agreement in the Council's By-Laws rather than in Argonne's Operating Policy, the Commission was continuing the historical practice of having two concurrent but not identical concepts functioning at Argonne. One was the contractual reality as represented in official government documents. The other was the university reality, as represented in the statements of the Participating Institutions, and in the public relations releases both of the Commission and of the schools. No one wanted to destroy the illusion of participation.

Organizational Schematic Based on *"Argonne National Laboratory Organization and Operating Policy,"* June 1, 1950

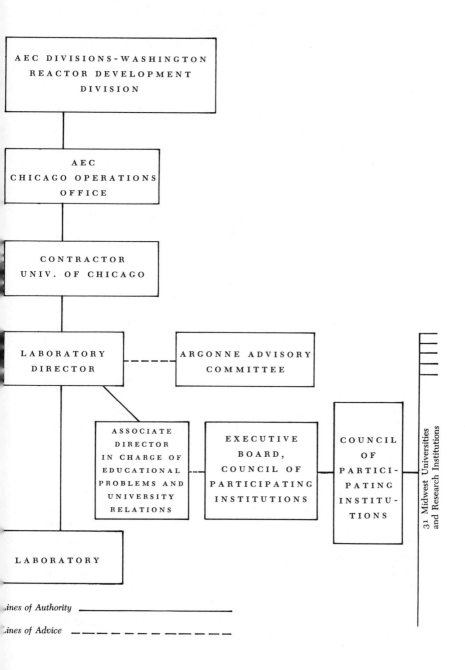

AEC DIVISIONS-WASHINGTON
REACTOR DEVELOPMENT
DIVISION

AEC
CHICAGO OPERATIONS
OFFICE

CONTRACTOR
UNIV. OF CHICAGO

LABORATORY
DIRECTOR

ARGONNE ADVISORY
COMMITTEE

ASSOCIATE
DIRECTOR
IN CHARGE OF
EDUCATIONAL
PROBLEMS AND
UNIVERSITY
RELATIONS

EXECUTIVE
BOARD,
COUNCIL OF
PARTICIPATING
INSTITUTIONS

COUNCIL
OF
PARTICI-
PATING
INSTITU-
TIONS

31 Midwest Universities
and Research Institutions

LABORATORY

Lines of Authority ——————

Lines of Advice — — — — — — — — —

All this loomed large to the participants. Those whose perspective went back to the end of World War II could see that the promised regional research laboratory with which they had started in 1945 had been transformed into a reactor development center whose principal mission was programmatic research that had little to do with academia, its needs or preferences. Their colleagues on the East Coast and the West Coast had fared much better. The Seventh Semi-Annual Report of the Commission, in January 1950, made this clear.

> In Commission laboratories, different practices are followed in the freedom of individuals to plan and carry out their own research. Brookhaven and the Radiation Laboratory allow maximum freedom. The success of these institutions in recruiting and retaining outstanding research scientists is undoubtedly due in part to this.

> Primarily concerned with basic research, these two laboratories also have important and specific research problems of a practical nature assigned to them.

> The two national laboratories at Argonne and Oak Ridge have a larger proportion of their personnel and facilities assigned to specific projects, and there are fewer opportunities for basic research. In each case, however, there is a substantial amount of basic research growing out of the interest and abilities of members of the staff.[11]

The preceding October, in a speech at Oak Ridge, AEC Commissioner Henry D. Smyth gave a more structured view of this difference. The Commission, he said, supported national laboratories for three reasons: "The first is to make more and better weapons. The second is to develop possible peacetime uses of atomic energy; and the third is to develop such scientific strength in the country as is needed in the long run to support the other two."

To reach these goals, Smyth saw three necessary conditions, all of which were supplied by national laboratories. "To summarize," he wrote, "the AEC needs the national laboratories because it needs secrecy and big groups of scientists who will take orders, and big equipment." Smyth then went on to show that he really meant Oak Ridge and Argonne, but that Brookhaven was a national laboratory of another type.

> [Brookhaven] really owes its existence to the recognition on the part of a number of people in the Northeast that there were

certain facilities which no one university could afford to construct but which were badly needed if the research departments of these universities were to continue to be first rate. . . . The other side of the picture was the recognition, first by the Manhattan District and later by the Atomic Energy Commission, that there was a large group of able scientific people in the northeastern area who in the long run could contribute greatly to the basic scientific problems facing the Atomic Energy Commission and were, therefore, worth supporting. Because of its origin, and because the hope is that the staff at Brookhaven will be largely a rotating staff, emphasis there should be principally on basic research.[12]

While the reasons for the distinction between the captive Midwest and the free coastal areas are difficult to accept at face value, the needs of the AEC for programmatic laboratories somewhere in its system can be attributed to the changes that occurred between January 1949 and June 1950, the period marked by Hafstad's appointment and the official adoption of his charter for Argonne. During these eighteen months, the Commission had come apart and had been put back together again. Of the original five Commissioners, only Summer Pike remained. Both David Lilienthal and Lewis Strauss had left shortly after, and partly because of, their internal struggle over whether the United States should develop a hydrogen bomb. There had also been the eroding politics of Senator Bourke Hickenlooper, his charges of "incredible mismanagement," and the public hearings that had occupied the Commission for three months during 1949. Hickenlooper's charge—"that the United States Atomic Energy Program is virtually a failure"—quickly became Hickenlooper versus Lilienthal, with attendant spectres of communism, security leaks, and waste. Even Argonne had its small role in the hearings. Zinn testified and retestified about some lost uranium-235, in what became known as "the case of the missing brown bottle," a mystery that was solved more by agreement that the brown bottle had really been a green jar than by finding the uranium. Several days were also spent by Laboratory security people discussing the seemingly lax access to the construction site permitted by a graded system of parking stickers. Though Lilienthal won the hearings, he subsequently resigned the chairmanship. In mid-1950, Gordon Dean was about to become Chairman, and the General Manager, Carroll Wilson, had resigned rather than serve under Dean.[13]

More important were international events. In the fall of 1949, the Russians had exploded their first nuclear weapon, long before they had been expected to do so. President Truman, with a strong assist from the Joint Committee on Atomic Energy,* decided that the safety of the nation lay behind an "atomic shield" of thermonuclear bombs. The Berlin Crisis, in which Russian troops isolated West Berlin and a United States airlift reconnected it, had helped change the tone of the times. So had the departure of Chiang Kai-Shek from the Chinese mainland, leaving Mao Tse-tung in control of what was suddenly the most populated communist country in the world. Worst of all, in the summer of 1950, the Korean War began.

What was the Laboratory doing during all this? The reactor development program had finally begun to move. The Materials Testing Reactor was under construction at the new testing grounds at Idaho Falls, Idaho; so was a land-based prototype of the submarine propulsion reactor; and the Experimental Breeder Reactor, after being designed and fabricated at Argonne, was also being built in Idaho. Back at Site D, the Quonset huts in the east area were the only working laboratories, but the permanent buildings were going up. The first, Chemistry, was almost completed. In between the construction areas, the old barns still stood.

*The Joint Committee, in turn, had been strongly persuaded by AEC Commissioners Lewis Strauss and Gordon Dean and by physicists Edward Teller, Luis Alvarez, and E. O. Lawrence.

PART TWO

The Executive Board
of
The Council of Participating Institutions
1950–1958

The Executive Board of the
Council of Participating Institutions
of Argonne National Laboratory
October 1950 to 1958

Name	Institution	Years Served
Warren C. Johnson	Chicago	1950–1951 Chairman 50–51
E. F. Barker	Michigan	1950–1953 Chairman 51–52
Edward Creutz	Carnegie	1950–1952
Titus C. Evans	Iowa	1950–1954
Andrew C. Ivy	Illinois	1950–1951
A. C. G. Mitchell	Indiana	1950–1952
John E. Willard	Wisconsin	1950–1953 Chairman 52–53
E. E. Dreese	Ohio State	1950–1954 Chairman 53–54
H. L. Friedell	Western Reserve	1951–1957 Chairman 55–57
W. F. Libby	Chicago	1951–1954 Chairman 54–55
A. L. Hughes	Washington Univ.	1952–1956
P. G. Kruger	Illinois	1952–1954
J. C. Warner	Carnegie	1953–1957
C. L. Critchfield	Minnesota	1953–1957
D. H. Loughridge	Northwestern	1954–1957
J. H. Jensen	Iowa State	1954–1958 Chairman 57–58
L. L. Quill	Michigan State	1955–1958
R. S. Shankland	Case	1955–1958
John Z. Bowers	Wisconsin	1956–1958
W. L. Everitt	Illinois	1957–1958
R. G. Herb	Wisconsin	1957–1958
Newell S. Gingrich	Missouri	1957–1958
F. Hovorka	Western Reserve	1957–1958

Secretary: Joseph C. Boyce, Argonne, 1950–1955
Illinois Tech., 1955–1958

CHAPTER 6

Beginning Again

Section V, Part 3, of the "Operating Policy of the Argonne National Laboratory," as approved by the Atomic Energy Commission on June 1, 1950, promised that "A mechanism to assure greater interaction between ANL and neighboring universities and research institutions will be established." The general types of interaction were specified: "interchange of personnel, for graduate students completing work at Argonne, for graduate study on the part of Argonne personnel, for mutual stimulation in basic research programs, and for assistance on the part of university engineering departments to the Argonne development program." In addition, the Laboratory Director was to "make provision for the accommodation of qualified research personnel as temporary staff members."

The instrument by which this interaction was to occur was a newly created position of Associate Director in Charge of Educational Programs and University Relations. The Liaison Director, who had functioned briefly as a transfer mechanism between the Laboratory administration and the old Board of Governors, had vanished more mysteriously than the brown bottle of uranium-235. Into the new post, in July 1950, came Joseph C. Boyce, Zinn's consultant on university affairs the previous year.

The extent of interaction when Boyce came to the Laboratory is reported in a summary prepared for the General Advisory Committee six months after he became Associate Director. In January 1951, seven faculty and nine graduate students were temporarily in residence. They came from seven of the thirty-one Participating Institutions. That month, sixty-seven university people visited the Laboratory. In addition, seven irradiations were performed, while film badge services were provided to eighteen institutions.

Boyce did not regard this as sufficient. In his report he tried to explain the low figures. The number of temporary faculty was attributed to the large student enrollments at universities, which made it difficult for faculty to take leaves. The number of visitors was attributed to security regulations which made "Q" clearance, the AEC's requirement for access to information about restricted data, including nuclear weapons, the standard required for visitors to all divisions except the biology group. Typical of the problems this presented was that of the faculty visitor who was not allowed to attend a lecture because his security clearance was from the Navy and not from the AEC.[1]

When the Council Executive Board, which was to represent the schools in their relations with Argonne, held its first formal meeting in October 1950, it had to resolve a year-long controversy over a security clearance requirement for graduate fellowships. The Board wanted students to have the fellowships but did not want to participate in the enforcement of the AEC's security requirements. Its solution was to ask the AEC to administer fellowships directly without using the Board as an intermediary.

The question of the effectiveness of the relationship between the Laboratory and the schools was raised by Boyce at this first meeting. To appraise the program, the Executive Board asked Boyce to prepare two lists: one in which he did the normal thing—list all the examples of participation—and the other in which he listed all the requests from the Participating Institutions that had not been granted. The thought was to present them to the Council at its March 1951 meeting, a presentation that never occurred.[2]

The Board met again in January 1951, to adopt a revised set of By-Laws. Though the Council, at the meeting at which it had dissolved the Board of Governors, had already adopted By-Laws, these had not been accepted by the AEC. Instead a redraft had been proposed through the Chicago Operations Office. The changes were minor with one exception—the provision for an Argonne Advisory Committee. In the proposed version, the Executive Board, instead of naming two of its members directly to the Advisory Committee, would nominate them for appointment. The difference is indicative of the type of wordsmanship continually reflected in the documents that balanced authority at Argonne. The Executive Board approved the new By-Laws, and in March the Council did the same. The document was then signed by Warren Johnson for the Council, Walter Zinn for the Laboratory, William Harrell for the University of Chicago as contractor, and Alfonso Tammaro for the AEC. Norman Hilberry commented that because of the agreement the University of Chicago "holds full contractual responsibility for the operation of the Laboratory for the first time since its reorganization in 1946." At the same Council meeting, Johnson told the representatives that "the Participating Institutions Program was now underway as a real program on a substantial basis under the direction of Mr. Boyce."[3]

The relationship between the schools and the Laboratory became formal. A Memorandum of Agreement between the Laboratory and the Council was drawn up to provide a guide for sub-contracting with individual faculty and students who would be coming to the Laboratory either to pursue their own work or as consultants. It was concerned with such routine but necessary matters as who would pay salary and travel and what rules governed patents and publications. Still, the old problems remained to erode any optimistic forecasts. The security problem was loosened in ways more for public relations than research. At the Council meeting in March 1951, it was announced that the reactor had been partly declassified, and that two visiting days had been set aside for students whose fields were directly related to reactors. Cleared faculty could accompany the students, but the names of all visitors had to be submitted to Boyce at least two weeks in advance. At the June meeting of the Executive Board, there was a report on the tour: one hundred and eighty uncleared visitors had been escorted through the Laboratory to see the reactor and the Van de Graaff generator. The tour, one Board member said, "was much appreciated." Another responded, "It is hoped this opportunity may be offered once a year."*

The attempts to expand temporary staff programs fared no better than the attempts to soften security. Hilberry announced at the June meeting that because of military and Commission budget shifts, the openings for temporary staff from the schools would be cut from thirty to twenty. When either number is placed against the permanent scientific staff of six hundred, the cut does not seem relatively important. Both figures were small. Boyce's reaction was that the program had been "short-changed."[4]

Boyce had an opportunity to expand on this view two months later. Gordon Dean, the Chairman of the Commission, visited Argonne and criticized the Participating Institutions Program for not being sufficiently broad. Zinn, in turn, asked Boyce for a summary

*Chicago news commentator Paul Harvey, who had been a critic of the "inadequate" security procedures at top secret laboratories, had a different view of Laboratory security. Harvey, one winter day, was caught climbing over a fence at Argonne. He was questioned but not detained by the FBI. The United Press reported on February 9, 1951, that Harvey claimed to have been working with investigation divisions of several federal agencies.

report on the previous year, Fiscal 1950–1951. Boyce provided the usual data:

28 in residence—17 faculty, 11 graduate students;
215 visitors, excluding those from the University of Chicago and the special reactor-day tour;
75 irradiations;
film processing for 18 schools, an average of 300 badges per week;
approximately 44 consultants hired by the Laboratory.

Chicago statistics were excluded "as the relations with that institution are close and continuous." The suggestion is that the figures were not easily obtainable, and if they were, it would demonstrate that participation by University of Chicago staff was out of proportion to its position as one of the thirty-one institutions sharing in the program.

More interesting than the report were Boyce's accompanying comments. He had obtained comparable figures for Oak Ridge, Brookhaven, and Argonne on the numbers of faculty and students in long-term residence.

Residence for Over Three Months

	ANL	BNL	ORNL
Faculty	8	10	21
Students	9	15	20

Residence for Summer Only (1951)

Faculty	4	46	73
Students	1	37	—

Boyce offered as the principal reason for the difference between Argonne and Oak Ridge the qualitative differences of the schools in the respective geographic areas. He cited statistics to the effect that of the 11,927 Ph.D.'s awarded in 1949 and 1950, thirty-five per cent were in the Argonne area and only nine per cent in the Oak Ridge area. The difference between Argonne and Brookhaven had to be explained on different grounds, since the Brookhaven area had accounted for forty-three per cent of the Ph.D.'s during that same period. The villain, Boyce said, was the lack of on-site housing for visiting staff and their families.

Boyce then went on to put the ultimate blame on the Commission, charging that if they really wanted the program expanded, they would not have cut the proposed budget for Fiscal 1952 by three-quarters of a million dollars. The effect of the cut had been to reduce the possible number of temporary staff from thirty-six to seven. Since commitments had been made to twenty people, the Laboratory had made up the difference out of divisional budgets. Boyce listed five "imperative" steps for the Commission to take:

1. restore the budget so as to support the original thirty-six visiting staff members;

2. provide funds for ten summer positions in 1953 and twenty in 1954;

3. provide funds for an on-site Guest House;

4. provide housing for the families of five faculty coming to the Laboratory for a year;

5. give a clear directive to facilitate visits to unclassified experimental facilities and to seminars on unclassified topics.[5]

Boyce did not get what he wanted. The budget stayed cut. And in the spring of 1952, Boyce was still telling the Executive Board that the factors that limited the Participating Institutions Program were the lack of housing and restricted access to unclassified work. Little had changed. When Zinn spoke at the spring meeting of the Council on the Experimental Breeder Reactor attaining criticality and producing electricity, the minutes contained the notation, "Members of the Council are reminded that Mr. Zinn's remarks are classified." A general account had already appeared in the Semi-Annual Report of the AEC, published in January 1952.[6]

The pattern continued during that year. When the Executive Board met in October, the same ground was replowed. Boyce reported and the Board members expressed disappointment. Once again the question of the relationship between the Laboratory and the Participating Institutions was raised. In effect, the Executive Board had been serving the function that Hafstad had prescribed for it—it was advisory not to the Laboratory Director but to an associate director, who was without authority to implement change, who could only coordinate within limitations set for him, not by the schools but by the Commission and the Laboratory Director. In this role, the Executive Board had concerned itself with such knotty questions as the control over publication by graduate students, the need for patent waivers, and the establishment of criteria for electing new members of the Participating Institutions.

The Laboratory's business had gone on without them. The Commission had authorized a new research reactor (May 1951) which was to be the CP-5, the first reactor to be built on the Du Page site. General construction had progressed to where the buildings originally planned had been finished. The Laboratory existed physically and continued to be Hafstad's major arm of development. Out in Idaho, the first Experimental Breeder Reactor had successfully been brought to criticality in December 1951 and had even produced that initial token bit of electricity. But military defense dominated the Washington perspective. The keel for the *Nautilus* was laid in June 1952, even though the reactor prototype was still being pieced together in Idaho. Zinn was asked to direct the development work toward a new generation of more efficient plutonium-producing reactors. The prospect for power reactors that produced economical electricity was tagged to the breeder concept and projected as reality for sometime between 1970 and 2000.

In 1952, the United States could count twenty reactors operating or under construction. Argonne, at the Laboratory and at the Idaho proving grounds, had six. Brookhaven had one, Oak Ridge one, plus three of what were called "small reactor experiments." Knolls Laboratory had a prototype of a submarine reactor, and North Carolina State University was building the first campus reactor for teaching and academic research. The remainder in the total of twenty were at Hanford and Savannah River producing plutonium for bombs.

Their product was in demand. The Nevada testing grounds had been opened in 1951, and three series of weapons tests, totaling twenty explosions, including one public performance, were held there. More significant was a test at the Monte Bello Islands, Australia, in October 1952, that announced Great Britain's advent into the nuclear-bomb powers. At the end of the month, the United States secretly detonated its first thermonuclear device, a 10.4 megaton explosion that erased a small Pacific atoll and created new parameters for instant destruction.

It was also in October 1952, at the quarterly meeting of the Council Executive Board, that an anonymous member asked the penetrating question, "Has the Argonne Advisory Committee been appointed?" The answer was, "No." Two and one-half years after the Board of Governors had abdicated, there had been no move by Zinn to implement the Committee that was supposed to advise him on broad policy matters. Apparently, there was neither desire nor need.[7]

Of and by itself, the revelation might have caused a stir or two, but it is unlikely, considering the past decline of the influence of the schools at Argonne, that any change would have been forthcoming had not a simultaneous movement begun—the planning by high energy physicists to build an accelerator in the Midwest.

CHAPTER 7

Organizing for High Energy

In the fall of 1971, if everything goes well, what will be for at least a brief period the world's highest energy proton accelerator, a 500-billion electron volt machine, costing in excess of $250 million, is to begin operation at a new national accelerator laboratory thirty miles west of Chicago. The laboratory, named in honor of Enrico Fermi, is operated by Universities Research Association (URA), consisting of forty-nine universities in the United States and one in Canada. It is expected to have a permanent staff of sixteen hundred and fifty people, with an additional temporary staff of three hundred and fifty visiting scientists.[1]

Twenty years earlier, in the fall of 1952, physicists from Midwestern universities first began to consider how to build a large particle accelerator in the Midwest. The political story of their failure has been told in broad form by D. S. Greenberg in *The Politics of Pure Science*.[2] The acronym formed by the name of the physicists' organization, MURA, for Midwest Universities Research Association, has become a catchword that calls up a confusing story of controversy between Argonne National Laboratory and physicists at the universities of the Midwest, and eventually between Congressmen from the Midwest and President Lyndon Johnson.

Building an accelerator became a regional issue primarily because of the earlier failure of Argonne National Laboratory, the University of Chicago, and the universities of the Midwest to develop a mechanism through which the schools had an authoritative role in determining Laboratory policy. It continued to be a problem because the parties could not resolve this question of authority, could not reverse their earlier patterns of behavior. MURA became the focal point for discontent directed toward Argonne in particular and the Commission in general. It also became a vehicle for reform. An interim by-product, which paralleled an interim solution of the MURA dispute, was the formation of a new university arrangement *vis-a-vis* Argonne that replaced the Council of Participating Institutions with the Associated Midwest Universities.

In 1952, when the question of building an accelerator in the Midwest was first raised, the country was neatly balanced by particle producers. On the West Coast, the University of California's Radiation Laboratory was finishing its Bevatron, a $9,000,000, 55-foot radius, six billion electron volt proton machine that would go into operation in 1953. On the East Coast, Brookhaven National Laboratory had already begun initial operation of its Cosmotron, a 30-foot radius, three billion electron volt proton accelerator that cost a mere $7,000,000. In the middle of the country, however, there were only smaller machines on the order of Mev's, millions, instead of Bev's, billions. These were on a few campuses, Michigan and Chicago, for example. Argonne, though a national laboratory, had only a 60-inch radius cyclotron under construction which, when completed in late 1952, would produce particles with energies of 30 Mev. It was a machine that was in no way meant to support the type of research that physicists have in mind when they talk about "exploring frontiers." Since the truism holds—that what matters most to high energy physicists is high energy—the Midwesterners felt that there were certain inequities in the national distribution of particle producers.

Walter Zinn always maintained that he initiated the first discussions on the possibility of an accelerator for the Midwest, and various documents produced within Argonne say that he sounded out Enrico Fermi on the subject in November of 1952. Other sources credit Fermi and P. Gerald Kruger (Illinois) with having originated the idea, independent of the Laboratory. There are references to a series of informal meetings among physicists both in and out of Argonne in December 1952 and January 1953. Given the operating reality of Brookhaven's Cosmotron (its dedication ceremonies were held on December 16 and 17) and the impending operation of Berkeley's Bevatron, it is more than likely that building a billion volt accelerator in the Midwest was a common thought among the area's high-energy physicists.[3]

The first formal meeting to discuss the possibility took place on January 30, when nine physicists met at Argonne and wrote a "Dear Tom" letter to T. H. Johnson, the Director of the AEC's Division of Research. The letter stated their belief that the maintenance of a high level of nuclear physics in the Midwest required a cosmotron-type machine, that such a project was too large for a single university or organization to undertake, that a cooperative effort was desirable, and that they hoped the AEC would support the study, design, and construction stages of such a project. The letter went on to say, "As one of the interested parties," Argonne had "offered to sponsor preliminary meetings to crystallize plans" under the ANL Participating Institutions Program, and proposed that the work be "guided by a Midwest Cosmotron Committee, whose membership will include, but would not be limited to, the individuals sending you this letter." It was signed by "S. K. Allison, E. Fermi, R. G. Herb, P. G. Kruger, J. J. Livingood, A. C. G. Mitchell, L. A. Turner, J. H. Williams, and W. H. Zinn," in alphabetical order, and without titles or organizational references. Allison was Director of the Institute for Nuclear Studies at the University of Chicago, Fermi the Institute's most distinguished member. Herb was from Wisconsin, Williams from Minnesota. Kruger, who was from Illinois, and Mitchell, from Indiana, were also members of the Council Executive Board. Livingood, Turner, and Zinn were from Argonne.* The group simultaneously approached David Saxe, Acting Manager of the AEC's Chicago Operations Office, to ask if the AEC would consider the initial study of an accelerator to be "a proper and desirable use" of the Participating Institutions Program. Saxe said yes and added that Argonne's basic physics budget possessed enough flexibility to permit assistance in the exploratory stages. He gave approval to use approximately $10,000. Alfonso Tammaro, Manager of the Chicago Operations Office, saw the proposal to build an accelerator as a clear test of the viability of the Participating Institutions Program. In a memorandum to Lawrence Hafstad outlining practical steps for reducing the security requirements during the planning stage, he wrote, "If we are unable to accommodate such a project both in the initial stages and in its actual operation, we should recognize that the Participating Institution Program is going to remain largely limited to such activities as service operations and reactor irradiations."

Tammaro's response was more constructive than T. H. Johnson's. The Director of Research answered the January 30 letter by posing a number of broad policy questions: How rapidly should the Commission provide facilities in various high energy ranges? Should all possible research at a low energy be "exhausted" before moving up to higher energies? Should large machines be restricted to national laboratories? If not, is there a danger of the government favoring one university over another? How much parallel high energy work should be supported? How much should accelerator research "be

---

*Turner, who had been a member of the Board of Governors, was now the Director of Argonne's Physics Division. Livingood was the Laboratory's senior accelerator physicist.

allowed to divert attention from other important areas?" Though these are all important questions, they became secondary to a much smaller question, namely, who would control a Midwestern accelerator, the Laboratory administration or the physicists who used it.[4]

The January 30 letter to Johnson marked the high point of cooperation on this issue between Argonne and the physicists of the Midwest, but even then its unanimity was partly illusory. Both Kruger and Mitchell had already raised the question of operating such an accelerator apart from Argonne, claiming that because of the Laboratory's security regulations it would not be readily accessible to users.

The nature of an alternative to Argonne was spelled out in a letter from F. Wheeler Loomis, Chairman of the Physics Department at Illinois and a member of both the December 2 Committee and the old Board of Governors. Loomis felt the ideal physical location was on Argonne land, but only under certain conditions.

> In the important matters of control and management and policy, however, my prejudices can perhaps be summed up by saying that the Brookhaven pattern is appropriate to the purpose and the Argonne Pattern is wholly inappropriate.
>
> By the phrase "Brookhaven pattern" I intend to imply all, or nearly all, of the following points:
>
> 1. Actual management and control by representatives of a *small* group of institutions which serves as the contractor.
>
> 2. A program in which pure research has the highest, if not sole, priority.
>
> 3. Entirely unclassified and open, with its own security officers.
>
> 4. Its own director, separate from the Argonne. Who this will be is probably *the* most important problem.
>
> 5. Separate grounds, facilities (within reason), services, telephone, cafeteria, etc.
>
> 6. Separate budget.
>
> I realize that some of the above will present formidable difficulties and that there will be a natural tendency to drift toward the Argonne pattern because of contiguity and precedent. All the more reason to establish the intended pattern firmly from the beginning.

Loomis's letter had been in response to an inquiry that Boyce had sent to physics departments of the Participating Institutions.

Further opposition to an Argonne pattern of administration was reiterated at the spring meeting (March 1953) of the Council Executive Board. It was apparent, Boyce reported, that there was "considerable difference of opinion as to the suitability of locating such a machine at Argonne." The solution offered by some Board members was to make the accelerator project part of the Participating Institutions Program "under the directorship of a Cosmotron Board made up of physicists from the universities most concerned." Ultimately, it would be a separate division of Argonne, somehow free from security requirements and the proverbial red tape. The unifying organization would be the Participating Institutions Program, a single strong program in the Midwest.

At this meeting, the Council Executive Board was asked to nominate two members to the about-to-be-formed Argonne Advisory Committee. This was the body that three years earlier was to have begun advising Zinn on matters of policy. Its initiation at this time was partly in response to the disgruntled query posed at an earlier Council Executive Board meeting, but it was also partly an attempt by Zinn to demonstrate that the Laboratory was administratively responsible to the Council. The Board nominated Erwin E. Dreese (Ohio State) and Kruger, a balanced slate, since Dreese was to favor the accelerator program being administered through Argonne while Kruger wanted it run by a separate organization.

At the annual Council meeting the next day, the proposed accelerator was again debated. Frederick Seitz (Illinois) "urged strongly that the Cosmotron be operated by a separate inter-university corporation, independent of the Argonne National Laboratory." Boyce, on behalf of the Laboratory, replied in a formal and precise statement of policy.

> The Laboratory would be glad to take part in the Cosmotron project if the universities of the area wish it to do so. The Laboratory can make no comment on the proposal for a separate organization for the management of the Cosmotron since that is clearly a matter between the several universities and the Atomic Energy Commission. The Laboratory has grave reservations about the wisdom of locating the machine on the Argonne site if it were to be managed by a completely separate organization. Irrespective of the decision on the ultimate management of the machine, the Laboratory is glad to offer its services to facilitate the preliminary technical planning on a cooperative basis with university physicists of the region.

The Council then passed a motion endorsing the project "irrespective of the ultimate decision as to its management."

The movement for an organization separate from Argonne grew rapidly. A series of meetings was held in the spring on both technical and policy questions. The technical sessions generally agreed on studying a type of accelerator, developed at Brookhaven, that incorporated the concept of strong focusing. The policy sessions reiterated the need for a separate organization in which Argonne was a partner with no greater status than any university. Zinn consistently maintained the position that a study group and accelerator could be a separate division of Argonne, but otherwise would have to be subordinate to him as director and to the realities of the Argonne contract with the University of Chicago and the AEC.

On April 18, the differences were stated once again at a meeting of the policy group, this time against the background of an offer from the University of Wisconsin to provide a site for the machine and temporary housing for the study group. The three Argonne representatives, Zinn, Boyce, and Turner, eventually left the meeting. Those remaining, including two physicists from the University of Chicago, elected Ragnar Rollefson (Wisconsin) as Chairman and instructed him to seek an appointment with Commissioner H. D. Smyth to discuss an accelerator completely separate from Argonne National Laboratory. This meeting took place on May 1. AEC participants were Smyth, T. H. Johnson, and Hafstad. Johnson agreed to accept a request for a study group separate from Argonne, but insisted that the question of the ultimate location of the accelerator that would be designed should be left open.[5]

During the summer, a technical study group of sixteen people, under the direction of D. W. Kerst (Illinois), spent three weeks at Brookhaven studying the new accelerator that was operating there. In August, the group spent a three-week period at Wisconsin. The Brookhaven sojourn was paid for by Brookhaven funds, the Wisconsin time by the individual schools using their own money as well as AEC and Office of Naval Research funds that had been allocated to physics departments.

The support seemingly promised by AEC-Washington was not forthcoming. An overall budget cut due to the Korean War was offered as one reason. A policy decision by the General Advisory Committee not to fund major programs other than at national laboratories was the other. Johnson formally refused to support studies for the coming year that would have cost $135,000. As a result, the Midwest group approached the Ford Foundation, a move that initially was encouraged by the Foundation, much to everyone's surprise, but was soon refused, making the group dependent once again on either the AEC or its own devices.

Johnson, acting through Boyce, then offered to reconsider a proposal from the Midwest group if it accepted Argonne as the site for the machine and agreed to an early centralization of the design study. Boyce carried the message, which was declined. The Midwest group, instead, moved to incorporate. A meeting was held on November 19, 1953, to which the physicists of eight universities (Chicago, Indiana, Minnesota, Illinois, Michigan, Wisconsin, and both Iowa State College and the State University of Iowa) brought their institutions' chief financial officers.* With only Samuel Allison and William Harrell of Chicago abstaining, they formed an Organization Committee which began drawing up a document that would be entitled "Agreement for Cooperative Nuclear Research." The purpose was to organize a not-for-profit corporation, to "be known as 'Midwestern Universities Research Council, Inc.' or such other name as the Organization Committee may determine" in order to "acquire" a Cosmotron. This arrangement of one scientist and one administrator from each school was patterned after the Board of Trustees of the Associated Universities, Inc., which administered Brookhaven. The Agreement was formally signed on April 15, 1954, by the fiscal officers and the representatives of the respective governing bodies of the member schools. It was an impressive collection of Boards of Trustees and Regents and, for the two Iowa schools, the State Board of Education. Similarly impressive was the commitment of $10,000 from each school toward financing initial operation. It represented a substantial change from the uncommitted involvement that had been the pattern in the Council of Participating Institutions.[6]

The organization of a separate group did not go uncontested by Zinn and Boyce. At the June 1953 meeting of the Council Executive Board, Boyce attempted to rationally respond to the three major criticisms of the Laboratory as a potential site for the accelerator: security; emphasis on programmatic work as opposed to basic research; and red tape. He was always ready to offer statistical evidence that these negative conditions were not representative of the Laboratory; that there had been considerable progress

*The participants were P. G. Kruger and H. O. Farber, Comptroller (Illinois); Allan C. G. Mitchell and J. A. Franklin, Vice President and Treasurer (Indiana); John H. Williams and L. R. Lunden, Treasurer (Minnesota); J. M. Jauch and Fred W. Ambrose, Comptroller (State University of Iowa); Julian K. Knipp and Boyne H. Platt, Comptroller (Iowa State College); H. R. Crane and W. K. Pierpont, Vice President (Michigan); and Ragnar Rollefson and A. W. Peterson, Vice President (Wisconsin). Kruger was elected Chairman.

in diminishing security requirements so that between forty to fifty per cent of the work was not classified, that the basic research/programmatic research dichotomy was one people had difficulty defining, and that the elimination of "red tape" was something everyone wanted. What was needed, Boyce maintained, was analysis of these problems in order to rectify them.

None of this, of course, spoke to the real issue, which was authority. The position of the Midwest Cosmotron Group was always clear on this. Zinn and Boyce could be equally clear. The strategic response Boyce offered was that if a separate accelerator were built in the Midwest the Laboratory would have failed in fulfilling its purpose as a regional research center. The argument had unstated secondary conclusions. If Argonne had failed, then the Council and its Executive Board had also failed. This was not lost on the Executive Board, several of whose members felt that they and their schools had closer ties to Argonne than to the still amorphous Midwest Cosmotron Group.

Boyce broadened the attempt to persuade people that Argonne was the best answer. In July, he sent an informational letter to the physics departments of the thirty-two participating schools. His account of the origins of the accelerator movement and its progress was slanted toward giving the impression that the Laboratory had been the originator and prime sponsor. His letter also ignored the early divisiveness and its reasons. "Certain members of the group," he wrote without explanation, "are strongly opposed to this [Argonne] location and prefer that the whole project should be quite independent of the Laboratory. The prospect of immediate funds being so small, it seems more important now that technical problems rather than geographic or administrative ones be given priority."

Boyce's internal position, the one he adopted with Zinn, was not much different. He claimed not to understand why some people objected so strongly to locating the accelerator at Argonne; he felt that the Laboratory should push an accelerator only if there were "enthusiastic support" from the universities. Should the Midwest group be unable to find support outside the AEC, he said, the Laboratory should cooperate under the terms Johnson had outlined, with the clear understanding that if the machine were located at Argonne it would operate under the Laboratory's administration.

A more aggressive policy was advocated by Willard F. Libby, of the University of Chicago's Institute for Nuclear Studies. Libby, who was a member of both the General Advisory Committee and the Council Executive Board, wrote Zinn urging him to have the

Laboratory go its own way. "Grasp this firmly," he wrote, "and appoint Livingood to head accelerator work." Libby believed that a positive approach would consolidate the effort around Argonne. The Commission, according to him, was not supporting an accelerator for the Midwest because of the "dissaffection" and "illness" that had become so evident. Libby felt that the Commission would build an accelerator in the Midwest only if it were at Argonne or under Argonne's auspices. The reasons, while mainly financial, he wrote, were also motivated by a desire to make the relations with the Participating Institutions "more significant and useful." The way Libby explained it, Zinn owed it to the Midwest to start an accelerator program at Argonne, around which, Libby predicted, "everyone would rapidly rally."

Zinn did not immediately take up the challenge. At the Council Executive Board meeting in early October, he took the position that though the Laboratory was anxious to have the accelerator, he did not think it should "properly attempt to obtain the machine in the face of the considerable opposition which had been shown by the Midwest group." Moreover, he thought that the Commission's recent authorization of a 25 Bev machine for Brookhaven precluded starting another accelerator for several years.

Libby and John C. Warner, who was also a member of the General Advisory Committee, said that the GAC felt otherwise. David Saxe of the Chicago Operations Office said that he understood that the Research Division would support a machine at Argonne. At the end of the meeting, the Board adopted an ambiguous resolution that said go ahead without saying in what way.

THEREFORE the Executive Board of the Council of Participating Institutions strongly urges that the Argonne National Laboratory take a vigorous positive position in support of the project for the design, construction, and operation of a Cosmotron in the Middle West. The Laboratory should also strongly seek the cooperation of the Midwest Cosmotron Group now actively engaged in solving basic problems in the design of such machines. To accomplish this, the Laboratory should offer the services of competent physicists and engineers from its staff and should arrange an acceptable administrative organization for guiding the design, construction, and operation of the machine.

Part of the reason for the ambiguity was that Kruger, one of the Cosmotron Group's leaders, was still a member of the Executive Board.[7]

Zinn, told to be positive, was. Livingood and M. Hamermesh began an "Indoctrination Course on Cosmotrons," the purpose of which was to upgrade the Laboratory staff prior to bringing in experts from universities and other laboratories. Simultaneously, Boyce began to plan for giving visiting physicists open access to the library, the cafeteria, and the seminar rooms. Livingood's first lecture on Cosmotrons was given the same day that the formal Organization Committee that would lead to MURA met for the first time.

In mid-December, the Argonne Advisory Committee* came into the picture. According to Zinn, the Committee unanimously recommended that he undertake those steps within his power to:

1. bring about a Cosmotron in the Midwest,

2. establish an accelerator group at the Laboratory whose ultimate purpose is to bring about the construction of a Cosmotron at the Laboratory with AEC funds,

3. attempt to arrange for a combined effort with the Midwest Cosmotron Group.

That this was unanimous, as Zinn claimed, is dubious since Kruger was at the time a member of the Advisory Committee. He resigned in February, claiming a conflict with his position as a member of the Organization Committee of the Midwest Cosmotron Group.

Zinn sent a proposal to T. H. Johnson on January 27, 1954, specifically asking permission to alter the Laboratory budget for fiscal 1954 and fiscal 1955 to allow a group of eight to ten people to begin accelerator studies under Livingood's direction. The cost would be about $225,000. Zinn promised to "explore means by which this group can work with the Midwest Cosmotron Group." He had been assured, he wrote, that physicists from the University of Chicago would participate. Zinn, however, made it clear that the ultimate objective was a specific proposal to build a Cosmotron at Argonne. "I could not have any considerable interest," he concluded, "in setting up this group with the intention of having it assist in the construction of a Cosmotron elsewhere. I feel very strongly that if the AEC is to construct a Cosmotron in the Midwest

---

*In addition to the Council Executive Board's nominees, E. E. Dreese (Ohio State) and P. G. Kruger (Illinois), members included Ovid W. Eshbach (Northwestern), Enrico Fermi (Chicago), Lawrence A. Hyland (Bendix Aviation Corporation), Cecil M. Watson (Minnesota), and John E. Willard (Wisconsin).

and is to support Argonne, the needs of all would be best served by having the machine at this location."[8]

What happened to Zinn over the next two months exemplifies why administrators grow old rapidly. On February 1, Zinn received a phone call from Washington and then wrote a memorandum to his file. "Dr. [T. H.] Johnson has received my Cosmotron letter. He indicated that his division would react favorably." On February 12, Zinn received another phone call and wrote his file another memorandum:

> Dr. Johnson is writing me a letter in which he, General Nichols [the same General Nichols from the days of the Manhattan Project and now the AEC's General Manager], Dr. Hafstad, Dr. Henry Smyth, and Dr. J. C. Bugher [Director of the Division of Biology and Medicine] have all agreed to these points on the Cosmotron:
>
> *a.* They will not commit themselves now to try to get the money for a Midwest Cosmotron at any time in the future.
>
> *b.* They do commit themselves now that if they can ever have the money it will be for a Cosmotron to be built at Argonne.
>
> *c.* The study that I proposed is being authorized provided it does not require additional funds in fiscal 1954 and 1955.

On February 26, Johnson sent Zinn a copy of a letter he was sending to the Chicago Operations Office saying all the above a little more circumspectly and adding a paragraph on the importance of a favorable research environment. "Future planning will therefore depend in substantial measure upon the success realized during the ensuing months in enlisting the interest and cooperation of the Midwest accelerator scientists in the Argonne program." There was one small hitch. Johnson was sending the letter prior to receiving approval for transmittal. His haste was so Zinn could have it in hand on March 1, when he was to meet with the Council Executive Board. That day Johnson called Zinn and retracted the letter. At the Executive Board meeting Zinn reported that he had made the proposal and that, according to the minutes, "negotiations are in progress but a formal authorization has not yet been received."

On March 8, Johnson wrote rather succinctly:

> In response to your letter of January 27, I have had further discussions of the Midwest accelerator with Drs. Smyth, Nichols, Bugher, and Hafstad. We felt unanimously that if we were to

recommend an accelerator in the Midwest it would be for the Argonne. However, until we can see more clearly that such an accelerator should be built I am not prepared to authorize the initiation of the design study project proposed in your letter.

Zinn came right back. He wrote Johnson that he wished to raise a question "before giving wider distribution to your decision." Since the accelerator proposed was approved by the several groups that advised the management of the Laboratory, "the inference will be quickly drawn that the Atomic Energy Commission is not much interested in having a university participating program at Argonne." Zinn then proposed to interpret the decision as "an indication that we should attempt to draw up a brief indicating why a Midwest accelerator is a necessity." But he would do so only if it were "what is needed in order to permit a decision on the larger question."

Johnson replied, "The General Manager still has this question under study and I would suggest withholding, if possible, your report to your advisory groups that your proposal has been rejected." The reason he offered was that General Nichols was interested in seeing the report of the National Science Foundation's newly formed Advisory Panel on Ultrahigh Energy Nuclear Accelerators.[9]

The use of the Participating Institutions as a lever to hold off a final negative decision was not entirely unwarranted. The Executive Board at its March 1 meeting and the Council at its March 2 meeting had spent a great deal of time discussing the ramifications of the accelerator issue. "The time had come," the Board reported, "for a reexamination of the place of the Participating Institutions Program." The Board supported building the Cosmotron at the Laboratory, and spoke about making its own role more important. Hafstad had come to the Council meeting. "Any criticism that ANL is not a suitable site for the Cosmotron," he said, four years after he had engineered the Hafstad Charter, "implies that it is not doing properly one of the jobs for which it was established." Kruger stood alone at these meetings, reiterating again the desire of the Midwestern Cosmotron Group for a Brookhaven organizational pattern in which the schools, acting through a Board of Trustees, hired the Director, chose the site, and controlled the operation of the accelerator.

The NSF Panel did little to resolve the issue. Its May 2 report, the first in a series of attempts to clarify priorities in the building of high energy machines, was far too general to point a clear path. The most specific recommendation was Number 6—"That no fixed general policy be made with regard to the location of new accelerators at individual universities, national laboratories or other research establishments, but that each proposal in the future be reviewed on its merits. . . ." As an addendum, the panel made easy access by qualified scientists from other organizations a criterion for choosing sites.[10]

Four days after the NSF report was issued, Kruger, as Chairman of Midwest Universities Research Association (MURA), requested a meeting with the Commission (it was referred to in Commission literature as an "audience") to discuss financing an accelerator. The response of the General Manager, K. D. Nichols, was to have Johnson prepare a formal proposal for the Commission recommending that they authorize Argonne to start a design study of "a high energy accelerator which might satisfy the needs of the Midwest region." This proposal, AEC document 603/17, was circulated to the Commission for a decision during the week of June 7. The MURA people were scheduled to meet with Nichols on June 10.

The argument presented in the Johnson proposal harked back to the original concept of developing Argonne as a regional laboratory, a concept that General Nichols himself had been working toward during the last days of the Manhattan District.

"If the Laboratory has fallen short of its goal in this respect," the report argued, "while winning its laurels in the field of reactor technology, it does not necessarily follow that the plan was unreasonable and should now be given up." This section concluded:

If ANL should now be allowed to embark on an accelerator study it would have a new opportunity to demonstrate its adaptability to the role of a regional laboratory. Any other course would further alienate the midwest scientists from the Argonne and it would be difficult in the future to return to the original plan. On the other hand if developments during the next few years indicate that ANL will be fully occupied with reactor projects and that a new site for a high energy laboratory is preferable, that choice can be made with unanimity.[11]

The Commission approved the proposal. When Nichols met with the MURA group on June 10, he told them either to cooperate with Argonne or get no machine. When the MURA people raised the possibility of an AUI Brookhaven-type management for Argonne, they were told that the AEC would not "close its mind to the possibility," but that the AEC was in no way critical of the management being provided by the University of Chicago. The

MURA people, faced with no alternative, agreed to meet with ANL and University of Chicago representatives as soon as possible to see if a cooperative arrangement could be worked out.[12]

The unsuccessful MURA attempt to get AEC support had been a scene played to the side of much more dramatic events. Nichols delivered his ultimatum to MURA on June 10, 1954. On June 12, he wrote a letter refusing J. Robert Oppenheimer's appeal of the majority decision of the AEC's Personnel Security Board. On June 29, the Commission, led by Chairman Lewis Strauss, concurred with Nichol's opinion that "Dr. Oppenheimer's clearance should not be reinstated." Only Commissioner H. D. Smyth dissented.*

The Oppenheimer case, the lengthy hearing in April and May of 1954, which gave portentous meaning to the innocuous phrase "In the Matter of . . . ," was the peak in a security-phobic period. Julius and Ethel Rosenberg had been executed in June 1953 for transmitting nuclear secrets. The investigation of "subversion" at Fort Monmouth by Senator Joseph McCarthy, that would lead to his own condemnation by the Senate at year's end, was underway. More than two thousand federal employees, President Eisenhower announced in his State of the Union message, had been "separated" from the government during 1953. Visas to visit America and passports to leave it received special attention if the applicant was a scientist.

The phobia during Eisenhower's first two years in office ran parallel to movements exactly opposite in spirit. The Joint Committee prepared a revision of the Atomic Energy Act that became law in August of 1954. It increased industrial participation in the development of nuclear power, permitted international cooperation on peaceful applications, and loosened restrictions on the availability of technical information. The new law made possible the implementation of Eisenhower's "Atoms For Peace" proposal, which would eventually populate underdeveloped nations with research reactors and, more significantly, gave impetus to the development of nuclear engineering at American universities.

Internationally, CERN, the European Organization for Nuclear Research, EURATOM, and the International Atomic Energy Agency were being organized during this period. Public attention, however, focused on weapons. Russia exploded its first H-bomb in

---

*Two hundred and fourteen Argonne scientists also dissented. They had written a letter to the Commission expressing their concern, as government-employed scientists, that "unpopular" or "unwise" decisions would now be labeled "disloyal."

August of 1953, while in March 1954, fallout from the United States' tests in the Pacific caused radiation injuries to twenty-eight American participants, twenty-three Japanese fishermen on the *Fukuryu Maru* (Lucky Dragon), and two hundred thirty-six Marshallese from the nearby islands of Rongelap and Utirik.

The Atomic Energy Commission had its preoccupations in subsequent months. The Oppenheimer hearings left a legacy that is still being analyzed and judged. The fallout in the Pacific caused protests and concern about the carefulness of the Commission's self-regulation. The AEC even got itself into another perennial controversy, public versus private power, when it transferred a contract to purchase electricity from TVA to a power group that came to be known as Dixon-Yates.

In competition with such rich dramas, the struggle to gain a larger accelerator installation in the Midwest for research of a most basic nature seemed a problem that could certainly be resolved in friendly cooperation.

CHAPTER 8

ANL versus MURA

Walter Zinn announced the Commission's authorization of an accelerator design study to the Council Executive Board in a letter on June 17, 1954. He outlined the steps he proposed to take to implement the authorization, both those he could take independently and those that required the cooperation of MURA. Internally, at Argonne, he was going to establish a Study Group, headed by John Livingood and including five scientists from the Laboratory and five from the Participating Institutions. The group would be given space in an "open" area to eliminate visiting problems, except for "aliens."

His proposals for cooperation with what he still called "the Midwest Cosmotron Group" reiterated former positions: that the Cosmotron Group be established as a separate division of the Laboratory; that the head of the division be appointed by the Laboratory after "soliciting suggestions" from the Council Executive Board and the Midwest Cosmotron Group; that the technical direction of the Cosmotron project be delegated to the division director; that a Technical Steering Committee be created to provide liaison with the Participating Institutions to aid and advise the director of the Cosmotron Division and "to report to the Director of Argonne on the adequacy of the program."

Most members of the Board replied to Zinn's letter by indicating their unreserved approval. C. L. Critchfield, a physicist from Minnesota, approved, provided the "tentative nature" of the proposals for cooperating with MURA was made clear. John C. Warner, President of Carnegie Institute of Technology, approved and suggested that an attempt be made to explain the situation to the presidents of some of the MURA schools in order to make certain they understood the problems of establishing good relations with the Cosmotron group. Only P. G. Kruger was perturbed, and he asked for a special meeting of the Council Executive Board. It was arranged for July 8, when the General Advisory Committee would also be meeting at Argonne, thus assuring that Warner and Libby could come. On the day before, July 7, Zinn took the first of the independent steps he had proposed and officially established an Accelerator Study Group within the Physics Division of Argonne.

The purpose of the July 8 meeting, as stated by Libby, was to consider the external proposals by Zinn for cooperating with MURA. The issue went quickly from Kruger's assertion that the proposed Technical Steering Committee had no authority and no responsibility to his proposal that a Brookhaven-AUI type of management be established for all of Argonne instead of the contract with the University of Chicago. When Kruger received no support from his fellow board members, he retreated to seeking a means for controlling only the accelerator. Again he received no support, and the board passed a motion, with Kruger abstaining, "That Mr. Zinn go ahead to explore cooperation with the Midwestern Group along the lines of his letter of June 17." The vehicle would be a joint meeting of the Council Executive Board, the MURA Board, representatives from Argonne, the University of Chicago, and the AEC's Chicago Operations Office.[1]

The gala affair, held on July 16 and attended by no fewer than twenty-four people, represented an impressive amount of scientific and administrative talent. The result of the meeting was total impasse; Zinn and Kruger would communicate with one another in the indefinite future if and when they had something to communicate. To reach this inconclusive end, the group spent four hours, interrupted by lunch, in circuitous discussion. Zinn's proposal turned out to be "only a suggestion" that was nonnegotiable. MURA's counter-proposals ranged from a subcontract from Argonne to build and operate the accelerator to a primary contract from the AEC for operating all of Argonne in lieu of the University of Chicago. There are five written versions of this particular meeting, each representing a different point of view as to what was important. The negative results, however, are made clear in each. The only accomplishment was a hardening of positions. The MURA people wanted control of the accelerator by the operating physicists. Zinn wanted no second authority on Argonne land. The AEC wanted the accelerator at Argonne. The Council Executive Board wanted to retain its semblance of participation. The University of Chicago wanted its prime contract.[2]

The direct attack on the University of Chicago's role brought forth a policy statement from the University that it would carry out whatever administrative changes were required by the Council

Executive Board that were within the framework of the contract with the AEC, and that it would seek AEC approval of those changes that were not permissible under the contract.

Zinn formally submitted his earlier proposals to Kruger on August 4. They were politely and formally rejected on October 1 by the MURA Board of Directors. Kruger promised to send Zinn a counter-proposal if one could be formulated and hoped that technical cooperation would continue. Since MURA had a virtual monopoly on high-energy physicists in the Midwest, members from the University of Chicago and Northwestern being the exception, it was to the Laboratory's advantage to continue the technical liaison.

The administrative impasse became more impassable. MURA incorporated; Kruger resigned from the Council Executive Board. Lewis Strauss, Chairman of the AEC, sent A. L. Hughes (Washington University), the Acting Chairman of the Council (he had replaced Willard Libby, who was now an AEC Commissioner), a letter clearly stating that the Commission intended to build the accelerator at Argonne.

> . . . The Commission would hardly be consistent with its stated objectives for Argonne, nor would it be keeping faith with the staff at Argonne and the many midwestern institutions which have contributed to its growth and success, if it were to establish a major particle accelerator research center elsewhere in the Midwest than at Argonne.

All that was needed before construction could begin at the Laboratory was a little consistency with the national interest. The Council Executive Board appointed J. C. Warner as an ad hoc committee of one to work with the University of Chicago to resolve the Argonne/MURA problem. The MURA technical group held a meeting at Argonne under security restrictions. Six young physicists from the University of Chicago offered to jump over the administrative disagreement if an operational agreement could be reached. They proposed to work on an accelerator at Argonne provided: three-fourths of the scientific personnel on the project were university faculty; access to the Laboratory was not limited by security or nationality requirements; faculty were free to bring students.[3]

Negotiations for resolving the impasse began in December 1954, and were a year in concluding. On December 6, Warner and L. A. Kimpton, the Chancellor of The University of Chicago, met with the presidents of several MURA schools. The result was to ask the MURA physicists to prepare a position paper.* This document, entitled "The Desirable Conditions for a Midwest Laboratory," began with the basic premise that "the desirable laboratory derives its strength and vigor from the participation of university and college research departments in the Midwest." It concluded by taking a "firm stand that both responsibility and authority for the operation of a cooperative laboratory should be vested in the universities which are to use it." The summary listed six conditions: 1) commitment to fundamental research; 2) minimal security regulations since all the work should be unclassified except under extraordinary circumstances; 3) free access; 4) majority of scientists must be university faculty; 5) community living facilities; 6) the universities "must have adequate control of the project."

This document became the central point for future discussions. By implication, it asserted that Argonne was not desirable because it possessed the opposite characteristics. The major problem was the definition of "adequate" control. It was Samuel Allison's opinion that contractual or financial responsibility could be separated from technical responsibility, but this was a long-standing illusion of people who tried to mediate between the Laboratory and MURA. Zinn and Kruger both understood that authority meant just that and nothing less. When the Council Executive Board met on January 17, 1955, it discussed the "Desirable Conditions" document with Zinn. His responses were to claim that points one through five were already being met by the Laboratory and to reject the possibility of point six—control by the universities. Zinn would accept no mechanism for implementing point six other than his proposal of a Technical Committee advisory to him, an idea that already had been rejected by MURA. Following the discussion, the Council Executive Board went into executive session. What came out was an ambiguous document that appeared to support Zinn's organizational suggestion while at the same time it expressed a desire to satisfy the six requirements of MURA. The Executive Board suggested that two meetings be held, the first a meeting of the presidents of the MURA schools and the second the presidents of the participating institutions. It was further suggested that subsequent to these meetings, Zinn create a new administrative position, Research Director,

---

*The authors were S. K. Allison (Chicago), H. R. Crane (Michigan), R. H. Hildebrand (Chicago), D. W. Kerst (Illinois), J. K. Knipp (Iowa State College), K. R. Symon (Wayne), and J. H. Williams (Minnesota), Chairman.

the holder of which would "also have prime responsibility for the development of the accelerator."

Zinn did not respond to this proposal for three months, and when he did, it was with a sense of pessimism, indignation, and impatience. He felt that meetings of presidents of universities would not bring about a working arrangement. He also felt that the appointment of a Research Director, who would be required to head the accelerator group, would dilute the accelerator work. More importantly, the idea that a Research Director was needed implied that the basic research of the Laboratory was negligible, quantitatively and qualitatively. Zinn protested this and offered to have staff presentations made to the Executive Board. His final thrust was to say that the Laboratory's accelerator program was being hampered by the delay in setting up a Steering Committee, and that he proposed to take steps to obtain such a committee, with or without MURA, as soon as the Board had met in May.

Zinn's delay in answering was paralleled by an inability of the university presidents to arrange the suggested meetings. A meeting of Kimpton of Chicago with Presidents Hancher of the University of Iowa, Morrill of Minnesota, and Warner of Carnegie Institute of Technology finally occurred on April 13. Out of it came only the agreement that more proposals for cooperation would be proposed.[4]

On May 6, MURA submitted to the AEC its "Proposal for Cooperative Research in High Energy Physics Through the Establishment of a Laboratory in the Middle West Which Will Serve Best the Educational and Scientific Needs of That Area," a title with all the flavor of the eighteenth-century "Projectors."* The proposal called for building a 20-Bev Mark V accelerator, based on the Fixed-Field Alternating Gradient principle, at a cost of $17.3 million to be spent over a five-year period. T. H. Johnson, the AEC Director of Research, refused to consider it "unless the Argonne Laboratory is in the picture." He advised Kruger to work with Zinn through the Council of Participating Institutions.

Johnson's rejection was sent two days after the Council Executive Board had finally concluded that MURA and ANL could not

*"Projectors" were forever devising schemes to improve society. Daniel Defoe, in his Essay on Projects, exemplifies the more reputable "projectors." The more infamous floated stock promotions with titles like: "Company for creating and maintaining certain engines for raising sand and stones out of rivers and harbours, for the better cleansing and the rendering the same more navigable," or "Company for erecting houses and hospitals for maintaining and educating bastard children, by which all the parishes of England will be eased of a vast charge."

cooperate at the administrative level. The Board also had decided that its own future responsibilities were intertwined with the question in ways that required it once again to contemplate its own relationship with the Laboratory. The members of the Board could not agree on the precise relation or solution. R. S. Shankland (Case Institute of Technology) proposed a separate Institute for Nuclear Studies within Argonne, run by a governing board chosen from the larger schools of the area. The Institute would initially be responsible for high energy work, but would gradually take over everything but reactor and development work. A. L. Hughes wanted to separate the Argonne-MURA deadlock from the Argonne-Participating Institutions problem. He felt that the Executive Board had allowed its own problems to affect its decisions on the MURA deadlock. Hughes wanted the Council Executive Board to have more direct responsibility for operating Argonne. H. L. Friedell (Western Reserve University) saw the MURA "dissidence" and the Participating Institutions' status as interlocking. MURA, he felt, had been organized because of the Participating Institutions' "lack of proper concern and responsibility." This was very different language from the acquiescence through which the Executive Board had come into existence five years earlier when L. R. Hafstad had insisted upon emasculating the Board of Governors. But Hafstad was no longer in the picture. He had left the AEC the previous January to join the Chase National Bank of New York.

In July 1955, Zinn sent a "preliminary proposal" to Johnson for development of an Argonne accelerator, a 25-Bev tandem machine based on the Fixed-Field Alternating Gradient principle that was being developed by MURA. The budget, which did not include construction costs, was $2.5 million. Zinn asked Johnson to review the proposal and give his "advice as to the appropriateness of submitting it." It was a fishing expedition to which Zinn received no answer.[5]

The reason for the silence was that other fishermen were also out, and in deeper waters. The President of the University of Michigan, Harlan Hatcher, acting on behalf of the MURA presidents, had formally requested a meeting between the Commissioners of the AEC and the presidents of the MURA schools plus Chancellor Kimpton of The University of Chicago. The purpose, he wrote, was "to explore the whole matter *de novo*." Commissioner Strauss set the date for August 3 and added to the participants the presidents of several non-MURA schools—Case Institute of Technology, Notre Dame, and Washington University. Strauss proposed that they meet without staff in order to have the freest discussion possible, but at the same time indicated that he wished to define the parameters of the discussion by the AEC's commitment to Argonne. "Can we suppose, therefore," he asked, "that our discussion will take place around the question, 'How can we create a center of basic research for the Midwest at the Argonne National Laboratory which will serve as a coordinated source of benefits to all concerned?'"

The meeting was attended by twelve college presidents from the Midwest, one comptroller, one dean, three AEC Commissioners (the other two, including Strauss, were in Geneva for the First International Conference on the Peaceful Uses of Nuclear Energy), and the new General Manager, Kenneth E. Fields.* The meeting began with a statement by Commissioner Libby of the AEC's position, that it would not be desirable to construct a second national laboratory in the Midwest, that any regionally based accelerator would have to be at Argonne. President Hatcher led the opposition.

Hatcher: The Midwestern situation was different from that on the East and West Coasts, particularly Brookhaven. The Midwestern universities were primarily interested in developing a similarly productive arrangement with the AEC along essentially the same lines. Specifically, would the AEC support a high energy accelerator in a cooperative research center?

Kimpton (Chicago): The question of constructing a high energy accelerator has become the symbol of the universities' interest in the broad question of developing a satisfactory relationship with the AEC.

Libby (Acting Chairman of the AEC): The AEC has a big investment in Argonne; it would like very much to make the Laboratory the center of Midwestern basic research. There basic work and development work could flourish side by side.

Glennan (Case Institute): Argonne's reactor development program, which is highly classified, did not encourage close relationships.

Hovde (Purdue): Scientists now apparently have no effective means of bringing about cooperative contacts.

Kimpton: There unquestionably exists a prejudice against

---

*The university representatives were Herbert O. Farber (Comptroller, Illinois), Edwin B. Fred (Wisconsin), T. Keith Glennan (Case), Virgil M. Hancher (University of Iowa), Harlan H. Hatcher (Michigan), T. M. Hesburgh, C.S.C. (Notre Dame), James H. Hilton (Iowa State College), F. L. Hovde (Purdue), Lawrence A. Kimpton (Chicago), James L. Morrill (Minnesota), Esthan A. H. Shepley (Washington), J. C. Warner (Carnegie), Herman B. Wells (Indiana), and Dean Donald Loughridge of Northwestern. The Commissioners were Libby, Thomas Murray, and J. von Neumann.

Argonne on the part of universities, and this prejudice is mutual to some extent.

Morrill (Minnesota): Continuing the present relationship would not be satisfactory. A major reorganization of the Laboratory would be required if it is to become the center of Midwestern research.

Kimpton: If a high-energy particle accelerator is built at Argonne, a separate division of Argonne would be established. A Steering Committee could be established that would advise and assist the director of the new division. The Steering Committee would have two executive tasks: to approve the design of the accelerator; to approve the scheduling of research. In all other matters, it would advise and assist. Similar arrangements could be set up in other fields. The important question really was what depends on the good will of the director, what on the good will of the committee.

Wells (Indiana): We do not like dependence on good will.

Hatcher: We want a Brookhaven-type of organization.

Hesburgh (Notre Dame): A proper research environment could be obtained by the universities assuming responsibility for the Laboratory's programs.

All of the Presidents (except Kimpton): Independent management!

Hatcher: Propose that a committee of University presidents and Commission staff recommend a solution.

All: Agreed.

Kimpton: I could not approve any steps which might adversely affect the continued success of the Laboratory's operation.

The next day Hatcher wrote Commissioner Libby to say that the presidents had become a committee of the whole with Warner, Hovde, and Kimpton as a drafting subcommittee. While a solution was not yet obvious, the unanimity of the opposition to the existing administration was. Argonne, and with it the University of Chicago, had become isolated from the other schools. Kimpton's presence on the subcommittee was a mechanism for ending that isolation as painlessly as possible.[6]

To Zinn, the future seemed apparent. He told Strauss that he would resign, but at Strauss's insistence held back the formal letter pending Commission proposals to resolve the situation his way. "I must reaffirm," he wrote Strauss, "that the creation of two separate operating organizations at this location is not something of which I wish to be a part."

Strauss countered with a phone call. "Would Zinn stay on if the AEC established an accelerator elsewhere?" Zinn responded that the establishment of laboratories was the Commission's business, not his. What concerned him was whether such a decision would exclude Argonne from building an accelerator.[7]

On November 8, 1955, four presidents (Hatcher of Michigan, Hovde of Purdue, Father Hesburgh of Notre Dame, and Kimpton) met with Commissioners Libby, von Neumann, and Strauss. Libby announced the proposed compromise—a second major accelerator installation that would be separate from Argonne. Argonne, however, would also get an accelerator. The proposal was specifically tied to competition with Russia, which was currently building a 15-Bev machine which, when it operated, was expected to be the world's largest. The Commission proposed that Argonne build a 12-Bev machine on a crash program. It would be an enlarged version of Brookhaven's 3-Bev machine, which had been operating for three years. Thus, according to Strauss, the problem was one of scale rather than design. The Argonne machine, which would be ready in three years, would answer short-range needs. On the other hand, the Midwestern universities would be asked to "start planning the best accelerator the world has ever seen." Strauss called it the "Dream of the World's Finest." Location, Libby said, was not a problem. It did not have to be at Argonne, though they hoped it would be near. The presidents, including Kimpton, agreed with the proposal. Hatcher pushed for a clear picture of the AEC's attitude toward MURA, but the Commissioners adopted a "hands-off, that's-up-to-the-schools" attitude. "Is MURA the organization the AEC wants to operate the new accelerator facility?" Hatcher asked. "It's the type of organization," was the best answer Strauss would give.

Five days later, on Sunday, November 13, a large, formal peace gathering was held at the University of Chicago with nine presidents, the MURA board, physicists from the MURA schools, and AEC staff. The AEC proposal was presented by Commissioner Libby. President Hatcher then posed four questions to the MURA board:

1. Did MURA accept the AEC proposal to design "a dream machine"?

2. Did MURA accept a proposal for a joint six-member committee of university presidents and MURA board members to represent the various groups in continued negotiation with the AEC?

3. Was MURA prepared to present budgetary requests to the AEC?

4. What action did MURA wish to take on a site?

The MURA people then met separately in two groups, the physicists first and then the entire Board. They returned to report that they had unanimously agreed "to assume the responsibility for the design, construction, and operation of a 'dream' machine in the Midwest, with the understanding that the presidents of the universities involved will support this action. . . ."

The six-man negotiating committee was formed on the spot—J. Williams, H. Farber, and A. W. Peterson from MURA; Hovde, Hancher, and Warner from the presidents. Hatcher announced "that a Midwestern universities association would be established in the fullest sense of the term." Allison said the Chicago physicists wanted to join MURA. Kimpton said he hoped Chicago would become a member. The AEC representatives then returned to the meeting and expressed their satisfaction. Libby hoped that the Midwest universities would continue to support programs at Argonne. There is no record of a pipe having passed around the table.[8]

Official action was taken by the Commission on November 23. Strauss wrote Hovde, who was chairman of the six-man MURA-presidents committee, that Argonne would be asked to build an accelerator as soon as possible to "give us program superiority over the Russians during the next dozen years or so." MURA would be asked to intensify its work "looking forward to the construction of what we all hope will be for many years the world's finest accelerator." The selection of site, he said, should be deferred until authorization by Congress. He concluded by asking for development budgets.

The peace was not deeply rooted. Kimpton, Harrell, Zinn, and Livingood immediately went to Washington to see Strauss in order to try to modify the Laboratory's assignment—to build a beefed-up Cosmotron—which Zinn and Livingood did not feel was reasonable. Technically, such a machine would be halfway between what already existed, the 6-Bev machine at Berkeley, and what was already under construction at Brookhaven, a 25-Bev machine. They wanted to build for the higher energies—either 15 or, preferably, 25 Bev. On the policy side, Zinn tried to have a reservation placed in any instructions to MURA, which would make it clear that construction of a MURA accelerator was contingent upon a review of its technical feasibility. Without this, Zinn felt, the Laboratory would be in an unfavorable position in recruiting staff. There were other bickerings. When a special meeting of the Council Executive Board was called on December 7, Zinn declined to come on the grounds that he had no clear statement on a Commission decision on the accelerators. Harrell reported on what he termed the "current trend

of AEC thinking," essentially a review of the two-accelerator proposal that had actually been approved by all concerned. The Board
then held an introspective discussion that progressed through six
issues:

1. Can the Board make any recommendation until this question of the nature of the Argonne accelerator is settled?

2. What are the chances that a big machine will be built at
Argonne—and, if so, to what extent will university physicists
participate in its construction and use?

3. Is there technical manpower for two large accelerator projects in the Middle West?

4. Could not the Laboratory render its present types of services to the university communities without the present formal
Participating Institutions Program?

5. What is the future of MURA?

6. Should the Council Executive Board resign?

The discussion departed from the pattern of earlier discussions
in that the role of the University of Chicago was increasingly questioned, i.e., did Chicago really want participation or did it want
Argonne to be its own special bailiwick? The Executive Board
moved that the University of Chicago appoint an ad hoc committee
to study the future relationships between Argonne National Laboratory and the university community. They hoped for a report by
July 1956.[9]

During the next several months, there were numerous public
announcements that let everyone in on what many people already
knew. The AEC announced the funding of both the Argonne and
the MURA design groups.[10] Zinn submitted a letter of resignation to
Harrell on January 27, and it was accepted "with sincere regret" on
February 7, to be effective June 30.

Three years of bickering and infighting were over. Zinn, the
principal protagonist, was leaving the scene. It must have appeared
to the MURA people that they had won a substantial victory and
were on the way to having a Midwest research center controlled by
the universities. The Council Executive Board was about to experience a second study of the relationship between the schools and
Argonne. In the three years during which this dispute had evolved,
the Laboratory had settled into its own routines. The CP-5 research reactor had begun operating in 1955. The total staff had

dropped from three thousand to twenty-five hundred, but the scientific staff had grown to thirteen hundred. The number of summer faculty was up to thirty-eight. The reactor development program had many accomplishments. Idaho, with its boiling water reactor experiment, was a fact. Borax-III, as it was called, had even supplied the town of Arco with electricity before the reactor was purposefully destroyed in an experiment to calculate the extent to which reactors could "run away." Nuclear propulsion of submarines was a bigger fact. The *Nautilus* made its maiden voyage in 1955, and eight more submarines were being built. The development of electricity-producing reactors, while not pursued as aggressively as the Joint Committee on Atomic Energy would have liked, was opened to private utilities through a civilian power reactor program. At Shippingport, Pennsylvania, the first large pressurized water reactor was being built to demonstrate the practicality of nuclear power. Construction permits had been issued for two more utility-owned reactors, one in Illinois, the other in Massachusetts.

Private ownership of power reactors had been made possible by the Atomic Energy Act of 1954. This major revision of the McMahon Bill had also strengthened the role of the Joint Committee by giving it the authority to approve all AEC appropriations for acquiring property and for building facilities, a power that established the Committee as a court to which the development decisions of the Commission could be appealed. At the time, the relevance to particle accelerators was not apparent. The two machines in the Midwest had entered the design phase. There was continued backbiting, but it did not really matter since everyone assumed that he was going to get what he wanted. The bitterness and the organizational hassles would not reappear until it was time to request funds for actually building the yet-to-be-determined multi-Bev machine.

The Council Executive Board in this period of relative quiet undertook to set its own realities straight.

CHAPTER 9

The Rettaliata Report

The committee to reexamine the relationship between Argonne and the university community was appointed on March 23, 1956. It had a representative membership—a professor from the University of Chicago, a division director and a scientist from the Laboratory, three members of the Council Executive Board, and as chairman the President of Illinois Institute of Technology, John T. Rettaliata, a man who fit the criteria established for the job, i.e., he "had not previously had any active connection with either the Laboratory, the MURA group, or the Participating Institutions Program." *

The University of Chicago set up the committee reluctantly. At the Executive Board meeting on March 16, Chancellor Kimpton expressed the hope that the Board would develop plans for more effective university participation. Harrell was blunter. He asked if, in light of Zinn's pending resignation, the Board would reconsider its request for an *ad hoc* committee. The answer was "no," and for emphasis, the Board suggested an appropriate composition for the committee. As a second gesture toward establishing a new role in Argonne affairs, the Board also established a subcommittee to discuss the candidates for the directorship with Harrell.

The charge to the Rettaliata Committee, as it was soon called, was general, a request to review and recommend, but with the promise that its recommendations would receive attention. "We shall use our best efforts," Kimpton wrote Rettaliata, "to provide effective implementation."[1]

*The committee members were H. L. Friedell (Western Reserve), J. H. Jensen (Iowa State), and Robert S. Shankland (Case Institute) from the Council Executive Board, Stephen Lawroski and Oliver Simpson from Argonne, Mark Inghram from the Physics Department at the University of Chicago, and Rettaliata.

84

The first task the Rettaliata Committee set for itself was to solicit comments, to take an opinion poll from university presidents and Council members.

"I do remember quite well when our . . . relationships with Argonne were originally established and when we had high hopes of these which subsequent developments disappointed."

". . . Very satisfactory. . . ."

". . . So-called Participating Institutions had no part whatever in the participating program."

". . . Good for the Midwest. . . ."

". . . Universities have no real stake in the operation. . . ."

". . . Pleased. . . ."

"In the original thinking . . . the Laboratory would be a focal point for Midwest nuclear scientists to work on problems of their own design using the research facilities of the Laboratory. However, this appears never to have been the case."

"Very pleased."

"The Council of Participating Institutions is a travel and listen group."

"There is nothing not adequately handled."

The positive responses were mostly from smaller schools or from departments, such as medicine, within the larger schools, whose needs and aspirations were significantly less than those of the larger MURA schools and the physicists. Balanced and weighed, the responses were of little value. The Committee was essentially dependent on its own internal views.

The Committee members from the Council Executive Board had the dominant opinions. J. H. Jensen, who was Provost of Iowa State College, offered a maxim that is proverbial among university administrators—that any system will work if the people concerned want to make it work and that any system will fail if the people are not concerned with "fairness." His viewpoint essentially placed the burden for failure on the University of Chicago at the same time that it minimized the advantages of changing the present form of operation. Chicago, Jensen felt, should have seen to it that the Argonne Advisory Committee operated and functioned in a meaningful way. R. S. Shankland (Case Institute) similarly saw Chicago as a negative factor, but also included the AEC, which, he felt, had never made a clear commitment to the principle of university participation in Argonne. He felt a need for some structural changes that would improve the likelihood of participation, for example, that the policy-setting board meet not with the chief business officer of the University of Chicago but with the principal administrator—the Chancellor, that the Laboratory have an overall director who was not in charge of a particular development division the way Zinn had been in charge of reactor development, and that the Participating Institutions have an executive officer of their own supported by the AEC.[2]

The final report was a blending of these views. A year after the original request had been made, President Rettaliata put together his Committee's consensus. There were nine recommendations affecting three of the four parties to the Argonne complex.

For the Laboratory, the Committee recommended the creation of three associate directorships, one for education, one for research, and one for development. The Laboratory was also told to channel through the contractor, i.e., the University of Chicago, all communications of a major policy nature between the AEC and ANL. This Zinn had ceased to do. During his last years, he had been acting as an independent entity to the point that his initial moves to use the threat of resignation were made directly to the AEC's Chairman, Lewis Strauss. In the end, however, it was to Harrell that Zinn had to send his letter of resignation, and it was Harrell who accepted it.

Two other recommendations to the Laboratory were of the exhortative type—"to devote a proper proportion of the total effort to educational and fundamental research activities," and to "maintain close and cooperative relationships with the Participating Institutions." What was proper, close, and cooperative was not defined.

For the Participating Institutions there were two specifics and one exhortation—to have its own full-time staff administering its own "positive" program; to locate the staff at the Laboratory and support it with money from the schools and "other agencies;" to "maintain close and cooperative relationships with ANL."

The recommendation to the University of Chicago was that it create "a high-level correlating mechanism" between the Laboratory and the Participating Institutions called the Policy Advisory Board that would be advisory to the contractor and possess "a prominent voice in advising on matters of policy concerning the operation of the Laboratory." The Board would consist of nine people, five appointed by the Participating Institutions and four by the University of Chicago. The Chancellor of the University and the

Chairman of the Council of Participating Institutions would attend the quarterly meetings.

A flow chart at the end of the report showed where everyone would belong in the proposed hierarchy. There were lines of authority and lines of communication. It was the latter that connected the Laboratory to the Participating Institutions and the Participating Institutions, through the Policy Advisory Board, to the University of Chicago.[3]

The Rettaliata Committee made no recommendations to the AEC.

Kimpton called the Rettaliata Report "sound and constructive." "In my opinion," he wrote Shankland, "the report represents a significant contribution not only to the welfare of the Laboratory but to science and engineering in the Middle West."

The report was circulated, and the returns began to come in. The first significant response was from Alfonso Tammaro, now the AEC's Assistant General Manager for Research and Industrial Development. He reported that the Commission "welcomed" the report and its guidelines, was "particularly pleased" with the concept of a full-time staff for the schools, and was "interested" in the Policy Advisory Board. "In this connection, however, one word of caution is advisable," he wrote to Kimpton. "The Argonne National Laboratory is one of the principal instruments for implementing the United States atomic energy program. As in the past, the Commission will continue to direct the program and establish policies to be followed in many areas of research and development. We do feel, however, that there are many segments of the basic research program which can benefit from the counsel of the suggested board."

When Kimpton formally presented the Rettaliata Report to the Council Executive Board, there was little doubt the Board would approve it. After all, three prominent members had helped write it. Tammaro's letter, which Kimpton read to the Board, was the only sour note. Was Tammaro's letter, the Board members asked, "intended to declare a significant segment of the Laboratory program as being beyond the purview of the Policy Advisory Board?" Their own answer was yes, and with an acquiescence that was at least historically consistent they accepted their own answer. The minutes of the meeting report:

Although it was recognized that it was not appropriate for the Policy Advisory Board to intervene in the development program of the Laboratory, it was clear that the Policy Advisory Board must be kept informed of all major decisions in the de-

Relationship between Atomic Energy Commission, Contractor,
Argonne National Laboratory and Participating Institutions
(Rettaliata Report)

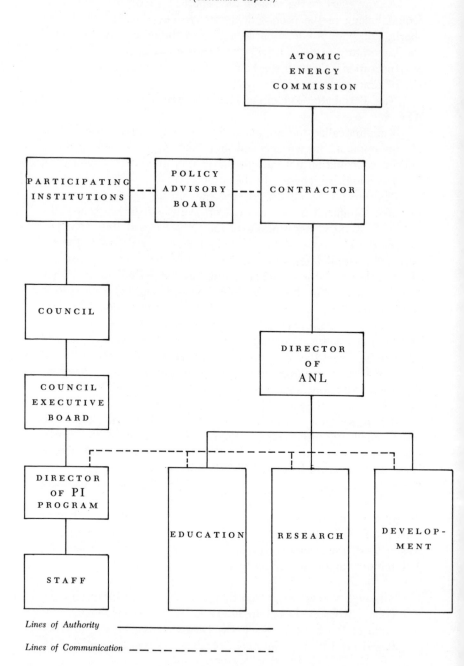

Lines of Authority ——————————

Lines of Communication — — — — — — — — — — —

velopment program. In this relationship, it would not be tolerable for the Policy Advisory Board to be kept in ignorance of major decisions. The Board expressed the hope that the Commission would make a clear statement on this point.

The desired statement was delivered by J. J. Flaherty, Manager of the Chicago Operations Office. He wrote:

> I . . . can assure you that it is not the AEC's intent to limit the scope of the policy board's interest in the program of the Laboratory. To be effective, such a board clearly must be empowered to look at all facets of the work. On the other hand, it should be equally clear that some portions of the work of the Laboratory are segments of a coordinated national development program on which the AEC sets target dates and assigns responsibilities. . . . I am sure that the University of Chicago, as contractor for the Laboratory, will welcome advice on all aspects of the Laboratory's program, but it should be equally clear that the University's ability to accept and act on the advice received is far more restricted in many areas of the development program assigned to the Laboratory than it is in the basic research program.

Flaherty offered to discuss the statement further "if the AEC attitude on this point is still not clear."

Clarity, however, was not a problem. Harrell wrote to J. H. Jensen, Chairman of the Executive Board, "We believe that we can function effectively under the interpretation of Mr. Tammaro's letter set forth in the letter from Mr. Flaherty. . . ." Harrell's view became the Board's view. In mid-April, the Rettaliata Report was sent to the presidents of the Council institutions and to Council members. A special meeting was called for May 20, at which the Executive Board announced it would recommend that the Council adopt the Report. The Laboratory administration also approved of it. Norman Hilberry, Associate Director of Argonne since its inception as a national laboratory and recently appointed Director, had reviewed it together with "key members" of his staff.

The only dissent came from J. L. Morrill, President of the University of Minnesota. "I have been frankly perplexed," he wrote to Kimpton, "to know how to reply usefully and cooperatively. . . ." Morrill expressed "considerable doubt as to whether the reorganization will actually effectuate the purposes which you have in mind. . . ." and said it was his "impression that the new plan really does not come to grips—indeed bypasses—the MURA enterprise which has been so central in our minds and hopes all this time. . . ."

I am perfectly aware of the AEC "facts of life" about MURA although personally still indisposed to accept them as final— and I think all of us have sort of hoped that with your influential assistance we might still through the Argonne National Laboratory have worked out some feasible approach to the MURA endeavor. I cannot discern in the proposed reorganization any real recognition of the MURA problem or any feasible avenue for its solution. I have the feeling that the Rettaliata Committee itself might well have had a larger representation within its personnel from the MURA institutions and that the committee might have faced up more straightforwardly to that issue.

It seems to me also that in the proposed plan of reorganization the lines of communication between the Universities and the Laboratory are so tenuous, and the powers of the Policy Advisory Board and of the director of the participating institutions program are so minimal that no really major changes are proposed in the presently existing pattern of participation.

Morrill's reference to the "AEC 'facts of life' about MURA" reflected the deterioration of the AEC-MURA relations that had occurred between the December 1955 agreement with the presidents and the spring of 1957.[4]

Morrill, unfortunately, could not attend the Council meeting on May 20, but said his "misgivings" would be presented by J. H. Williams, a member of Minnesota's Physics Department and the President of MURA. Williams did just this, but received no support from other Council members. Norman Hilberry pledged the Laboratory's future cooperation. The Council approved the Rettaliata Report 29 to 0, with three abstentions, and immediately elected five members to the proposed Policy Advisory Board. They were an interesting selection, for among them were Farrington Daniels, who had been Chairman of the first Board of Governors, Frederick Seitz, who had strongly favored building a Midwest accelerator separate from Argonne, and Williams.* The public announcement of the approval of the Rettaliata Report was full of hyperbolic predictions—"a major step forward," "one of the most significant steps in the history

---

*The other two elected were John Cooper (Northwestern) and A. G. Norman (Michigan).

of this Laboratory," "a major contribution to the progress of science in America."[5]

A committee on incorporation was appointed in June and given a target date of July for a first draft of the Articles of Incorporation and the By-Laws for the new university organization that would replace the Council. The deadline was met, and the Council Executive Board reviewed and generally approved the documents. Among the disagreements, all minor, was the name for the new organization. A point on which the Board did agree was that security clearances would be needed for the officers and directors. A second draft was approved by the Executive Board in September, at which time the name Associated Midwest Universities was chosen. Because of the possible confusion with Midwest Universities Research Association, the Board moved to inform MURA of its choice.

On October 15, the Council met to formally approve the incorporation of AMU. It decided that the executive officers or governing boards of twenty institutions would have to approve the change, request membership, and send in the $1,000 annual dues in order to officially make the change from a Council of Participating Institutions to an association of Midwest universities. Membership was open, according to Article I of the By-Laws, to those schools who "demonstrated active interest in basic science research by offering graduate research programs of good quality leading to doctorates in at least three of the four broad fields of biological science, chemistry, engineering, and physics."* Getting the required number did not prove difficult. Minor modifications in the By-Laws were proposed by a number of schools, but by mid-April, twenty-two had sent in their dues and four more had indicated that they soon would. Only the University of Pittsburgh declined to join.

The incorporation papers, filed in Illinois on April 16, 1958, listed as the purposes of the new organization:

a. To promote, encourage and conduct education and research in all branches of science, including, but not limited to, nuclear science in relation to all other fields of science;

b. To establish means for facilitating the use of the Argonne National Laboratory and other laboratories by duly qualified personnel and students from the several cooperating institutions and other research and educational institutions;

*Two original Council members who did not meet the educational requirements, Battelle Memorial Institute and the Mayo Foundation, were allowed to join.

c. To establish, maintain, and operate laboratories and other facilities as necessary for research and education.*

The Secretary of State of Illinois questioned the proposed organization on the grounds that both its name and objectives were similar to those of MURA. However, H. R. Crane (Michigan), the new President of MURA, sent a letter saying MURA had no objection to the incorporation of AMU or the use of the name. The certificate of incorporation was issued on May 2.

The Executive Board of the Council of Participating Institutions held its last meeting on May 8, scheduled a final meeting of the Council for June 10, and then transformed itself into the Board of Directors of Associated Midwest Universities. The new directors elected officers—J. H. Jensen, President; L. L. Quill (Michigan State University), Vice President; and as Secretary, Joseph Boyce, who was now Vice President at Illinois Institute of Technology.

The new era that was to start with AMU began officially on June 10, 1958. The Council of Participating Institutions met. The Executive Board moved that the Council dissolve its organization and transfer its activities to the Associated Midwest Universities. It did. The meeting adjourned, and Jensen immediately called to order the first meeting of the Council of Sponsoring Institutions of Associated Midwest Universities.

The event was hailed publicly with appropriate remarks from AEC Chairman Lewis Strauss, from James R. Killian, President Eisenhower's Special Assistant for Science and Technology, and from the Joint Committee on Atomic Energy. It was, they said, "perfecting the means," providing "new impetus" and "a major step forward" in bringing the universities and Argonne together.[6]

*The incorporators were: J. H. Jensen, Frederick Seitz, John Cooper, and Joseph Boyce.

CHAPTER 10

The Dream Machine

The Policy Advisory Board, proposed in the Rettaliata Report, had actually begun to function before Associated Midwest Universities came into being. In addition to the five members elected by the Council of Participating Institutions, the University of Chicago appointed four members: Rev. T. M. Hesburgh (Notre Dame), Dean G. A. Hawkins (Purdue), Professor H. R. Crane (Michigan), and Robert Gunness (Standard Oil Company of Indiana). It was a diversified group, not only geographically but academically. There were two physicists, a chemist, a biochemist, a botanist, two engineers (one academic and one industrial), and a university president.

The first meeting, held July 17, 1957, was in every way an impressive start. The Policy Advisory Board voted to invite to all of its meetings the Chairman of the Council of Participating Institutions, the Director of the Participating Institutions Program (when he was hired), the Director of the Laboratory, and any University of Chicago staff Chancellor Kimpton felt were appropriate. They appointed search committees to look for candidates for three associate directorships of the Laboratory that had been recommended in the Rettaliata Report—Education, Research, and Development. Most significantly, they set up eight review committees, one for each division of the Laboratory—for example, the Applied Mathematics Review Committee, the Reactor Engineering and Remote Control Review Committee, and the High Energy Physics Review Committee. The purpose of each was "to consider and advise on the work" within the particular division, the advice going to the University of Chicago, and from the University, at its discretion, to the Director of Argonne. To show that the Policy Advisory Board was responsive to what was still the key emotional issue in the Midwest, it appointed J. H. Williams, the President of MURA, and Kimpton a subcommittee to consider any opportunities "for closer

93

working relationships or for integration of the high energy group at Madison with the high energy group at the Laboratory."[1]

What had happened to the truce agreement of December 1955 was that the AEC had unilaterally reverted to its original position of making Argonne the only accelerator center in the Midwest. The reversal had been gradual in coming, or at least in becoming apparent. In February 1956, the Commission went before the Subcommittee on Legislation of the Joint Committee on Atomic Energy to request authorization for the Argonne accelerator. Under the Atomic Energy Act of 1954, appropriations for "acquisition or condemnation of any real property or any facility or for plant or facility acquisition, construction, or expansion" required specific legislative approval. This meant that the AEC's budget, after review by the Bureau of the Budget, would go to the Joint Committee, which would send a recommendation to the Appropriations Committee, which in turn would report it out to Congress for enactment. The Joint Committee, however, could recommend more or less than the budget submitted to it, a power of review and initiation that made it a potential vehicle for maneuvers, protests, and changes.

At the February 1956 Authorization Hearings, the AEC's General Manager, K. E. Fields, explained the decision of the preceding December to build a $15 million accelerator at Argonne and to support design and development work by MURA. The decision was justified by Commissioner Libby in terms of competing with the Russians for high energy machines. The Argonne accelerator, he told the Joint Committee, would cut down the Russian lead over the United States to only two or three years. The Joint Committee, and subsequently Congress, on May 3, 1956, approved the $15 million. The location, however, was not specified in the authorization act, an omission that was an exception to the practice for unclassified projects. What this authorization meant was that the AEC was now free to allocate funds up to $15 million to Argonne, or for that matter to any organization, for the specific purpose of building a high energy accelerator, and at any time that progress warranted. As for MURA, until the AEC requested construction money, the financing of MURA's development work was an internal AEC affair which did not require the overt public commitment of the Joint Committee, of Congress, or of the President.[2]

In the fall of 1956, the National Science Foundation Advisory Panel on High Energy Accelerators once again reviewed the state of particle machines. On the Panel were both Seitz and Williams. The report was essentially a panegyric that called for annual expenditures of between $60 and $90 million by 1962 from a combination of federal agencies. Two recommendations were relevant to the Midwest: that support be given to development of new types of accelerators, and that no fixed general policy be made with regard to the location of new accelerators. Both could be interpreted as non-specific support of MURA. There was also in the report, in a section on implementation, an injunction that the lack of an accelerator in the Midwest "be remedied" and, in an appendix, that "the most important recent development in accelerator technology" was the Fixed-Field Alternating Gradient (FFAG) principle being developed principally by MURA. The essential feature of the FFAG machine would be the creation of an intense beam, of an order not producible in current machines, and allowing two separate beams, from two tangentially located machines, to collide so that the sum of their kinetic energies would be available. "It is important," the report said, "that the development should proceed as early as possible to a large working model in order to place the whole FFAG development on a firmer foundation." Table II listed the multi-Bev installations under construction, in design, or under consideration in the world. Argonne was credited with a 15-Bev Synchrotron in design status, MURA with two 15-Bev colliding beam synchrotrons in study status. Unfortunately for MURA, one beam "in design" was worth more than two colliding beams "under study."[3]

When the Joint Committee's Subcommittee on Legislation met on April 10, 1957, they were asked to approve authorization for "Project 58-g-1, High Energy Accelerator, Argonne National Laboratory, Illinois, $27,000,000." General Manager Fields described it as "the principal project in physical research" and justified the increase from $15 million to $27 million on the basis of the NSF Panel report that a "more powerful machine would be a sounder investment." The Congressmen had memories and the minutes of old meetings. They started to recall the discussion a year previously about Russia and $15 million. Chairman Holifield was under the impression that what had been approved the previous year was a MURA accelerator. After being disabused of that idea and educated on the importance of higher intensity, the Committee came back to MURA. The Executive Director of the Joint Committee, James Ramey, began and the AEC Director of Research, T. H. Johnson, answered.

Mr. RAMEY. What is the status of the MURA?

Dr. JOHNSON. That project has been going ahead in the study phase during the past year and I feel that they have demonstrated the validity of the principle that they were working on, but I do not believe that we could foresee building such a machine at the present time. We would not know whether this is the kind of machine that we would want to build or not. It takes time to consider these things. And I am quite sure we would not think of going ahead with a machine of that kind for a number of years even if the money were available.

Representative HOLIFIELD. Was that the project that Dr. Zinn proposed?

Dr. JOHNSON. No, that was Midwest University Research Association.

Representative HOLIFIELD. The one he opposed?

Dr. JOHNSON. I do not think it is fair to say he opposed it.

Representative HOLIFIELD. It was rumored he resigned because of Commission rejection of the original Argonne accelerator proposal. Is there any truth in that?

Dr. JOHNSON. Indeed I do not know the truth of the rumors.

Representative PRICE. This is the same program.

Mr. FIELDS. It is the same program you heard about at the time he resigned, yes, sir.

Representative PRICE. Universities like Midwestern, [sic] Ohio, Illinois, Notre Dame.

Mr. FIELDS. Yes.

Dr. JOHNSON. It might interest you, we have been surveying the scientific community to see what substantial interest there was back of this Argonne plan and I have a number of letters already available, one just came in which is typical of the majority that have been received so far. I cannot put my finger on it but I will just quote from memory.

The head of the physics department at the University of Iowa closed his remarks by saying that he thoroughly endorsed this program that we are contemplating at Argonne Laboratory.

Representative HOLIFIELD. This was the project last year you were going to put—

Dr. JOHNSON. At Argonne.

Representative HOLIFIELD. At Argonne.

Dr. JOHNSON. Yes.

Representative PRICE. The universities do not want it at Argonne. There seems to be a little battle among universities as to where they actually want it but they do not want it at Argonne.

Dr. JOHNSON. There is a difference of opinion, Mr. Price, but let me quote this letter from the head of the department of physics at the University of Iowa. I think they heartily endorsed the university program providing it was also the decision of the Commission to locate the 12½-billion volt weak focusing machine at Argonne National Laboratory to satisfy immediate requirements.

Representative PRICE. That is under the department of physics, and I happened to serve on the Board of Visitors of West Point, and the dean of engineering of Iowa was on the Board and he indicated that he wanted it at Iowa. There are differences of opinion in the Middle West.

Representative HOLIFIELD. The universities wanted it in the Midwest; did they not?

Mr. FIELDS. Yes; and they wanted it—well, the project was a long range one to begin with. They wanted it to go forward. They wanted an installation, separate from the Argonne National Laboratory, which would, in effect, amount to another national laboratory.

Representative HOLIFIELD. Which would be free from interference of Commission direction.

Dr. JOHNSON. That is right.

(Discussion off the record.)

Dr. JOHNSON. There was a substantial body of opinion in favor of putting this MURA project at a new site, but it was by no means unanimous.

Mr. RAMEY. It is not going to be authorized or planned for some years?

Mr. FIELDS. We have no plans to request authorization, and, as a matter of fact, we are working with them, I think you should know, to see how their efforts can be welded into the Argonne effort and bring these things together. We believe there should be a high energy physics program in the Middle West because it is an area where there is probably the greatest congregation of physicists in the United States. We believe that with the right kind of collaboration it could be extremely productive. You do not have any installations in the Middle West like the Radiation Laboratory on the west coast; nothing like the Brookhaven Laboratory on the east coast. We really feel there should be this collaboration. It is going forward very effectively and there are some proposals that the chancellors are proceeding with now that would provide more effective arrangements for participation of all the universities. And we feel that, given a little time, this is all going to be pulled together quite effectively.

Representative HOLIFIELD. But it will be located at Chicago?

Mr. FIELDS. It will be part of the Argonne Laboratory program—

Representative HOLIFIELD. Do you think that is isolated far enough from the collection of scientists in and around Chicago and that area; that they will not get the maximum utilization of it?

Mr. FIELDS. These big machines have to be isolated, it seems to me, from all but the operating installation itself. If you put it on a university campus it is good for that university.

Representative HOLIFIELD. I was thinking of the distance from the scientists rather than any other point of isolation.

Dr. JOHNSON. The Argonne Laboratory is about as centrally located as you could find. It is close to the Chicago Airport.

Representative HOLIFIELD. That is what I wanted to point out.

Dr. JOHNSON. About equal distance from everybody.

Representative PRICE. I think what they are more interested in than anything else are the facilities to which they have exclusive use where they do not run into allocations of time as against Commission scientists and the university people for working.

Mr. FIELDS. I think we are going to get the right kind of collaboration on this in due course.

Representative COLE. I do not understand. You say you are not asking for this thing you have been talking about and I understand you have been talking about the thing you are asking for.

Mr. FIELDS. No, sir. The reference last year was to the so-called dream machine.

Representative COLE. Dream?

Mr. FIELDS. Dream.

Representative COLE. This $27 million is not the dream machine, then?

Mr. FIELDS. No, Sir.

The result was Public Law 85–162, Sec. 107(b), which amended the previous year's authorization "By striking therefrom the figure '$15,000,000' for Project 57–d–1, High Energy Accelerator, and substituting therefor the figure '$27,000,000.' "[4]

Between the hearings and the passage of the new authorization act, Father Hesburgh, the President of Notre Dame and a University of Chicago appointee to Argonne's Policy Advisory Board, sent a letter to Minnesota's President Morrill which he entitled "A Possible Statement of Policy on the Future of Science in the Midwest." He asked Morrill to circulate it to the presidents of the participating institutions for signatures. Morrill, in turn, asked six presidents, including Kimpton, to join with him in signing before he circulated it.

The statement was strong and pointed. "We assume initially that universities are the prime centers of talented scientists. . . ." it began. ". . . No one university in this region can assemble or finance fully adequate facilities in all of the sciences. . . . Expensive facilities must be largely financed with the assistance of the federal government."

The statement then pointed out that two patterns of management existed—in the east, Associated Universities Incorporated, which operated Brookhaven; and in the West, the University of California at Berkeley, which operated the Radiation Laboratory. The Midwest had a third pattern—the designation of the University of Chicago as contractor with participation by other schools. "We . . . believe," the statement said, "that this participation will be largely nominal and superficial unless it is patterned after the model of the Associated Universities Incorporated of the Eastern universities."

At issue was whether the university-government relationship in the Midwest would be "national-laboratory centered or university centered."

If national-laboratory centered, this will mean that the scientific talent will either be drawn out of universities where it is not centered in research and educational functions, or it will be diverted to other more promising regions because these scientists are unwilling to be commandeered and prevented from pursuing the most promising scientific research endeavors under the most favorable conditions in a university atmosphere, joined to an educational endeavor.

If it were to be university centered, then six principles would have to be put into effect:

1. The Midwest should have its share of costly research facilities.

2. Wherever possible, they should be located on or adjacent to campuses.

3. "The program planning and research organization of these inter-university research and education centers should be the common concern of all the competent scientists and administrators in all of the universities. Participation should be vital, truly inter-university on the level of planning, programming, researching, and educating, and not merely nominal."

4. Business administration should be located at the facility.

5. Educational functions should remain the prerogative of the universities.

6. It was time to face these issues.

Hesburgh and Morrill thought it was time. The others didn't. Kimpton replied.

Since I am moving heaven and earth to try to make the Argonne Laboratory a great center in the Midwest for basic and applied research, I do not believe I can appropriately join you in your letter. Since research, particularly in physics, requires increasingly larger and more expensive equipment and, since the government in general and the Atomic Energy Commission in particular have indicated that they wish to concentrate such facilities on one site, I see no alternative but to try to make at the Argonne a great scientific center.

The authorization hearings showed the AEC's position. The response to Hesburgh's policy statement brought forth Chicago's. The logical place to resolve the problem, to prevent the hardening of positions, was in the Policy Advisory Board. It held its first meeting the week after Morrill sent Hesburgh's letter to Kimpton. Williams and Kimpton were appointed a committee of two, but whether it would be possible to work out the problem was dubious.

As John Cooper (Northwestern) wrote to Kimpton, "One of the principal weaknesses in previous years has been the lack of a definite understanding of the missions of the Laboratory. . . . There may, in fact, be four different concepts of the missions: the Laboratory's, the University of Chicago's, the Participating Institutions', and the Atomic Energy Commission's."[5]

The Congressional authorization for the $27 million accelerator was approved in late August. The draft of the Associated Midwest Universities By-Laws began to circulate in September. The incorporation of AMU was approved by the Council in October, and in December the Atomic Energy Commission announced authorization of the new 12.5 Bev proton accelerator to be built at Argonne. The official press release, dated December 12, 1957, also declared the December 1955 agreement with the presidents of MURA null and void. It explained that MURA, which had received support of more than $2 million from the Commission, was working on a third demonstration model.

> Should this model demonstrate that a large accelerator based on the MURA concept is technically feasible and more attractive than possible alternative designs, and depending on construction authorization and the appropriation of funds for such a machine now estimated to cost about $100 million, the Commission will consider construction of a large accelerator of this type. In the utilization of such a machine, large supporting facilities in many scientific fields are required. The Commission, therefore, believes that if a large accelerator of the MURA type is to be built in the Midwest, it should be located at a site where such facilities already are in existence; namely, the Argonne National Laboratory.

That Lewis Strauss was still Chairman, that Willard Libby was still a Commissioner apparently made no difference.

The Policy Advisory Board, at its next meeting, passed a motion supporting MURA. "The Argonne Board strongly urges the early construction in the Midwest of this super-accelerator provided that the recent advances in design principles . . . are fully validated and supported by the reviewing scientists." The last qualification became extremely important.[6]

On February 13, 1958, the MURA plans got a public airing at the hearings on the AEC's Physical Research Program that were held by the Joint Committee. Keith Symon (Wisconsin), Technical Director of MURA, was invited to explain just what the FFAG accelerator was. He did, proceeding from the concept of colliding beams produced in separate accelerators to what was the current objective—a model in which two beams would circulate in opposite directions simultaneously within one accelerator. It wasn't long into the hearing before the Congressmen began asking questions about sites and getting answers about administration. Symon made it clear that he thought MURA wasn't getting enough support for its development work, but more important, when Representative Price of Illinois asked if MURA were ready to start immediate design work, Symon answered, "Yes, sir, I think we would."

"That would indicate, then," Representative Price continued, "that a failure to get approval of the proposal at the present time is the only thing holding you back."

To which Symon responded, "Yes, or at least it begins to hold us back if it is delayed much longer."[7]

The formal revised MURA proposal, which incorporated the concept of two counter-rotating beams in one machine, was sent to the AEC on March 14, 1958. In mid-April the Division of Research sent the proposal out for technical review to fifty-nine scientists. The man sending it was the new Director of Research, J. H. Williams, who had stepped into the position from his dual role as President of MURA and as a member of Argonne's Policy Advisory Board.

At the May 27, 1958, Authorization Hearings, the Atomic Energy Commission reported that both the MURA proposal and one from Stanford University for a mile-long linear accelerator were out for review.* General Manager Fields announced that they were not requesting authorization for either during fiscal 1959. The next witness before the Committee was Senator Alexander Wiley from Wisconsin who began by saying:

> My purpose is simple. I am here respectfully to recommend that you direct the Atomic Energy Commission to reexamine immediately its decision which was, unfortunately, not to request the authorization of funds for the construction of the high-speed accelerator near Madison, as recommended by the Midwest University Research Association. In my judgment, if the Atomic Energy Commission refuses to reconsider its position, the result will be a national tragedy.

And so MURA began the first of its political efforts, through the congressmen of the Midwest, and from them through the Joint Committee, to reverse the decision-making process within the AEC.

*The Stanford proposal was reviewed by seven physicists.

"The issue," Wiley said, was "when it would be built, and whether it will be built in the freest possible atmosphere of a university, where you have minds that explore and reach out to understand the meaning of life and the meaning of these new things and new forces as against the more closed atmosphere of a Federal laboratory." Wiley brought with him R. Rollefson, the Director of MURA; H. R. Crane, the President; and K. R. Symon.

Rollefson, in his opening statement and under questioning, reviewed the problems with Argonne over site location and over administration. Symon reiterated his earlier statement that they were ready to go ahead with the engineering design. Crane summed up that there was no way for MURA and Argonne to devise an organizational arrangement that would suit both parties.

What the MURA people really wanted was not the $82 million they now estimated it would cost to build their FFAG machine, but $1.4 million to build a laboratory on their Madison site. The laboratory was important not only as a place to work, but more as an assurance that the MURA machine would really be built, and built at Madison. MURA's basic need was to boost its own morale.

Representative Holifield avoided the direct request for laboratory funds by indicating that the normal route would be for the Committee to authorize the full $100 million for the entire project and have the AEC dole out what was needed along the way. Holifield then asked Williams, the new AEC Director of Research, to speed up the technical review so that they might have it before Congress adjourned in the summer. Fields indicated that the Commission had not decided on the relative priority of the MURA machine and the Stanford machine. The hearing closed with a sandwiching statement of protest against the AEC by Wisconsin's second Senator, William Proxmire.

The technical review was sent to the Committee at the end of June. Unfortunately for MURA, it was, at best, equivocal. The AEC's summary said:

Summarizing, the question of technical feasibility seems to be uncertain with reviewers' opinions split about 50–50, although many of those expressing belief in feasibility based this on confidence in the successful outcome of future development. The feasibility of the high-intensity single-beam device seems to be much better established. One-third of the accelerator builders recommended that at least the success of the 50 Mev. model be awaited before the construction authorization of the whole machine was made. The research value of the single-beam high-intensity machine was uniformly acclaimed, but several noted that if this were the main objective of the machine, it could be achieved at a lower cost than the clashing-beam machine; while opinions on the research value of the clashing-beam device were split about 50–50. The reviewers agreed uniformly on several points: (a) The excellence of the existing MURA group (but many emphasized the necessity of need for more staff, particularly on the engineering side, if construction is undertaken); (b) the underestimation of the construction cost estimates, and many believed that the operating costs were underestimated; and (c) the necessity for the continued support of the MURA group.[8]

When the Joint Committee reported out the authorization bill, there were no MURA construction funds. MURA's first effort at politics had gone for nought. Its future as a builder of accelerators was already its past, but as a catalyst toward changing the relationship of the universities to Argonne National Laboratory it was to prove extremely powerful. The MURA failure hung as a backdrop through the entire history of the Associated Midwest Universities.

PART THREE

The Board of Directors
of
Associated Midwest Universities
1958–1968

The Board of Directors
Associated Midwest Universities
May 1958 to June 30, 1968

Name	Institution	Years Served
John Z. Bowers	Wisconsin	1958–1960
W. L. Everitt	Illinois	1958–1965 President 61–62
Newell S. Gingrich	Missouri	1958–1959
Raymond G. Herb	Wisconsin	1958–1960
Frank Hovorka	Western Reserve	1958–1961
James H. Jensen	Iowa State	1958–1965 President 58–59
Laurence L. Quill	Michigan State	1958–1064 President 59–60
Robert S. Shankland	Case	1958–1965 President 60–61
A. B. Cardwell	Kansas	1959–1963
W. D. Armstrong	Minnesota	1960–1964
W. R. Marshall	Wisconsin	1960–1966 President 62–63
J. Russell Bright	Wayne State	1961–1966 President 63–64
Bryce L. Crawford	Minnesota	1963–1967 President 64–65
John A. D. Cooper	Northwestern	1964–1968 President 65–66
Edwin L. Goldwasser	Illinois	1964–1967
William Kerr	Michigan	1965–1968 President 66–67
Frederick D. Rossini	Notre Dame	1965–1968 President 67–68
Warren F. Stubbins	Cincinnati	1965–1968
A. H. Emmons	Missouri	1966–1968
Armon F. Yanders	Michigan State	1966–1968
John R. Pasta	Illinois	1967–1968
William R. Savage	Iowa	1967–1968

Secretary: Joseph C. Boyce, Illinois Tech., 1958
John H. Roberson, AMU, 1959–1968

Treasurer: Joseph C. Boyce, Illinois Tech., 1958
Arthur T. Schmehling, Northwestern, 1958–1968

Officers of the Council of Associated Midwest Universities

Chairman	Vice Chairman	Year Elected
Thomas H. Osgood Michigan State University	Adolf Voigt Iowa State University	1958
Adolf Voigt Iowa State University	Thomas Read University of Illinois	1959
J. Russell Bright Wayne State University	Alfred H. Weber St. Louis University	1960
Alfred H. Weber St. Louis University	Warren F. Stubbins University of Cincinnati	1961
Warren F. Stubbins University of Cincinnati	Titus C. Evans University of Iowa	1962
Titus C. Evans University of Iowa	Philip N. Powers Purdue University	1963
Philip N. Powers Purdue University	Marvin T. Edmison Oklahoma State University	1964
Marvin T. Edmison Oklahoma State University	Ross J. Martin University of Illinois	1965
Ross J. Martin University of Illinois	Herbert D. Rhodes University of Arizona	1966
Herbert D. Rhodes University of Arizona	William J. Argersinger University of Kansas	1967

Secretary: Joseph C. Boyce   1958
Illinois Institute of Technology

            John H. Roberson   1959–1968
Associated Midwest Universities

Policy Advisory Board of
Argonne National Laboratory
May 1957 to 1966

Name	Institution	Organization	Years Served
J. A. D. Cooper	Northwestern	Elected by Council of Participating Institutions	1957–1963
Farrington Daniels	Wisconsin	Elected by CPI	1957–1962
A. G. Norman	Michigan	Elected by CPI	1957–1964
Frederick Seitz	Illinois	Elected by CPI	1957–1961
		Appointed by Chicago	1961–1966
John H. Williams	Minnesota	Elected by CPI	1957
		Returned by agreement between Chicago and AMU	1960–1966
H. R. Crane	Michigan	Appointed by Chicago	1957–1966
Robert C. Gunness	Standard Oil Co. of Indiana	Appointed by Chicago	1957–1966
George A. Hawkins	Purdue	Appointed by Chicago	1957–1966
T. M. Hesburgh, C.S.C.	Notre Dame	Appointed by Chicago	1957–1960

Frederick D. Rossini	Carnegie Inst. Notre Dame	Elected by CPI	1958–1966
Laurence L. Quill	Mich. State	Appointed by Chicago	1960–1966
James H. Jensen	Oregon State	Elected by AMU	1961–1965
Joseph Hirschfelder	Wisconsin	Elected by AMU	1962–1966
J. C. Warner	Carnegie Inst.	Elected by AMU	1963–1966
Titus C. Evans	Iowa	Elected by AMU	1964–1966
W. R. Marshall	Wisconsin	Elected by AMU	1965–1966

Chairman: Lawrence Kimpton, Chicago, ex officio   1957–1961
          George Beadle, Chicago, ex officio   1961–1966

Secretary: James Gilbreath, Argonne   1957–1965
          Richard Adams, Argonne   1965–1966

CHAPTER 11

Beginning Once More

The differences between 1946, when the Council of Participating Institutions had been created, and 1958, when Associated Midwest Universities was formed, were vast. In 1946, atomic energy was a Commission-owned activity, newly inherited from the Army, a classified subject conducted behind security fences at four guarded installations. In 1958, atomic energy had been indiscriminately tracked around the nation and the world. Indices were everywhere. A total of one hundred and eighty-one reactors were operating in the United States; eighty-nine others were under construction; and sixty-seven more were in the planning stages. Eight of those operating were non-military power-producing reactors, two of which were feeding electricity into commercial grids. Ten of the operating reactors were for research and training at schools, including three AMU institutions. Selective radioisotopes were being used routinely in industry and medicine by thirty-five hundred civilian licensees. The nation actually possessed something called an Atomic Energy Industry made up of some old corporations changing with the times and some new ones sired by the technology. Large and small, they tried to make money from trafficking in radiation, its development, its instruments, and its use.

Military growth was equally extensive. The *Nautilus* had logged fifty thousand miles and sailed under the polar ice cap. The *Sea Wolf* was operational; more submarines were being built along with nuclear-powered surface vessels. There was even a large program to build a nuclear-powered plane, which was to be terminated several years later by President Kennedy. Weapons development was a major occupation. A series of twenty-four nuclear bombs, euphemistically called "devices," were detonated in 1957 at the Nevada test site in Operation Plumbbob, and a series of ten larger tests, in the megaton range, were held in 1958 at the Eniwetok proving ground in the Pacific. There was much national and international concern about fallout, and the extent to which radioactive isotopes entered the food cycle and eventually the bones of children. World maps showed the separate fallout belts from the tests of the Russians, the English, and the Americans. Roentgens and microcuries were household words; people knew there was tritium in the snow and strontium-90 in the milk.

The International Atomic Energy Agency had formally come into being in 1957, with fifty-nine charter members. By 1958, the United States had already exported six research reactors and was building nineteen more for shipment to other countries. The AEC had cooperative agreements with thirty-seven nations covering not only the exchange of information but also the leasing and, in some cases, the transfer of reactor fuel and radioisotopes intended for peaceful uses of nuclear energy.

All this had been accompanied by the decline of classification. Nuclear energy was not an entirely open field, but there had been attempts to declassify and release technical papers. In part, this was due to the Atomic Energy Act of 1954; in part it was because classification had ceased to be an effective way to keep the world from knowing what it already knew. Technical competence no longer resided solely in government laboratories, nor for that matter, as the Russian and English bomb tests proved, in the United States. International competition, moreover, was no longer solely nuclear. The Russians had developed intercontinental ballistic missiles, and in October 1957 had launched the first satellite, *Sputnik I.*

By 1958, a new academic discipline, nuclear engineering, was well established in American colleges. Between 1957 and 1962, an average of one hundred and ninety-six Master's degrees and twenty Ph.D.'s were granted annually by departments or divisions of nuclear engineering, which themselves grew from eighteen in 1957 to forty-six in 1962. The AEC's direct assistance to colleges and universities in all nuclear-related areas, for purchasing equipment, for building facilities, totaled $3.4 million in 1957. The list of unclassified sponsored research projects in the physical and biological sciences at schools took up thirty-three pages of small type in the Commission's Semi-Annual Report to Congress in January 1958.[*][1]

---

*The AEC was not the only federal agency sponsoring university research. A 1958 report from the National Science Foundation claimed that the federal dollars given annually to schools for research had grown from $15 million in 1940 to $440 million in 1957. All the money, however, was not directly beneficial to schools. Included in this total was $175 million for the operation of "research centers," one of which was

Even Argonne had drastically changed. From the potpourri on the Chicago campus and Site A in the Cook County Forest Preserve, it had grown into mature size on the 3,700-acre tract in Du Page County. On the one site there were four separate laboratory areas: the original Quonset huts in the east area which housed the administration together with some research; the main research area to the north with permanent facilities for physics, chemistry, chemical engineering, biology, and reactor engineering; the "hot" area in the south with the CP-5 research reactor, the Juggernaut Reactor, the Experimental Boiling Water Reactor, the facilities for fuel fabrication and waste processing; and between the three, the much sought after new housing, a residential motel with seventy-two bedrooms to sleep twice that number of off-site visitors. By 1958, the value of the facilities at Argonne was nearly $88 million. Under construction or authorized was an additional $100 million worth. The annual operating budget for fiscal 1958 was nearly $34 million. The staff totaled around thirty-one hundred, of whom eight hundred were designated as either scientists or engineers and the rest assigned to supportive services, including administration.

Argonne's top personnel had also changed.* Norman Hilberry, the new Director, had been a member of the original Met Lab since its organization in 1942 and had served as Compton's assistant throughout the war. In this capacity he had been the compiler of many of the staff reports on postwar planning and had written an extensive summary of 1945 thinking on postwar laboratory organization. When the Met Lab was reorganized into the Argonne National Laboratory in 1946, Hilberry was appointed Associate Director and was given, among other duties, the responsibility for maintaining a relationship with the Board of Governors. In 1949, when Argonne's focus shifted from being a regional laboratory to a reactor develop-

---

identified as Argonne National Laboratory, operated by the University of Chicago. The main purpose of the report was to raise questions. Did federal support threaten the independence of universities in selecting research? How much did the availability of funds determine a school's growth in a particular area? While the report concluded that government influence had not been "detrimental" to the schools, it attempted to look critically at what had been happening in the interface between the campus and Washington. (NSF 58-10)

*The AEC itself had changed. Admiral Lewis Strauss had been replaced as Chairman by John McCone, a change that marked the end of an era in which the personality of the Chairman was a key factor in the development of nuclear energy.

ment center, Hilberry became Deputy Director. Upon Zinn's resignation in 1956, he assumed the Acting Directorship and eventually, at the time the Rettaliata Report was being implemented, the Directorship.

As a result of the Rettaliata Report, the Laboratory administration had been slightly restructured to create an Associate Director for Education and an Associate Director for High Energy Physics. Beneath this level were the original Laboratory divisions, of which the most recently created, the Particle Accelerator Division, was about to become the most important. The construction of the Zero Gradient Synchrotron was slated to begin in fiscal 1959 and would give Argonne a new experimental area comparable to the existing three research sites. The Associate Director for High Energy Physics was Roger Hildebrand, a physicist from the University of Chicago, while another Chicago high-energy physicist, Albert Crewe, was Director of the Particle Accelerator Division.

The Associate Director for Education in 1958 was Frank Myers, a physicist and former Dean of the Graduate School at Lehigh University. Under his jurisdiction were programs by which people at various educational levels, undergraduate through postdoctoral, came to the Laboratory to be trained. They came from government, from industry, and from universities, regardless of whether or not their schools were in AMU. The most publicized educational program was the International School of Science and Engineering, which had begun in 1955 as part of President Eisenhower's Atoms for Peace Program. It brought to the Laboratory scientists from many countries, who received advanced training and participated in research. In reverse, some of Argonne's own employees took courses, both on and off site, a few of which carried college credit. The announcement of Myers' appointment to the associate directorship promised that he would "implement a new and aggressive program in cooperation with universities and colleges of the Middle West to use the Laboratory's resources and the talents of its personnel to spur science education."[2]

In 1958, reactor development was no longer central to the Laboratory's purpose, not just because Zinn was gone but because reactor development was occurring in other sectors of the scientific community, both civilian and military. Argonne, if it were to remain as large as it was, finally needed the shift into the more basic research programs that people had long spoken of and edged toward. The largest pending project was the accelerator, in a sense the only contemporary project that looked forward to the 1960's. Another brief companion was a proposed high-flux research reactor that had the cute name of "Mighty Mouse." The estimated cost of $80 million killed it from the start, though another reactor proposal appeared three years later much diminished in cost and with a less figurative name.

Into this environment so different from what had existed twelve years earlier came the Associated Midwest Universities, expected to amend the record of the past and yet not particularly equipped to do so. The contract between the Atomic Energy Commission and the University of Chicago contained a section on cooperation with research and educational institutions that emphasized AMU but not in a crucial way. There should be, it said, "a broad program of cooperation with the university community, particularly as represented by the Associated Midwest Universities, but also including other interested colleges, universities, and nonprofit research institutions." AMU, of course, had its own charter, its Articles of Incorporation, in which it could say all that it wanted to about its own purposes at Argonne. Not until January of 1960 would AMU have a contract with the AEC which would give it money for programs and, more importantly, some contractual recognition of its functional role at the Laboratory.

Unfortunately for the new organization, the one aspect of Argonne that had not changed by 1958 was the deadlock between the Laboratory and MURA. In need of easing, it was about to get tighter. In September 1958 a new report came from the NSF Advisory Panel on High Energy Accelerators.* Among its general recommendations was a repetition of an earlier panel's advice that no fixed policy be made as to site location of future accelerators. This was clearly an attempt to counter the policy statement made by the AEC when it announced authorization of the Zero Gradient Synchrotron (ZGS). Specific recommendations, however, were not as favorable to MURA. The Panel said that the Stanford Linear Accelerator should be built as soon as possible, but that the MURA proposal should be deferred until a series of intermediate proving steps, all of a study nature, could be undertaken. It urged that the MURA group, but not its machine, be supported on a continuing basis.[3]

The NSF report was rapidly followed in November by a report from a special panel that was set up by the President's Science Ad-

---

*This Panel had originally been formed in 1954. It reported that year, again in 1956, and for a final time in 1958. By then accelerators had become so expensive and the debates over their construction so intense that the NSF Panel was succeeded by a panel sponsored by both the General Advisory Committee and the President's Science Advisory

visory Committee and the General Advisory Committee. Named the Piore Panel, after its chairman, Emanuel Piore, it was a Presidential-level committee which could be expected to have a strong effect on policy.* It reviewed the national accelerators, set priorities, and made unequivocal recommendations, of which the eighth was, "Reject the present MURA accelerator proposal but continue to provide adequate support and encouragement to the MURA development group."[4]

Though the Piore Report was not released publicly until May 1959, its contents were known in the high energy field in November 1958. As a result of the two reports, only the most optimistic theoreticians could continue to bank on a MURA-operated accelerator. The rest had to revert to an appraisal that had been made by a group of Midwestern physicists the year before—that the "outlook for MURA is now hopeless" and that the only chance for a Midwest accelerator was to support Argonne's project. Their tactical response, in 1957, was to attempt to place on the proposed Policy Advisory Board some people favorable to the cooperative use of the Argonne accel-

---

Committee. The membership of the NSF Panel is interesting because of the number of physicists who were also involved in the controversy between Argonne and MURA.

1954	*1956*	*1958*
S. K. Allison (Chicago)	Allison	H. L. Anderson (Chicago)
H. A. Bethe (Cornell)	E. J. Lofgren (U. of Cal.)	Lofgren
L. J. Haworth (Brookhaven)	Haworth, Chairman	Haworth, Chairman
W. K. H. Panofsky (Stanford)	Panofsky	R. R. Wilson (Cornell)
I. I. Rabi (Columbia)	Rabi	
M. G. White (Princeton)	White	White
J. H. Williams (Minnesota)	Williams	H. R. Crane (Michigan)
J. R. Zacharias (M.I.T.)	Zacharias	B. T. Feld (M.I.T.)
R. F. Bacher (Cal. Inst. of Tech.), Chairman	F. Seitz (Illinois)	Seitz
	R. Serber (Columbia)	Serber
	A. Roberts (Rochester)	

*The other members were: Hans Bethe, L. J. Haworth, Jesse W. Beams, and Edwin M. McMillan.

erator, an attempt that succeeded partly through the cooperation of the University of Chicago, which appointed a MURA physicist to the PAB.[5]

A more direct route to cooperative use was initiated by the Laboratory. Roger Hildebrand, the Associate Director for High Energy Physics, announced at the November 1958 meeting of the American Physical Society that an Argonne Accelerator Users' Group was about to be formed. Edwin L. Goldwasser of Illinois did the actual organizational work. The members, Goldwasser wrote in his invitational letter, would come largely from the MURA schools and from those schools not having formal working arrangements with the accelerators at Berkeley or Brookhaven.[6]

The initial meeting, held in mid-January 1959, was attended by nearly seventy physicists. They were told by Hildebrand that more than half the research on the Argonne accelerator would come from physicists not directly associated with Argonne. The Users' Group immediately began to work in an advisory capacity on specific problems such as the design of the experimental area, the methods of beam separation, and the choice of bubble chambers. An interesting aspect of the Users' Group was that, though it had been initiated by ANL, it remained essentially an informal group held together by a common interest in the ZGS. It was not officially responsible to Argonne, nor to AMU, nor to MURA, but it was intertwined with each.

The Board of Directors of AMU, at its December 1958 meeting, invited Goldwasser to have the proposed Users' Group function under the auspices of AMU. While this invitation was rejected, the Users' Group used the administrative services of AMU's office and its new executive director. In 1960, one of the first contracts AMU received from the AEC was to pay for the expenses of the Users' Group without its being a formal part of AMU. This was a new pattern for participation, which allowed the Users' Group to be financed but to remain independent in policy matters. In Goldwasser's words, the Users' Group was an "anarchistic, yet responsible, authorityless, yet effective, organization."[7]

The Executive Director for AMU assumed the new post in February 1959. He was John H. Roberson, a physicist who had worked in both the research and operational divisions of the AEC. As stipulated in the Rettaliata Report, his office was located at Argonne in the Administration Building. His direct liaison proved to be the Laboratory's counterpart, the Associate Director for Education, Frank Myers. Roberson's constituency, however, was back on the campuses. Except for site visits during the quarterly meetings of the Board of Directors, the officers of AMU were at their individual schools. Roberson was the Executive Director of an amorphous organization.

AMU had only one standing committee, the Nuclear Engineering Education Committee, which it had inherited from a status somewhat similar to the Users' Group. The Committee's origin went back to 1955, when a group of engineering deans and faculty met to discuss the newest of the engineering disciplines. Out of this came a proposal to build a nuclear engineering teaching facility at Argonne that was never implemented. The group was reactivated by Norman Hilberry in early 1958 and transferred to AMU in the fall. The NEEC, as an AMU committee, met once in 1958, at the University of Michigan. During 1959, it drew up an extensive statement of purpose and made plans for a conference to be held at Argonne the following year.

AMU was off to a start that was more typical of an organization just beginning rather than one that had a history behind it. The first annual report of the Board of Directors presented to the Council admitted that much of the first six months' effort had gone into the search for a director. As for programs, it had sponsored a conference on the use of isotopes in agriculture.

CHAPTER 12

Elephants and Committees

Over the next four years—1959, 1960, 1961, 1962—the history of the relationship between Associated Midwest Universities and the Laboratory occurred through parallel but essentially separate group developments. It is reminiscent of the fable of the five blind men feeling an elephant, each one touching a different part of the body and getting a different impression of what the beast was like. There were even, to maintain the analogy, five groups: the Laboratory administration, as represented by the Director's office; the Policy Advisory Board, which was advisory to the President of the University of Chicago; the Accelerator Users' Group, which was responsible to the high-energy physicists of the Midwest; the Board of Directors of AMU; and its only standing committee, Nuclear Engineering Education.

The Laboratory administration's impression can be traced through a formal procedure initiated in August 1958, when the AEC's Chicago Operations Office asked the University of Chicago for a five-year plan for Argonne. The request came at a time when the directors of all the AEC laboratories were trying to agree on a policy statement in hopes that the AEC would give them a basic charter.[1] Argonne's response was a two-volume Laboratory imprint entitled *Long Range Program* (March 1959), which purported to plan for the decade ahead. Volume I, essentially written by Norman Hilberry, presented a picture of a strong Laboratory staffed by people comparable in ability to those at a university and judged by similar standards of publication, research, and even teaching. The objectives of the Laboratory were, first, basic research on "a broad interdisciplinary front" and, second, "short range application projects." The Laboratory's role in education was to provide university staff access to unique facilities such as the Zero Gradient Synchrotron and to make available both graduate and postdoctoral appointments.

The report projected an increase in total staff from a current 3,439 to 5,850 in 1964 and to 6,700 in 1969. Scientific staff was projected to grow from 885 to 1,650 to 1,925. Building plans, both immediate and long-range, called for two additional research reactors, both high flux, a low-energy accelerator, and numerous buildings. The total cost was estimated at $118 million, which when added to what was already under construction would mean tripling the existing facilities.

The significant point for university relations is the cursory mention of the cooperative program and the lack of specific mention of AMU in the main report. The appendices made up for this, but not in a strong way. The section on "Education, Training and University Cooperation" hoped that ten years hence, if AMU were successful, there would be "several dozen faculty . . . at any given time . . . spending their periods of leave at the Laboratory." Cooperation with AMU, however, was only part of the overall pattern of activities involving universities. AMU's particular area of competence was identified as "research cooperation," primarily through the ZGS and the contemplated high flux reactor. The actual involvement of faculty, according to tables published in the appendix, though growing, was small in proportion to the Laboratory staff. The following table compares the total number of faculty at Argonne on both short- and long-range appointments to the number of salaried scientific staff, i.e., people who would be considered comparable in status and ability.

1951	1952	1953	1954	1955	1956	1957	1958
6/513	8/521	13/519	14/488	26/531	40/577	50/698	67/800

Comparison to the same ratio at the perennial model, Brookhaven, is telling. In 1958, Brookhaven had three hundred visitors spend at least one-third of their time at the laboratory, plus seventy full-time postdoctoral appointments. Together they outnumbered the permanent scientific staff of three hundred.[2]

The Long Range Program proved to be a convenient document. In June 1959, the Joint Committee asked the AEC to report on present and projected plans for all its laboratories. Argonne submitted its report, with summary statements on its research programs. In this revised version, the Laboratory administrators recognized four functions for Argonne:

1. providing objective and competent technical advice to the Commission;

2. providing the mechanism necessary to establish and execute the research and development programs necessary for the Commission to attain its objectives;

3. providing the means for mobilizing the research and development potentials of both universities and industry in support of AEC objectives;

4. providing a mechanism for the dissemination of information. . . .[3]

The AEC's full report, entitled *The Future Role of the Atomic Energy Commission Laboratories,* was submitted to the Joint Committee in January 1960. In it, Argonne was first categorized as a "multiprogram laboratory," a term that has stuck for differentiating between a laboratory like Argonne and project engineering laboratories (Knolls), production plant laboratories (Hanford), and university laboratories (University of Rochester Bio-Medical Center).

The totality of AEC research support appeared impressive. In 1959, the Commission spent $525 million on research and development that was not connected with nuclear weapons. The budget for 1960 was $100 million larger. The value of the Commission's research facilities was $1,124 million with an additional $707 million authorized. Argonne's share was a substantial $35 million in operating costs in 1959, and completed facilities that were valued at $104 million.

The AEC report on Argonne contained one reference to AMU:

The growing activities involving joint Argonne-university relationships are facilitated by Associated Midwest Universities, Inc., a recently organized non-profit group of universities. Although the schools making up Associated Midwest Universities are located in the Mississippi Valley states, opportunities for participation in the Argonne program by university researchers are not limited geographically.

In Argonne's future, the report predicted a moderate expansion of staff to implement existing projects, among which the new accelerator was foremost. The ZGS, it said, "is intended . . . to be available to qualified high-energy physicists of the nation or of the free world" and added that "about one-half of the available time" would go to non-Laboratory experimenters. In all other areas—the chemistry of plutonium, solid state studies, reactor development, and biological effects of radiation—there would be expansion and shifts, but within a basically stabilized Laboratory. Argonne could look forward to ZGS and little more additional growth.[4]

The AEC's report was circulated by the Joint Committee to selected members of the nuclear industry, to schools with strong research programs, and to the laboratories themselves, asking for detailed comments. The report and the comments on it were officially published in October. There was about the finished document, as there is about much that comes out of the government's writing apparatus, an air of unreality, in which words are used so as to mean as many things to as many people as possible. Still, this report contained in summary fashion some hard figures that described the parameters of the AEC research effort in dollars, people, and facilities, and projected a limited future.

Three responses were directly concerned with the Argonne-AMU relationship. John Roberson, the Executive Director of AMU, wrote that "a clear, emphatic, and unequivocal statement by the government of the important role to be played by the national laboratories as an adjunct to the universities would encourage educators to find a way to exploit the laboratories." It would also, he said, enable laboratory staff to value their university-involved work.

Chancellor Kimpton of Chicago wrote about the strength of the laboratories requiring cooperation with universities and industry. AMU, he said, had "enhanced" the Laboratory-university relationship during the past two years.

Norman Hilberry wrote that Laboratory relationships with universities, particularly with AMU, "are steadily developing and are beginning to materialize in mutual programs of cooperation in which the Laboratory is playing a significant role in support of Midwest educational programs that could not readily be initiated without its collaboration."[5]

The report and its commentaries, bound together, were the public record, in the fall of 1960, the official structured view.

The Policy Advisory Board had a different perspective. As the high-energy physicists had hoped, the Board was initially concerned with the availability of the ZGS to university physicists. At a meeting in October of 1958, shortly after the NSF Panel and just before the Piore Panel recommended against supporting the MURA accelerator, Frederick Seitz asked the Laboratory to assure universities of a "fair share" of ZGS experimental time. He was joined in this request by H. R. Crane, who wanted AMU involved in working up a policy statement on accelerator use that would be issued jointly by the AMU Board and the Policy Advisory Board. Both men had been members of the NSF Panel.

A. Geoffrey Norman (Michigan), a botanist, saw a need for a broader statement covering the use of all Argonne facilities, not just the ZGS. He suggested this privately to Kimpton, who agreed in principle and said that he was awaiting the appointment of an AMU Executive Director. Kimpton promised that if an executive director were not appointed soon, Hilberry and Myers would pursue the matter directly with the AMU Board of Directors. However, the subsequent remarks to the Users' Group by Hildebrand about a potential 50–50 split of ZGS time took the place of such a policy statement.[6]

The Policy Advisory Board made its contribution to the attempts to define the role of the national laboratories during the next decade. The Board followed the pattern of much that had been said before both by its own members and by others—the bits about unique facilities and interdisciplinary research, and large projects, and striking a balance between basic research and development. More interesting was what the Board was against—terminating the Laboratory and transferring its research program to some other agency. It tried to define the point at which the Laboratory would be impinging on industry, by carrying development past some unclear line, and on universities, by teaching and training at some unspecified academic level.[7]

The Policy Advisory Board's main work lay in supervising the review committees which were set up for each of the seven research divisions of the Laboratory. These were composed of six to eight members, primarily university people, but also including some representatives from industry and even other AEC laboratories. Each committee had at least one ex officio Policy Advisory Board member. The committees followed a routine by which they reported to the Chancellor of Chicago, who in turn transmitted the reports automatically to the Policy Advisory Board and to the Director's office. The reports did not go to the various division directors nor to the Board of Directors of AMU. The accepted view was that these reports, as was the Policy Advisory Board itself, were the property of the University of Chicago and only of the University. When the AEC attempted, in early 1959, to send representatives to meetings of the review committees and to require copies of reports, the Policy Advisory Board said "no" on the reports and left the question of visitors up to the individual committees. When the AEC continued to press the point, objecting to receiving only excerpts or edited versions of the review committee reports, the University of Chicago decided to totally isolate the review committees by assuming the financial cost of the consulting fees that were paid to the reviewers.[8]

The concept that the Policy Advisory Board had a responsibility to the Midwest scientific community rather than to Chicago was submerged within the operational review procedure. It reemerged in late 1961, when the Laboratory received notice that the proposed operating budget of the ZGS for fiscal 1962 had been cut from $7.8 million to $6.3 million and the budget for fiscal 1963 from $15.6 to $12 million. Albert Crewe, who had just replaced Hilberry as Laboratory Director, and Roger Hildebrand, still Associate Director for High Energy Physics, described the cut as "a serious blow to the vitality of the Midwest's high energy physics program." The reality was there. Nineteen groups, twelve from schools, were planning experiments for the ZGS. The Policy Advisory Board concurred that the cut was critical and asked the new President of the University of Chicago, George Beadle, who was attending his first Policy Advisory Board meeting, to talk to the new Chairman of the Atomic Energy Commission, Glenn Seaborg. Ironically, at the same meeting of the Board, the Laboratory also presented its proposal for a new reactor— called the Argonne Advanced Research Reactor, or A^2R^2. It would cost only $25 million and, the Board was told, would improve both the neutron flux and the morale of the Reactor Engineering Division. The Board took no action on the proposal.[9]

The perspective of the Users' Group naturally centered on the ZGS. After the successful first meeting, Goldwasser, who had been asked by Hildebrand to call the group together, appointed a committee to "Establish Procedures for Selecting a Chairman." The committee, chaired by Hildebrand, did just that, the procedure being to have the Associate Director for High Energy Physics name a selection committee, which in turn would appoint a chairman for the Users' Group, subject to the approval of the Associate Director. The committee not only established procedures, it immediately followed them by appointing Goldwasser chairman for 1959–1960.

During that first year, the Users' Group supplied letters that Argonne used to seek AEC support for the experimental facilities that were to be appended to ZGS. In turn, Hildebrand announced a policy on machine use in which he now anticipated that from one-third to one-half the research would be from Argonne staff and one-half to two-thirds from universities. To implement the policy, he proposed to establish a scheduling committee and a "long range," "broad planning" committee of "senior scientists." The principal appointments to both groups were to be by him. A final policy concerned the use of the large detection equipment that would be needed to visualize the particles produced by the accelerator. A group was being formed within Argonne to build a hydrogen bubble chamber. The builders, Hildebrand announced, would formulate the policies for the chamber's use.[10]

These announcements were made to the Users' Group at its third meeting, on January 15, 1960. On January 11, MURA had formally submitted a proposal to the AEC for the design, construction, and testing of an intermediate-size, 28-inch, bubble chamber at a cost of $558,200. (Eventually, it would be 30 inches and cost $2.5 million.) "It is proposed," the transmittal letter said, "that this chamber be used in conjunction with experiments on the Brookhaven AGS accelerator and the Argonne ZGS synchrotron as well as eventually being used with the MURA accelerator."

The MURA proposal was approved by the AEC almost immediately, but not in the context MURA had wanted. The approval letter stated:

> It is to be understood that this bubble chamber will probably be used exclusively at Argonne National Laboratory with the ZGS. As a result, arrangements should be made for an ANL member to participate in the design of the chamber. . . . It is expected that ANL will provide a crew for the ultimate operation of the chamber. Present plans are that the chamber itself will be assembled and tested in Madison and then will be transported to ANL. The magnet, however, will be assembled at ANL. . . . It is also to be understood that the chamber will be considered to be a national facility when completed and will be available for the use of various research groups.

A month of negotiations changed the ground rules to allow the chamber to be built at Madison, to recognize the possibility of its use at a facility other than Argonne, and to acknowledge that its builders would be given "favorable treatment" by the ZGS scheduling committee. The main point, however, was not modified. "We intend," the AEC said, "that the chamber is ultimately to be a ZGS facility. . . ." MURA, its accelerator shelved for the foreseeable future, accepted the terms.[11]

The distinction made between the Argonne-built bubble chamber and the MURA-built bubble chamber was not overtly apparent except to the MURA members of the Users' Group. When one of them, Keith Symon, was chosen by the Selection Committee to succeed Goldwasser as Chairman of the Users' Group, he attempted to broaden the impact of the Users' Group on Argonne policy. In November 1960, he invited four physicists—Goldwasser (Illinois), F. Reines (Case Institute), Arthur Roberts (Argonne), and Kent Terwilliger (Michigan)—to be the initial members of a "Users' Advisory Committee." The committee's purpose was "to keep track of the

ZGS program," advise the chairman of the Users' Group, make recommendations to Hildebrand "on matters of interest to the Users," and "serve as the spokesman for the Users' Group" to the Argonne administration and the AEC. "I do not know of any immediate and pressing need for a watchdog committee," Symon wrote, "but the Users' Advisory Committee would certainly serve that function if it were necessary."[12]

The Advisory Committee held its first meeting on December 15, 1960, with Hildebrand and Crewe, who was still the Director of the Particle Accelerator Division and the man responsible for building the ZGS. A number of technical design problems were discussed both for informational exchange and to seek assistance. The touchy issue, however, was the policy of using bubble chambers and the distinctions that were being drawn between the MURA-built chamber that was to be "community property" and the Argonne-built chamber that was not. Though Hildebrand initially responded by saying he thought that practice would prove similar though policies were dissimilar, his final assertion was that the leader of the Argonne design group, Robert Thompson, would make the final decision on the Argonne chamber's use and that physicists wishing to use that chamber would have to join Thompson's group in order to do so.

The Advisory Committee objected strongly. They acknowledged that builders of bubble chambers had proprietary interests that included time priority, maintenance responsibilities, and even the power of veto over proposed experiments that might modify or damage the chamber. But, they proposed, the use of major equipment should be governed by the same criterion that decided which experiments got time on the accelerator, namely scientific quality. To this end, they began discussions with Hildebrand to modify his policy.[13] And modify it he did. In June 1961, after an open discussion at a meeting of the Users' Group, Hildebrand proposed a policy that would schedule experiments according to scientific merit, make all large detectors available for general use, give builders a "reasonable" fraction of time, and allow builders to pass on all modifications.[14] This represented a significant change, though it was not as meaningful as it might have been, since shortly afterwards the Argonne chamber was refused funding by the AEC. This left the MURA chamber the only one to be divided.

The Users' Group and its Advisory Committee was semi-officially placed into a schematic of Argonne's administrative hierarchy. The resulting configuration told part of the tale of why policy modification was not always easy.[15]

The ultimate in cooperation: the June 1967 ground-breaking ceremony
for the A^2R^2, Argonne's research reactor that never got built.
From left to right: William B. Harrell, Vice President, The University
of Chicago; Kenneth A. Dunbar, Manager, AEC Chicago Operations Office;
Milton Levenson, Project Manager, A^2R^2; Winston M. Manning, Acting
Director, Argonne National Laboratory; and Philip N. Powers, President,
Argonne Universities Association.

The dedication of the Experimental Boiling Water Reactor (EBWR), the first nuclear power system in the United States built for experimenting in the generation of electric power. From left to right: John M. West, EBWR Project Manager; Representative Carl T. Durham, Chairman of the Joint Committee on Atomic Energy; Chancellor Lawrence Kimpton, The University of Chicago; and AEC Chairman Lewis Strauss

Argonne Universities Association trustees and administrative officers in
1968. Left to right, front row: Harold E. Wittig, The University of
Wisconsin; D. Robert Thomas, AUA Counsel; Clinton T. Johnson,
University of Minnesota; Philip N. Powers, Purdue University; Howard
R. Bowen, The University of Iowa; Frederick D. Rossini, University
of Notre Dame; (back row) Murray Joslin, Commonwealth Edison
Company; Edwin L. Goldwasser, University of Illinois; Kent M.
Terwilliger, The University of Michigan; Novice G. Fawcett, The Ohio
State University; John A. D. Cooper, Northwestern University;
John L. Magee, University of Notre Dame; Armon F. Yanders, Michigan
State University; Laurence R. Lunden, University of Minnesota;
G. Baley Price, The University of Kansas; Anton Lang, Michigan State
University; W. R. Marshall, Jr., The University of Wisconsin; William
Kerr, The University of Michigan; and William B. Harrell, The University
of Chicago. Three trustees were not present: Wilbur K. Pierpont,
The University of Michigan; John C. Weaver, University of Missouri;
and George W. Beadle, The University of Chicago.

The Experimental Breeder Reactor-II was the site in September 1965 for a meeting of the first three Laboratory Directors: Norman Hilberry, Walter H. Zinn, and Albert V. Crewe.

Site A, location of the reactors, Chicago Pile 2 (CP-2) and Chicago Pile 3 (CP-3) in Palos Park Forest Preserve.

An aerial view of the "ZGS Complex." In the center, surrounded by an earthen wall, is the Zero Gradient Synchrotron (ZGS), Argonne's 12.5 billion electron volt particle accelerator.

This plaque on the wall of West Stands of Stagg Field was unveiled December 2, 1947, at the Fifth Anniversary reunion of those who participated in the event it commemorates. Present were (l to r) R. F. Bacher, USAEC Commissioner; Farrington Daniels, Walter H. Zinn, Enrico Fermi, and Robert M. Hutchins, Chancellor, University of Chicago.

Members of the new U.S. Atomic Energy Commission pay their first
visit to Argonne National Laboratory on The University of Chicago campus.
The date was November 20, 1946. (l to r) Sumner T. Pike and William
W. Waymack, members, AEC; Walter H. Zinn, Director, ANL;
David H. Lilienthal, Chairman, AEC; Farrington Daniels, Director,
Metallurgical Laboratory; Robert F. Bacher, and Lewis L. Strauss, members,
AEC; and Col. K. D. Nichols, District Engineer, Manhattan District.

An aerial view of Argonne National Laboratory. The area at the lower right houses administration and support facilities. The Zero Gradient Synchrotron, Argonne's $12\frac{1}{2}$ billion electron volt particle accelerator, is located at left center.

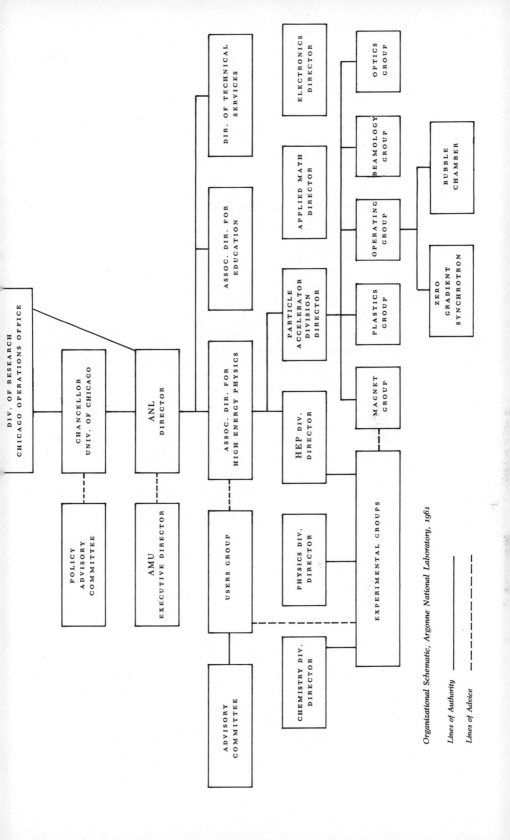

Organizational Schematic, Argonne National Laboratory, 1961

Lines of Authority ————

Lines of Advice — — — — —

The other part was told in the way the fiscal 1963 high-energy physics budget was cut by the AEC, without consultation with either Argonne or Chicago or any of the available university groups. It was presented as an accomplished fact. And though people like Goldwasser protested that the Midwestern community was continuing to feel cheated of its fair share of the high energy budget, the cut remained. The budget issue, in scale, was much smaller than the reactor development decision of 1948, but its procedures illustrated that the decision-making process that determined Argonne's actual operation had not significantly changed over the past thirteen years.[16]

Despite the fact that AMU's Executive Director Roberson served as a coordinator for the Users' Group, the AMU-Argonne relationship had not been particularly enhanced by the association. In January 1962, Hildebrand wrote Symon about four projects that he had been proposing AMU provide for the high-energy physics group ever since 1959. These were: housing, to be built with AMU funds; AMU automobiles for off-site dining; a chartered plane service to fly physicists from their home campuses to a small airport near Argonne; and a fund to support the travel of foreign users without requiring AEC approval. None of these, Hildebrand complained, had been provided by AMU.

> With only AEC funds it is hard to see what AMU can do for us that we can not do for ourselves with ANL or university contract money . . . With private money there is no end to the possibilities we might consider. We could, for example, have a cooperative research institute at or near Argonne suitable for some of our instruction leading to advanced degrees (this idea advanced by Alvin Weinberg has interested Al Crewe). But it is futile to think of such grand schemes if we can not find someone to buy us an automobile.[17]

Hildebrand's concept of AMU's appropriate level of cooperation did not exactly match the self-image of the Board of Directors. True, AMU had gotten off to a slow start. Its first year was spent finding a director and running a few meetings. But the question of some ideal working relationship between AMU, ANL, and the University of Chicago was never lost sight of. At the second annual Council meeting (May 1959), several Council members wanted to know about both the Policy Advisory Board's activities and those of the review committees. AMU's President, J. H. Jensen, who attended Policy Advisory Board meetings by virtue of his office, and Norman Hilberry, the Laboratory Director, responded that the

Policy Advisory Board and the review committees had been promised "sufficient privacy in what they said so that they would feel free to express themselves fully." However, since the Policy Advisory Board had been intended, in the words of the Rettaliata Report, "to serve as a correlating mechanism between the Sponsoring Institutions and the Contractor or Laboratory management," Hilberry agreed to look into the possibility of circulating "abstracts pertinent to university interests."

The Board of Directors, following the Council's lead, tried to relate the Policy Advisory Board to AMU. In October 1959, it requested the Policy Advisory Board to examine the university-Laboratory relationship in the relatively neglected area of biology and medicine. It also decided to ask members of the Policy Advisory Board to speak at the 1960 Council meeting on the Laboratory research program in their particular field of interest. What the Board of Directors desired was that the Policy Advisory Board members and the review committee members begin to stimulate some interest among their colleagues in using Argonne. The idea of having Policy Advisory Board members report to the Council did not work. Only one Policy Advisory Board member appeared at the 1960 meeting, and he spoke primarily about MURA, of which he was President. A different tack was then taken by the Council, and it decided to seek a joint meeting with the Policy Advisory Board during the next year. There was great truth in the remarks of Chancellor Kimpton when he welcomed the Council to the annual meeting. "This is the kind of enterprise," he said, "in which we must expect to make haste slowly."

The Board of Directors persisted. The minutes of the July 1960 meeting say only that "a lengthy discussion took place on the desirable relationship between the universities, Argonne, and participation by individual university personnel." But when the Board met again, in October, it decided that a review of what had been accomplished during AMU's first three years was in order, particularly to evaluate the reality against the expectations of the Rettaliata Report.[18] Since the Board knew what its own activities encompassed—a Conference on Nuclear Engineering Education that had been held in January, with a second planned for early 1961, an upcoming conference of the deans of the AMU graduate schools, and three contracts with the AEC to support its own conferences and the Users' Group meetings—what the Board was driving at was the eternal question of why it and Argonne existed side by side. This was the subject of a letter sent by AMU's new President, R. S. Shankland, to Warren Johnson, who was now a Vice President of the University of Chicago and the scientific half of Chicago's Argonne management team, Harrell still being the financial officer. The letter was the first shot in a new skirmish of an old war.

> The Board views the Laboratory as a supplement to the surrounding universities. . . . We expect that problems and conflicts will always exist as long as the Laboratory is conceived as a research institution, without full and equal emphasis being given at all levels to its responsibilities to work with the universities in research and graduate education.
>
> If the Laboratory is to function as a cooperator with the universities, and be an effective supplement to them, then its research program must be predominantly in those fields of interest to universities.
>
> If this idealized situation is achieved, university interests should have a strong voice in determining the basic research program of the Laboratory. . . . The permanent staff of the Laboratory should give due consideration to university interests and be careful to avoid conflicts with them.
>
> We recognize also that there exists in some universities the viewpoint which considers the national laboratories to be in competition with the universities for staff, facilities, program support, and recognition for research results. This attitude exists because the Laboratory has not fully achieved its role which was originally conceived to be *a regional laboratory designed primarily to serve institutions in the North Central United States.*[19]

The last sentence (with Shankland's added underlining and a change in capitalization) harked back to, and quoted accurately, the recommendations made to General Groves by the inter-university committee chaired by Arthur Holly Compton that had met on December 2, 1945. The Board of Directors of AMU suddenly had some sense of its origins, of early intentions and past recommendations. "What is urgently needed," the Board wrote in 1961, "is for the AEC, the Laboratory, and the universities to agree on a constructive plan for increased use of the Laboratory by the universities."

The May 1961 Council meeting brought together several tangential pursuits—the evaluation of how well the Rettaliata Report had been carried out, the scheduling of a joint meeting with the Policy Advisory Board, and the search for a concept of the "desirable relationship" of the Laboratory to the universities. The Annual

Report of the Board of Directors presented but came to no conclusion about the key question of whether the Policy Advisory Board was a link between AMU and Laboratory management. The answer, however, was in the presentation of the members of the Policy Advisory Board who spoke to the Council. Three of them, as the minutes reported, gave informational talks on "topics of national scientific interest." The fourth spoke briefly on "Laboratory-University Relations."

The third pursuit was more direct. Six speakers from different university associations spoke on their organizational structures and their problems. AMU was one; the others were Oak Ridge Institute of Nuclear Studies, Brookhaven National Laboratory, MURA, the Mid-America State Universities Association, and the Accelerator Users' Group. It was a lesson in organizational structure which was followed by a discussion of the AMU-Argonne relationship. Some hard truths were faced by the schools: that the Council was a heterogeneous group, some members of which could speak for their schools, others only for themselves; that representation ranged from faculty of large schools to presidents of small ones. How, it was asked, could such a group set common goals? There was also doubt whether the Policy Advisory Board members elected by AMU's Board of Directors could really affect Laboratory policy and bring it closer to what the Council might want. The Laboratory, it was suggested, might be working at cross purposes with the universities.

The Laboratory comments were equally frank. Argonne had other missions besides collaborating with universities. The Laboratory believed its long term future depended upon a complementary relationship with the Midwestern schools. A national laboratory had to have "something of the academic atmosphere and opportunities similar to those found on the university campus." While the Laboratory staff had "many desirable expansions" in mind, the AEC had proposed only a limited increase for the Laboratory during the 1960's.[20]

The total impression was that the relationship, with the exception of the still-to-be-finished ZGS, was essentially a static one, with little movement of university people to the Laboratory or of Laboratory people to the universities. During the preceding year, there had been a number of AMU-sponsored meetings: the deans of the graduate schools, the chairmen of chemistry departments; meetings on non-destructive testing, on heat transfer, on computers; AMU's standing committee on Nuclear Engineering Education was working on its third annual conference, and had study groups exploring joint university-Laboratory use of the Experimental Boiling Water Reactor, which in 1961 was no longer the unique demonstration facility it had been in 1957.

The trouble was that much of this activity was only surface action, removed from the decision-making process that determined Argonne's research programs. If, when the ZGS went operational, it proved to be a Midwestern accelerator, then part of the relationship would be considered truly cooperative. Until there was some operating experience, there was only past and present history to rely on. Part of this was the unsuccessful Laboratory attempt to secure a new and more powerful research reactor, the A^2R^2.

The proposal for A^2R^2, dated July 15, 1961, had been under consideration by the Laboratory for two years. Its predecessor was the quickly scrapped Mighty Mouse reactor of 1958 that was to have cost $80 million. In 1960, when the Laboratory began to consider a modest $25 million reactor, the question of university support was raised. What was interesting about the existing Argonne reactors, notably CP-5, was that there was no time-sharing mechanism, no users' group, as there was for the ZGS. Laboratory research needs took up almost all of the reactor research capability, with the exception of a few irradiations. There were no large university experiments which required additional machinery such as spectrometers and neutron choppers sitting on the experimental floor for considerable periods of time. The university people who wanted to use reactors as neutron sources for basic research simply did not enjoy the cooperative relationship contemplated for high energy physicists.

Yet, if Argonne was considering an additional research reactor, the concept of university users would have to be considered, both for its political value as a means of acquiring authorization from the Joint Committee and, later, should the facility be built, for its scheduling impact. The A^2R^2 proposal was "based primarily on the needs of Argonne's internal program," but recognized the potential for cooperative work with university people. The trouble was the absence of any mechanism for accomplishing this. The inclusion of possible university participation struck one member of the Nuclear Engineering Education Committee "more as an afterthought than anything else." The Committee discussed a review committee involving a number of disciplines which would assess university interest in all Argonne reactors. This was not immediately followed, primarily because of the attention that was to be paid to the overall question of AMU and Argonne.

The time was ripe for a retrospective view. AMU had moved, undramatically, into its fourth year, and everywhere there were personnel or structural changes. Albert Crewe had become Director of Argonne in November 1961. George Beadle had become Chancellor of Chicago in May.* Glenn Seaborg, who had separated plutonium in Jones Hall in the war-time era of the Met Lab, had been appointed Chairman of the Atomic Energy Commission by President John F. Kennedy. And in Washington there had been a shift in the AEC's organizational structure whereby Argonne Laboratory, removed from the reactor development hierarchy, now reported to a new Assistant General Manager for Research and Development.

The question of AMU's future was designated as the sole subject of a special Board of Directors meeting scheduled for January 5 and 6, 1962. This had been decided back in July 1961, without any broad implications or ominous portents. Though AMU's Executive Director, John Roberson, proposed that the meeting focus on some specific problems, it stayed general in format and just happened.

The retrospective was held away from both Argonne and the University of Chicago at the Allerton estate owned by the University of Illinois. The conference divided into three groups: physical science, nuclear engineering, and biology, each of which met separately and then came together for a general session. Common themes that attempted to put some balance into the relationship recurred in each group:

—that Argonne should have a life of its own;
—that Argonne staff should be recognized by honorary faculty appointments;
—that there should be opportunities for faculty to come to Argonne in the summer to do their own research rather than consult on Argonne's projects;
—that the "glamorous field" of high energy physics should be de-emphasized;
—that direct housekeeping services should be provided to faculty visitors;
—that joint pilot projects, e.g., in thermonuclear plasmas or biology, should be initiated to test the validity of the concept of cooperative programs.

Two additional themes proved to be more crucial in the subsequent months: the role of the Policy Advisory Board and its re-

*The title was officially changed to President in October.

view committees, and the educational function of the Laboratory. Crewe, the new Laboratory Director, responded negatively to the concept of the review committees having two separate functions and serving two masters. He felt that as long as the review committee reports did not go to Laboratory staff, and he did not want them to, then reports, however different in subject, should not go to university people.

On the educational role of the Laboratory, Crewe took a "no charity, please" attitude. The Laboratory had facilities the universities would never have. What he wanted was what Zinn had wanted ten years earlier, an exchange in which the best people moved in both directions. An educational alternative was touched on by Brookhaven's Director, Leland Haworth, who referred to a plan by Alvin Weinberg, the Director of Oak Ridge, that advocated turning national laboratories into universities. Haworth opposed this idea, primarily on the grounds that "the place for students is a well-rounded university."[21]

The report of the Allerton meeting was printed and circulated within a month. Though its suggestions were discussed at subsequent meetings of the Policy Advisory Board and the Board of Directors, not much came of them. The Policy Advisory Board decided that the review committees might include in their reports to the President of the University of Chicago comments pertinent to the ANL-university relations, and that the President in turn could transmit these, if he wished. This was nothing like the personal interaction AMU wanted. The Policy Advisory Board also discussed but failed to reach an immediate decision on letting AMU's Executive Director attend its meetings. This had not only been recommended by the Rettaliata Report, but also had been adopted, and quickly forgotten, as a routine procedure at the first meeting of the Policy Advisory Board five years earlier. Yet, in 1962, his presence was viewed as that of an outsider.[22]

The Board of Directors of AMU was no more successful in implementing the suggestions from Allerton. At its March 21 meeting, it heard a report from an ad hoc committee that had met with Argonne staff to discuss university participation in choosing faculty for the Laboratory's summer program. The committee reported back that there was "no basis for AMU participation . . . at the present time." A proposed committee to set up a pilot project in the biological sciences was deferred until the new Director of the Biological and Medical Research Division had come on site. The problem of cars for visitors was temporarily solved by having the AMU Executive Director volunteer his own automobile pending a more substantial solution. The only positive note was a decision to change the name of AMU to Associated American Universities, a last-hour recommendation at Allerton that was intended to remove any hint of geographic parochialism.

The question of changing the Policy Advisory Board's role was pushed during 1962 by the President of AMU, W. L. Everitt (Illinois). In a letter to Chicago's President Beadle, he pointed to the recommendation of the Rettaliata Committee that the Policy Advisory Board be a link of communication between the universities and the University of Chicago, and stated that this function had been lost. He also passed on to Beadle a request from the Nuclear Engineering Education Committee that one member of the committee attend the program presentations made by three Laboratory divisions to the review committees and that the committee receive relevant program information. Beadle responded by saying he agreed with establishing the communication function and asked Everitt to bring the question up to the Policy Advisory Board, which was currently reviewing the review committees. Internally, at Chicago, Vice President Harrell commented to Beadle that the proposed change would reduce the frankness and the effectiveness of the review committees. He suggested symposia as a better way of communicating between ANL and AMU staff.[23]

The May 1962 meeting of the AMU Council reported on the various conferences and meetings of the past year, raised the question of communication, but gave the impression of an active, ongoing organization that was seeking better ways to be more effective. Hilberry was given a citation for twenty years of service at Argonne and the Met Lab. Goldwasser made a speech on his emotional and intellectual ties to AMU that ended with a suggestion that the organization become financially independent of the AEC in order to have more initiative in its activities. And Arizona was admitted to the Midwest, as the Council voted to make the University of Arizona a member and at the same time retain the name Associated Midwest Universities.

During these initial years of AMU, the development of atomic energy, under John McCone's Commission and then under Glenn Seaborg's, was relatively quiet and productive. The emphasis was on power reactor development, nuclear propulsion, bombs, and fallout. The Joint Committee continued to push for a more aggressive power program, but in the other three areas had few complaints. The first Polaris submarine, the *George Washington*, armed with sixteen atomic-bomb missiles, went on patrol duty in 1960. The voluntary moratorium on atmospheric bomb tests that had begun in late 1958 was broken in 1961, initially by a series of thirty-one Russian tests, which included twenty-five and fifty-megaton bombs, and then by American tests that eventually detonated an H-bomb in Nevada.* Radioactive clouds drifted over the United States, and anyone who wanted to know what the fallout signified had only to read the two-volume edition of the Joint Committee's hearings on the subject.**

By now AMU was four years old, going on five, and yet in many ways just beginning to feel its way into the administrative structures of the Laboratory and the University of Chicago. At the July meeting of the Board of Directors, Roberson reported that he believed that the relationship between the universities and the Laboratory had "degenerated," that his "communications at the working level" were not good. He cited as an example "a proposal for a graduate center" that, he said, was "well developed" within the Laboratory but about which he had only hearsay information. Roberson told the Board that he was discouraged by the lack of progress and that the Board should find an additional staff member who could replace him if necessary. The probability of losing its executive director was a problem, but more important to the Board was the news that a "graduate center" proposal existed.[24] After all, back home at the campuses, there already were graduate centers. Tender nerves were touched everywhere, knees jerked, and a new crisis suddenly existed that called into question the integrity of the relationship between AMU and the University of Chicago.

---

*France, which ignored the moratorium, had exploded its first atomic bomb in 1959, followed with two more in 1960 and 1961.

**The most spectacular scientific event during this period was the April 1961 orbital voyage of Yuri Gagarin in Vostok I. John Glenn followed him into space in February 1962. The concept of traveling beyond the earth, of putting a man on the moon, captured the imagination of the public and of the people who formulated the nation's scientific priorities.

CHAPTER 13

The Argonne Graduate Center

The idea of transforming national laboratories into universities did not originate at Argonne. Back in November 1960, a Panel on Basic Research and Graduate Education that was appointed by President Eisenhower's Science Advisory Committee had issued a 31-page report entitled *Scientific Progress, the Universities, and the Federal Government*. The main point of the report was expressed figuratively in a slightly twisted metaphor:

> Basic research and graduate education, together, are the knotted core of American science, and they will grow stronger together, or not at all. . . . The Federal Government, by its varied missions and the size of its financial commitments, is the most powerful single force in this whole field, while the universities are the natural holders and custodians of the knotted core. Both have done much to strengthen, and something to weaken the common enterprise in recent decades. Both must do better in the years ahead.

Conclusion XI, of the sixteen conclusions that the Committee felt would mean doing better, was headlined "Scientists Outside Universities Can Be Fruitfully Connected to Graduate Education." The report specifically cited Argonne as an example of a "great government-supported" installation where it should be possible for "research scientists to contribute to the graduate programs of nearby universities." Later in the text it recommended "improving [the] connection" to graduate education, but never got more specific than either of the verbs "contribute" or "improve."

Glenn Seaborg, still Chancellor at Berkeley, chaired the Panel. Among its fourteen members were George Beadle, still at the California Institute of Technology, and Alvin Weinberg, the Director of Oak Ridge National Laboratory.

Weinberg carried these ideas to a more pointed conclusion in a speech, on January 16, 1962, to the National Science Foundation Monthly Colloquium. He proposed that "Big Science," in which category he included national laboratories, whose demands had created a shortage of scientific manpower, could rectify the situation by playing a greater role in education. Weinberg used Conclusion XI of the 1960 Panel report as his jumping off point:

> There are two symmetric routes to achieve this aim of encouraging both graduate science education and basic research. On the one hand, one can start with a good school and build up its basic research; or one can start with a basic research institute (a federal laboratory, for example) and adjoin to it a good graduate school. The former scheme is the one traditionally followed in our country. It is, however, the latter scheme which I propose here.

And later, in his speech, after listing the advantages (many) and the disadvantages (only one—that it "might divert the laboratories from their primary purpose of developing nuclear weapons or reactors or rockets"), Weinberg said, "What I am proposing is nothing less than a gradual conversion of our big federal laboratories, wherever possible, into M. I. T.-type institutions—into research institutions which participate integrally, not peripherally, in educating Ph.D.'s in the sciences."*

Short of this, he advocated joint institutes with existing neighboring universities. His proposals, he predicted, were "likely to be received with suspicion—in particular, perhaps, by the academic community, which might see in such a move an encroachment on the proper domain of the universities."[1]

Weinberg's speech was published in *Science* in April 1962. His ideas circulated widely, as Haworth's opposition at Allerton a week prior to the Washington speech indicated. His prediction as to their reception was an understatement. Only it wasn't Weinberg and Oak Ridge that made the trial run, but rather Albert Crewe and Argonne.

---

*An example of what Weinberg had in mind was the conversion of Rockefeller Institute into Rockefeller University, a graduate school in mathematics and the applied sciences, whose President in 1971 is Frederick Seitz. Weinberg, by 1965, felt that his proposal was "a mistake," which, if carried out, would have blurred if not eliminated the "precious" quality of the federal laboratory—their "mission orientation."

Crewe, though director of a national laboratory, was only thirty-five years old. A high-energy physicist educated at the University of Liverpool in England and acknowledged to be a capable project leader, he had been at the University of Chicago for seven years and at Argonne for two. The Laboratory's Associate Director for Education was Frank Myers, who had previously been Chairman of the Physics Department and Dean of the Graduate School at Lehigh University. Together, Crewe and Myers wrote "A Proposal for an Argonne Campus for the University of Chicago." It was this proposal that Roberson had called attention to at the July 17 meeting of the Board of Directors of AMU. Dated July 18, it made a very specific recommendation:

> It is recommended that the University of Chicago establish a major Graduate Center of Pure and Applied Science at a location convenient to the Argonne site.

> It is recommended that the University take full responsibility for the administration of the Graduate Center and that it call on the Laboratory for assistance in supplying the instructing staff. . . .

The courses taught at the proposed center would include physics, chemistry, biology, mathematics, and applied science (engineering). Total enrollment was projected at the equivalent of five hundred full-time students, with an actual total of seven hundred full- and part-time students. This was described as more than the number of graduate students enrolled at M. I. T. The staff was estimated at the equivalent of between seventy and eighty full-time faculty, with the Laboratory providing two-thirds and the University of Chicago the remainder. Argonne would have no trouble providing the faculty, as six hundred of its staff members held Ph.D.'s. The proposal even calculated the space needed for classrooms, a lecture hall, and a library—sixty-six thousand square feet.

The reasons cited to justify the center's existence were the recommendations of the 1960 Panel headed by Seaborg and subsequent extension by Weinberg. The proposal emphasized, however, that it differed from Weinberg's ideas on one important point. "We . . . do not propose that Argonne become a degree-granting institution, but rather that . . . degrees be granted solely by the University."

The advantage to the University of Chicago was cited as expansion. The advantages to Argonne were the retention of staff currently lost to universities and a steady supply of bright young research people who would not be permanent employees. Not mentioned was a reason that Weinberg had already paid much attention to in other speeches—the realization that the original purposes for which national laboratories had been established, their particular missions, were no longer so encompassing as to justify the continued existence of the laboratories, and that they had better find some new missions.

The proposal acknowledged that a Graduate Center "might alter and ultimately limit" the cooperative programs with AMU. While it tried to see the brighter side, to emphasize the gains and not the losses, the main point of its comments was that AMU played a minor role in the educational programs of the Laboratory. There were only thirteen thesis appointees at the Laboratory, not all of whom were from AMU schools. The report estimated the Laboratory could handle two hundred. There were twenty-five summer faculty appointees, less than half of whom were from AMU schools. There were forty-one postdoctoral appointees, of whom thirteen were from AMU schools. There were one hundred forty-two undergraduates employed as summer aides, less than half of whom were from AMU schools.

The message that emerges from these figures depends on the point of view. One extreme is that AMU was hardly using Argonne; the other that Argonne was not letting AMU use the Laboratory.

The conclusion of the report asserted that the potential gains from a Graduate Center justified trying to find solutions to the possible problems, and modestly suggested that the proposal was only a "point of departure."

Part of the reason that the news of the proposal was disturbing was that it clearly suggested a unilateral relationship between Argonne and the University of Chicago. AMU existed as part of a multi-lateral relationship in which Chicago was intended to play no greater role than Wisconsin or Michigan or Minnesota. Compounding this aspect was the secrecy with which the proposal was developed. In June, the new President of AMU, W. R. Marshall (Wisconsin), had visited Crewe to discuss AMU-ANL relations. One of Crewe's complaints was that the AMU Board met in private, to discuss matters pertaining to Argonne, but no one on the Argonne staff participated. Marshall agreed to rectify this, and proposed a series of changes to the Board of Directors—to have Laboratory representation at Board meetings; to prepare AMU publicity on ANL programs; to establish direct relations between AMU and the divisional directors, bypassing the Policy Advisory Board. "We should work together on a joint interest basis," Marshall's report to his Board concluded, "rather than on a conflict of interest basis." That the

Graduate Center proposal was being privately prepared by Argonne during this month undercut the changes envisioned by Marshall.[2]

Roberson, AMU's Executive Director, wrote about the problem to one of the members of the AEC's General Advisory Committee, J. C. Warner, a former member of the old Council Executive Board. Roberson mentioned that he had seen the Graduate Center proposal, but had no copies. He stated that he believed no "framework" existed which represented a mutual understanding of the relationship between the universities, the AEC, the Laboratory, and the University of Chicago, that there was "no common understanding" of the purpose of Argonne. He proposed that the various university organizations involved with the AEC's laboratories meet with the General Advisory Committee.[3]

The suggestion was taken up. The General Advisory Committee* scheduled a two-day meeting on "Interrelationships between the National Laboratories and the Universities." The laboratory directors were to meet with the General Advisory Committee on October 4; the several boards of Associated Midwest Universities, Oak Ridge Institute for Nuclear Studies, and Associated Universities, Incorporated on October 5. The Argonne-AMU problem was not the only reason. Oak Ridge had begun discussions with universities in order to seek some mutual teaching arrangement. The Los Alamos senior staff was supposed to be interested in educational activities, and California had reportedly established a separate campus at the Livermore Laboratory.

Marshall met with Crewe on September 22 to discuss the possibility of AMU and the Laboratory presenting a coordinated viewpoint. Crewe suggested instead that they exchange proposed presentations. Three days later he sent Marshall what he called "notes." "I realize that some of this will come as a surprise to you," he wrote, "and may, at first sight, cause you some concern." He suggested meeting privately with Marshall before the General Advisory Committee meeting. The "notes" were a revised version of the Graduate Center proposal, with some general introductory material on the Laboratory and minus some of the specific details on staff size and student enrollment. The most important change was the statement:

The University of Chicago and the Laboratory are actively considering the possibility of increased involvement of the Laboratory in graduate education and, in particular, we are at this

*Members were Kenneth Pitzer, Phillip Abelson, Manson Benedict, Willard Libby, Eger V. Murphree, Norman Ramsey, Eugene Wigner, John H. Williams, R. A. Charpie, and J. C. Warner.

time considering establishing close to the Laboratory a teaching center which may take one of the many forms ranging from a full-fledged campus to a graduate study center.[4]

The proposal made it clear that the University of Chicago would have full responsibility for the "Graduate Center."

Unfortunately, Marshall was out of town and did not see Crewe's letter until October 3, the day before Crewe was to meet with the General Advisory Committee. Marshall brought it with him to Washington, where two other members of the Board's Executive Committee, A. B. Cardwell (Kansas State) and W. L. Everitt, read it. Frederick Seitz, who was now President of the National Academy of Sciences, joined them for the General Advisory Committee meeting. The Graduate Center was the main topic, but the Board members did not make any statement as to its merits. The position they adopted was that they had no prior knowledge of the proposal and would have to withhold judgment until they could consider details.

Within AMU itself, the response was stronger. A committee that was to plan the Annual Council meeting in May decided that it was not possible to do so until what it identified "as a key problem dominating all other relationships could be cleared up." The Executive Committee of the Board of Directors discussed the Center at its scheduled meeting on October 16, by which time it had received copies of the proposal from Crewe as a "privileged communication."

Crewe came to the meeting to explain his position, as did Chicago's Vice President for Special Projects, Warren Johnson. "The sense of this discussion," the minutes read, "was that Dr. Crewe felt that ideas such as the graduate campus should be presented initially to the University of Chicago as the operating contractor for the Laboratory. Board members felt that the University of Chicago had a clear responsibility for Argonne in financial matters but had responsibility equal to that of other Sponsoring Institutions in certain non-financial matters, which included graduate education."

In an executive session that followed, the Board decided that the proposal for a graduate center at Argonne to be operated by the University of Chicago was not sufficiently developed to be endorsed, opposed, or even commented upon substantively; that when a definitive proposal existed, it would be examined, probably by a committee of graduate deans; that the Board interpreted the idea of integrating the Laboratory and Chicago as evidence that AMU had not demonstrated that adequate cooperation existed; that it was time to define Argonne's educational role; that the role of the universities in

Argonne's affairs also needed to be defined to avoid a repetition of the previous disagreements that had led to dissolving the Board of Governors, forming MURA, and disbanding the Council of Participating Institutions.

Specifically, the Board asked that the Policy Advisory Board invite AMU's Executive Director to attend all meetings, except executive sessions; that the University of Chicago establish a Review Committee on Education and Academic Affairs; and that the reports of all review committees be made available to AMU in a form to be decided by the University of Chicago.[5]

The Graduate Center was the topic of the Policy Advisory Board's meeting the next day, and posed to the members of the Committee the severest test of their multiple memberships and allegiances. President Beadle of Chicago began the presentation by personally assuming the primary responsibility for initiating the controversy. Ever since he had come to the University of Chicago, he reported, he had been involved in discussions for renegotiating the contract with the AEC; that as part of these talks, the AEC had asked about Chicago's "real interest" in Argonne. To this Beadle responded that the University was interested in the intellectual and scholarly work of the Laboratory. In July, he had asked Crewe to write up his thoughts on how the Laboratory might have a more direct relation with Chicago. The result was the July 18th proposal for a Graduate Center. Beadle stressed that the proposal had not been considered formally by the administration, the faculty, or the trustees of the University, that there was no attempt to do anything in secrecy nor to make Argonne less useful as a center of collaboration with other schools.

Marshall continued the discussion by stressing the seriousness with which AMU viewed an apparently formal intent to develop such a center with a single university. AMU should have been consulted on what was obviously a matter of "substantial educational content" and certainly before the proposal was discussed outside of the Argonne complex.

J. H. Jensen, the first president of AMU, reviewed the negative aspects of past university relations with Argonne—the dissolution of the Board of Governors because "it was presented with accomplished facts," the demoralizing ineffectiveness of the Council of Participating Institutions, and the attempt in the post-Rettaliata days to try again. The Center proposal, he said, showed a lack of mutual confidence.

Marshall then announced that the Board of Directors planned to distribute the proposal to presidents of the AMU schools. Seitz thought that distribution would be a bad idea, that it would only "stir things up," and aggravate a situation that could be brought under control. Beadle agreed with Seitz, seeing the proposal as a potential "drag" in the future. Marshall replied that since the document was known to exist, not circulating would make it appear that it was being suppressed. J. H. Williams saw the question as academic. Most university presidents, he guessed, probably had copies of the proposal.

Seitz's desire to cool the situation didn't mean he approved of what had happened. That the proposal had gone to the General Advisory Committee before the Policy Advisory Board even knew about it had caused him to feel "embarrassed not only for myself but for the whole community." Jensen and F. Rossini expressed similar ideas. Rossini said he found it hard to believe. To make the embarrassment worse, the Policy Advisory Board had met at Argonne on July 18, the day the Graduate Center proposal was dated, and Crewe had reported on the long range plans of the Laboratory without mentioning it. The proposal existed as the Board met; it was in the Graphic Arts Division being printed and bound; the University of Chicago knew of it; but no one had discussed it with the PAB.

Crewe attempted to explain. The idea of a Graduate Center was unanimously supported by the Laboratory division directors. Myers and he had drafted what they felt was an initial document, meant to stimulate discussion, not to be taken as definitive. He thought the proper procedure was to discuss it first with the Chicago administration, then with the Policy Advisory Board and finally with AMU, but he said he "could scarcely ignore the coincidental request of the General Advisory Committee to discuss the role of the national laboratories in graduate education." The University of Chicago had agreed to the presentation to the General Advisory Committee, a decision that was acknowledged to be "an error in communication."

The solution to the dilemma was one that has its counterpart in labor-management disputes. Williams moved "that the proposal to the University be withdrawn without prejudice pending further discussion and analysis." The motion was passed unanimously. So was the next motion to establish a Review Committee for Educational and Academic Affairs. But the final motion, that the reports of review committees be submitted in some diluted form to AMU, was successfully opposed by the Chicago administration.[6]

President Beadle officially withdrew the Argonne Campus proposal "without prejudice to merit" on November 5, but the general issues it had raised remained alive, and, to AMU's mind, unresolved.

Roberson saw two needs: a consistent Laboratory policy toward universities; a stronger concept of AMU's mission to its membership. Together they could provide the basis for trying again to establish a stable relationship. Moreover, before it would be possible to ask university people to work toward that stability, he believed a new statement of overall purpose was needed.[7]

A similar reluctance to participate until there was some clarification was expressed by the AMU Board to AEC officials in Washington on November 13. The conclusion to their meeting was a suggestion that AMU work with the University of Chicago to identify points of agreement and disagreement. To this end, there was a series of meetings between Marshall and Beadle, Crewe and Marshall, and the AMU Executive Committee. In the process, Beadle and the Policy Advisory Board rejected a proposal from Marshall that the Review Committee on Educational and Academic Affairs report to the AMU Board as well as to the University of Chicago. There was agreement, however, that the first task of the Review Committee would be to study the idea of a Graduate Center. Marshall emerged from the meetings "optimistic about the possibility of stronger and closer working relationships with Argonne during the coming year."[8]

The deans of the graduate schools of AMU got their first hand report at a January 1963 meeting. Crewe presented all the justifications—the shortage of trained scientists, the limitations of existing facilities at schools, the capability of the Laboratory to fill these needs. A major modification in his presentation was to propose that the faculty of the Center be drawn from both Argonne and the participating institutions. The unique role of Chicago had disappeared; the degrees would be granted by the participating universities, "the Laboratory becoming a part of each university."

The deans approached the issue from a substantive point of view, discussing some of the problems of off-campus study, the relative status of graduate students at a laboratory, quality control of the actual research. They came to no conclusion other than that if any plan was developed, they should be asked to review it. The sense of the meeting was that AMU and ANL needed one another, and that it should be possible to work out a mutually beneficial arrangement that would improve the quality and increase the quantity of graduate education in the Midwest.[9]

Mutual trust between AMU and Chicago, however, advanced slowly. The Policy Advisory Board decided to allow the AMU Executive Director to come to only that part of its meeting that concerned ANL-AMU interactions. As for review committee reports, the standard policy of keeping them private was modified only slightly; the Policy Advisory Board voted to abstract them for consideration by the AMU Board, but not for distribution. When the AMU Board proposed a new committee of faculty and Laboratory division directors, Crewe objected.[10]

The Review Committee for Educational Affairs was appointed during March and held its first meeting in April. The charge to the Committee was to advise on programs of cooperation not only with AMU but also with Associated Colleges of the Midwest and beyond. There was room in the charge to take up anything educational from a graduate center to high school tours of the Laboratory.[11]

The more university administrators heard that something resembling a graduate school at Argonne was being considered, the more disturbed they became. At the Annual Council meeting in May 1963, Crewe once again spoke of his plans and said that the new Review Committee, if it believes the objective reasonable, "hopefully would come up with detailed suggestions." He himself wanted more than joint ANL-school programs, and suggested formal courses which would be accepted for credit by participating schools. Council members reacted with more doubt than understanding. That the Review Committee reported to Chicago and not to AMU disturbed several of them, particularly if it were true that the Committee was going to prepare specific proposals for a graduate center.[12]

Actually there was no need for concern. The Review Committee for Educational Affairs spent a year essentially burying the Argonne campus. The position adopted by the Committee was that no proposal for a graduate center had been prepared that was sufficient in detail to allow value judgments to be made. Until such a proposal was presented, the Committee could only approve of and encourage the growth of existing programs such as on-site thesis studies, postdoctoral appointments and employment of undergraduates. Its report was delivered to the Policy Advisory Board in April of 1964.[13]

What came out of the Argonne campus proposal was an increase in the attention focused on both the formal and informal ties between the Laboratory and the schools of AMU. The Board of Directors, in its annual report of May 1963, stressed the need for improving communications, for acknowledging the reciprocal responsibilities of the Laboratory and AMU to assist each other.

The Board could point to the studies of possible joint research facilities—in plasma physics and electron microscopy—as a sign of encouragement. AMU had conducted or facilitated six conferences during the past year; plans had been made for an engineering practice school during the summer. The annual expenditures of AMU had grown from $353 in fiscal 1958 to $167,000 in fiscal 1963. The Board was considering establishing the Presidency of AMU as a permanent salaried position. However, it was also clear that much of the energy that might have gone into constructive activities had been dissipated by the controversy and distrust engendered by the graduate center concept. There were gaps everywhere—communication, credibility, participation. And, unfortunately, there had been little structural change that would preclude continued divergence. When an AMU Council member asked the Board of Directors to consider how it might actively participate in the review of academic matters, the Board responded that it was "depending on the good faith of the parties involved."

CHAPTER 14

MURA Reoriented

The official attitude of the AMU Board at the May 1963 Council meeting was one of determined optimism, a desire to believe that the system of which the Board and the Council were a part would work if only everyone made it work. A week later, on May 20, the report of yet another Panel on High Energy Accelerator Physics was made public. The report carried within it the issue that would hasten the end of AMU. It recommended that the MURA accelerator be built at Madison, Wisconsin.

This panel, sponsored jointly by the General Advisory Committee of the AEC and the President's Science Advisory Committee, was known as the Ramsey Panel, after its chairman, Norman Ramsey of Harvard. Among its ten members were E. L. Goldwasser, J. H. Williams, and Frederick Seitz.[*] The broad sense of the report was a projection of needs and priorities through 1981, looking toward a generation of accelerators beyond the Stanford Linear Accelerator. What the panel came up with has been described as an "$8 billion, 18-year shopping list." Specifically, there were three major contenders for authorization: a 200 Bev proton accelerator being designed at Berkeley, a 600 to 1,000 Bev machine in larval stage at Brookhaven, and the 10 Bev Fixed-Field Alternating Gradient (FFAG) accelerator proposed by MURA. The FFAG machine was known as a high intensity, as opposed to high energy, machine. The initial estimated cost was $120 million, with a seven-year construction schedule.

The Ramsey Panel made thirteen specific recommendations. The first three concerned the steps to higher energies:

---

[*] Other panel members were: Philip H. Abelson (Carnegie Institution of Washington), Owen Chamberlain (University of California), Murray Gell-Mann (California Institute of Technology), T. D. Lee (Columbia), W. K. M. Panofsky (Stanford), and E. M. Purcell (Harvard).

—the authorization at the earliest possible date of the 200 Bev Berkeley machine;

—the authorization of storage rings to raise the energy available from the Brookhaven AGS;

—support of Brookhaven studies for the 600 to 1,000 Bev machine.

The fourth and the most immediate in respect to time and feasibility was:

Authorize in fiscal year 1965 the construction, by MURA, of a supercurrent accelerator without permitting this to delay the steps toward higher energy. The energy of the MURA-FFAG accelerator should be 12.5 Bev instead of the 10 Bev originally proposed.

There is a well-known interpretation by D. S. Greenberg that what the Ramsey Panel "really" meant to say about MURA was quite different than what it seemed to say. According to Greenberg:

The panel, confronted by a tightening budget and a determination to pursue higher energies, was willing to throttle MURA. The problem at hand was how to do it without leaving fingerprints.

The solution, according to Greenberg, was "lethal faint praise" that "sealed the doom of MURA."

The sections which he felt did the job were:

The Panel has considered the great value of continuing the productivity of the major U.S. high-energy laboratories, in particular, the Brookhaven National Laboratory and the Lawrence Radiation Laboratory. The facilities and their research and support staff have evolved for a long period of time and are the principal source of U.S. leadership in high-energy physics. The Panel believes that its recommendations will preserve the vitality of these centers on the east and west coast while at the same time strengthening the contribution from the Middle West *through its recommendation of proceeding with the construction of the MURA accelerator.*

The Panel recommends the following single step with respect to the high intensity frontier:

A 12.5-Bev high intensity, FFAG accelerator should be constructed near Madison, Wis., by MURA. Since such an accelerator can cover all areas of research now being brought under investigation by the ZGS accelerator, the Panel recommends the development of plans in which the use of both accelerators would be coordinated by a single group. The plans for the FFAG accelerator are in the most advanced stage of any proposed machine, and construction of this accelerator could be started immediately. While the Panel knows of tentative plans for four so-called pion factories at different laboratories, each costing in the range of $40 to $50 million, it is expected that the 12.5-Bev machine would serve most of the high energy purposes of the pion factories. *The Panel recommends that authorization for construction of the FFAG supercurrent accelerator be given as soon as possible, provided this is not expected to delay significantly the authorization of the steps toward higher energy recommended above.*

The Panel considered recommending against the construction of the FFAG accelerator. However, we are convinced that there is a genuine, high intensity frontier at this energy range, particularly if the energy is raised from 10 to 12.5 Bev, and that development of the associated technology is of direct value. The principal argument against the construction of the high intensity accelerator are its cost and the consequent possible danger that it might delay the steps to higher energy. The Panel concluded that it should state clearly its views in this matter; namely, that the highest priority in new accelerator construction should be assigned to the recommended steps toward highest attainable energy, but that *a 12.5-Bev high intensity, FFAG accelerator is an essential component of a balanced program and should be constructed provided that it will not delay the authorization of the steps toward higher energy.*[1] (italics added)

There is no question that the panel said that the advance to higher energy was more important than the advance to higher intensity. There is also no question that the panel said it wanted both high energy and high intensity. The significant difference between the Ramsey Panel report and its predecessors was that it was saying support both the MURA group and the MURA machine. It was specifically recommending construction and in the next available budget year. Hearings on authorizing legislation for fiscal 1964 had already been concluded in early May. The next budget would be prepared in the fall, submitted to the review of the Bureau of the Budget and to President Kennedy's Science Advisor, Jerome

Wiesner. It would then have to go to the Joint Committee for reporting out to Congress. Final approval by Presidential signature was
a year away.

Understandably, the report had extra significance to Argonne.
The 12.5 Bev ZGS was expected to be finished in August; actually
it generated its first proton beam on September 18, 1963. A three-
month tune-up period was anticipated, followed by an initial experimental period of three months. The Program Committee had
already selected the first six experiments, of which only two, amount-
ing to 14 per cent of the machine's time, were Laboratory experiments.[*2]

When the Policy Advisory Board met on July 17, 1963, President
Beadle, noting that two PAB members, Seitz and Williams, were on
the Ramsey Panel, asked them to comment on the panel's recommendations. This they did. Seitz explained that the panel meant
just what it said about MURA—it wanted FFAG built provided
there was no need to choose between FFAG and the 200 Bev machine that was being planned by the Berkeley group. That high
energy machine, which Seitz said had to be a truly national facility, had first priority. The MURA machine, which provided high
intensity, was intended to balance the U. S. program.

The recommendation on coordination between ANL and
MURA, Seitz reported, was left purposefully vague, so that it would
be possible for the two to plan together. The Commission would
welcome ideas on how this could be accomplished.

In the subsequent discussion, old problems began to surface.
Crewe asked what the Ramsey Panel had in mind for ZGS when the
MURA machine was finished. Did they intend ZGS to shut down?
Warren Johnson of Chicago commented that if the Midwest had two
12 Bev machines and the future emphasis was on higher energies in
the 200 Bev and over category, this might mean that in ten years the
Midwest would be second rate once again. To both men, Williams
replied that he thought the Midwest would really enjoy two
machines.

Beadle raised the site issue. What about building the MURA

---

[*]During 1964, ANL staff accounted for twenty per cent of ZGS
time. According to H. Orlans, this was primarily due to a shortage of
staff. Argonne wanted additional staff to get up to thirty per cent and
eventually 50 per cent. The size of staff actually was not the only limiting factor. The Program Committee had rejected two other ANL proposals for the first three month period (*Contracting for Atoms*, p. 68).

machine closer to Argonne? The Ramsey Panel had specifically mentioned Wisconsin as the site. Seitz replied that a common community of users was more important than a common site.

As a result of the discussion, the Policy Advisory Board voted to ask Kent Terwilliger, the Chairman of the Accelerator Users' Group, to set up a meeting of Midwestern physicists to consider how one group could coordinate the use of both machines as well as promote more general cooperation between ANL and MURA on future designs.[3]

Old ideas, unfortunately, are old because they have staying power. Shortly after the Policy Advisory Board meeting, Beadle wrote to Seaborg conveying what he identified as Crewe's position. It would make sense, he wrote, for both ZGS and FFAG to be located at ANL and administered together. This, of course, meant by the Laboratory and not by some second group under a contract separate from that of the University of Chicago. He discounted the possibility of AMU managing the accelerator. It was "an unwieldy group to try to run a facility." If FFAG were at Argonne, the two machines could be coordinated by the Users' Group. The Laboratory and the University of Chicago were represented in the Users' Group as a minority, and so far, Beadle reported, all the parties seemed happy.[4]

Roger Hildebrand, Argonne's Associate Director for High Energy Physics, also supported the idea of the Users' Group coordinating research on the two machines, the need for which was, at best, seven years away. Hildebrand believed that the informality of the Users' Group might be a way of avoiding the politics that were implicit in a formal structure that would have to be tied to at least five administrative boards: AMU, the Policy Advisory Board, the University of Chicago Board of Trustees, MURA's Board of Directors, and the AEC.

Terwilliger interpreted the Policy Advisory Board's motion as asking whether there could be two laboratories relatively close to one another that had machines of similar energy and, if so, how was competition minimized? Terwilliger asked the Users' Advisory Committee, the smaller group of five physicists that had been set up to consider policy questions, to take a stand on the site issue.

The Advisory Committee met on August 6 under the impression that the AEC intended to submit the MURA proposal to Congress for authorization in fiscal 1965. All but one member agreed that FFAG should be built and at Madison. Their argument was partly technical—higher intensity would allow new experiments that would be impossible or too time consuming on the high energy accelerators

—and partly geographical—the Midwest needed more facilities. The Users' Advisory Committee saw both ZGS and FFAG as "indispensable for the foreseeable future" and offered to reconstitute the Argonne Users' Group into a Midwest Accelerator Users' Group that would coordinate research at both machines. Terwilliger conveyed the sense of the Committee to both the AEC and to the University of Chicago, but to Chicago he added that a higher level of coordination might be desirable.[5]

The one dissenting voice on the Users' Advisory Committee was that of Arthur Roberts of ANL. Roberts believed that building FFAG separate from Argonne would present a "clear and present danger" to the ZGS and would mean that a finite life time had been set for ZGS even before it had begun operating. "We should now be engaged in devising ways of nurturing our baby in every way," he wrote in his analysis, "not in preparing a coffin for its burial." Roberts sent his minority report to Paul McDaniel, the Director of Research at the AEC, together with two recommendations.

First, that representatives of Argonne and MURA work to set up a new Midwestern organization to operate both ZGS and FFAG, with FFAG to be constructed at Argonne. "Exclude from the negotiations . . . ," he wrote, "all persons who were involved materially in the MURA-Argonne wars of the mid-Fifties."

Second, if agreement is reached, construct FFAG; if there is no agreement, reject it, "on the grounds that it poses a threat to the course of high energy physics in the next decade."

Roberts claimed to represent a "significant fraction" of current Midwestern opinion. "Having canvassed a segment of opinion," he wrote, "I can now report that there exists a considerable body that wears only one hat, which feels that high energy physics in the Midwest ought not to be killed at Argonne to be reborn in Madison." He tried to broaden his significant fraction by circulating to the Users' Group both his analysis and his letter to McDaniel. Roberts' attack, for obvious stylistic reasons, served the opposite end. Its circulation to physicists and to AMU Council members reopened the old scars. Seitz commented that Roberts was "fishing in troubled waters," that his letter was "not good for anything except to stir up dissension." Beadle disclaimed it as representing neither an ANL nor Chicago position. Goldwasser wrote a long refutation which he circulated.[6]

Yet Roberts was not an isolated dissident. He chose to say publicly what Crewe was willing to say more reasonably in private. The Argonne physicists and administration, Crewe told the Policy Advisory Board, did not want FFAG built anywhere, but if it had to be built, then it should be at Argonne under Argonne management. Ideally, they wanted a high energy, not a high intensity, machine at ANL in the indefinite future.

In the Policy Advisory Board discussions, nothing new was added to the position adopted seven years earlier when Zinn had first hassled with MURA. Crewe felt the Policy Advisory Board should listen to the Laboratory. The Policy Advisory Board members, however, wanted to support MURA and, hopefully, work yet one more time toward that utopian vision of a unified Argonne-MURA high-energy physics program.

Chicago was again in the equivocal middle. "As the contractor for Argonne," Beadle told the Policy Advisory Board, "our primary interest is making ZGS maximally useful in relation to other facilities." The Policy Advisory Board unanimously passed a motion that both supported the construction of the MURA accelerator "in the Midwest as soon as possible" and at the same time urged maximum support of the ZGS.[7]

The Board of Directors of AMU, meeting the following day, passed a similar motion recommending implementation of the MURA proposal "and that both the new FFAG and the existing ZGS machines be vigorously supported." This motion was then circulated to the Sponsoring Institutions of AMU with the request that there be an indication of agreement or disagreement. Twenty-one institutions agreed, ten abstained, none disagreed.[8]

Two Policy Advisory Board members attempted to persuade Crewe to modify Argonne's opposition to MURA. A. G. Norman urged him to "review again with some of your staff their reaction to the recommendation of the Ramsey Panel." The overt opposition, Norman felt, would harm Argonne and the development of high energy physics in the Midwest. He saw one result being a lack of full support for ZGS. Seitz also tried. "It seems to me to be a pity," he wrote, "that the staff of Argonne regards the MURA machine with animosity, for I think if we get it, it will inevitably have an enormous positive and beneficial effect upon the future of Argonne wherever the MURA machine may be placed."

Crewe had similar responses to both. He denied that there was animosity. He described it, rather, as "disappointment" because the MURA machine was to be a high intensity rather than a high energy machine. If FFAG were built, he wrote Seitz, "there is a danger that the Midwest will once more become a community of second-class scientists because it will have second-class facilities."

"All of our senior staff," he replied to Norman, "believe that the MURA machine, if constructed at Madison, would not be in the best interests of the development of high-energy physics in the Midwest." The Midwest, he predicted, would be "fourth class."[9]

There was additional input on the Ramsey Panel recommendations from two review committees. The Technical Committee on High Energy Physics of the Federal Council on Science and Technology gave a general response that was termed "very favorable, although for each specific proposal there was some exception taken by someone." The specific comment on FFAG said, "There was considerable support for the MURA accelerator by those from the Midwest, but relatively little support from outside the region."

The second review committee was composed of accelerator users, generally a group of younger high-energy physicists. Their comment on FFAG was euphoric—"bold and imaginative while at the same time . . . soundly based and practical." Again, MURA got just a slight twist of dissent. "Although two-thirds of the group endorsed the MURA proposal, the entire group felt that its authorization should not be allowed to delay the next high energy machine by more than one or two years."

When this dialogue occurred, the ZGS was going through its tune-up period and FFAG was still a budgetary question in Washington. The meetings on MURA involved the Bureau of the Budget, Jerome Wiesner, the Joint Committee, and assorted congressmen from the Midwest. According to Greenberg, the Bureau of the Budget's Director, Kermit Gordon, opposed FFAG and used the Ramsey Panel's phrase "without permitting this to delay the steps toward higher energy" as his rationale. Authorization would delay the high energy machines. The ZGS at Argonne, Gordon maintained, was intended to serve and "would serve the needs of the midwestern universities." The Ramsey Panel was reconvened on November 16 and 17 to give a more precise interpretation of its recommendation on MURA. It declined the opportunity. Instead, the panel retracted its recommendation on raising the energy level of FFAG from 10 to 12.5 Bev, retracted its recommendation that the machine be built at Madison and substituted "Middle West" instead, and then stated, "The panel wishes to reaffirm its general position in regard to the value of the high energy and high intensity frontiers in elementary physics."[*][10]

The decision had to be made at the executive level by President Kennedy. His term had been marked by nuclear-related events: the resumption of atmospheric bomb tests in 1961; the Cuban missile

---

[*]D. S. Greenberg reported that the eight members of the Panel who had met split 4–4 on MURA. (*Science* 143, January 31, 1964, p. 451.)

crisis of 1962, during which the public tasted the fear of nuclear attack; the period of rapproachment that followed, in which the AEC and Russia's Board for Peaceful Uses of Atomic Energy signed agreements for cooperative research, and, more importantly, in which a limited test ban treaty was approved by the Senate and signed by Kennedy on October 7, 1963. There was a sense of appropriate correction in the AEC's decision to give J. Robert Oppenheimer its highest honor, the Enrico Fermi Award. People who wanted to guess how President Kennedy would decide the MURA issue could point to the economic bluntness with which the nuclear powered aircraft project had been terminated or to the fiscal largesse of the space program. In a speech to the American Academy of Sciences, on October 22, 1963, Kennedy emphasized the importance of basic research, but also the necessity for its practitioners to make its value understood. His assassination, one month later, passed the MURA decision to the unexpected president, Lyndon Johnson.

On December 19, President Johnson met with both representatives from MURA and congressmen from the Midwest and rejected the MURA accelerator. There was a resultant flurry of letters, newspaper articles, editorials, but the decision was fixed. There would be no MURA accelerator anywhere, at any time. It was finally and irrevocably finished, in fact but not in spirit.

The scientific community of the Midwest—which was primarily the ANL-University of Chicago-AMU-MURA complex—had to find a way to live with only one machine—the ZGS at Argonne. January 1964 was a month of meetings. On January 8, Beadle brought together the top officials of MURA and AMU, ostensibly to unify high-energy physics in the Midwest. Robert Sachs, a former Wisconsin physicist who had just become Argonne's Associate Director for High Energy Physics, proposed involving MURA in ANL operations and spoke in favor of a new advisory board. Beadle acknowledged that having the University of Chicago as the single operator of Argonne might no longer be the best arrangement. They should, he said, be open-minded and look at other possibilities. Still, there lingered some last wisps of desire. President Fred Harrington of Wisconsin asked Argonne and the University of Chicago to disassociate themselves from the opposition to FFAG. Elvis Stahr, the President of both the University of Indiana and of MURA, said he was going to Washington to see Seaborg on the 14th for one last attempt to lobby for MURA. He wanted Beadle to go with him and lend his support. William Harrell, Chicago's Vice President for Business, expressed a view similar to Beadle's. They were, he said, in a situation like that which had existed in 1955, when the MURA dispute had previously peaked, and that what was needed was a new Rettaliata Committee.

The Washington meeting with Seaborg was well attended— Stahr, Beadle, Harrell, Crewe, Harrington, Seitz, Sachs, Goldwasser, and Bernard Waldman (Notre Dame), the Director of MURA. The meeting began with an administrative dance. Seaborg would not exactly say the MURA proposal was dead, but he would say that a good supposition to work on was that FFAG would not be in the budget. That having been made clear, the group discussed the next question—what could be done to bolster high-energy physics in the Midwest and keep the key MURA people from departing to the East and West Coasts, where the action was going to be. Crewe proposed a joint ANL-MURA project, preferably at Argonne, that would design a high energy machine that could be proposed two years from then. Seaborg's response was that this would only recreate the same box they were in now. In 1966, there would be Berkeley's proposal for a 200 Bev machine and a Midwest proposal competing for one decision. He pushed for an alternative that did not involve designing or building accelerators.

This left policy as the only place for change. The point was made that the universities had no guaranteed rights at Argonne—the graduate center proposal was cited as an example of the frailty of the universities' claim on Argonne. When Crewe responded by pointing to the Users' Group, Goldwasser, who had set up the Users' Group, said it did not have this type of authority. Seaborg agreed with Goldwasser's view and said there should be an arrangement guaranteeing the rights of university users in ZGS. He suggested that the University of Chicago, as contractor, set up a committee to study the problem of the management of the high-energy physics program and come up with an appropriate plan. The committee, Seaborg continued, should not be an advisory committee. It was to resolve the problem. Beadle agreed to set up the committee.

Crewe met the next day, January 15, with the AMU Board and proposed a committee jointly sponsored by Chicago, AMU, and MURA "which would concern itself with high energy physics at Argonne." The Board, after an executive session, agreed "in principle" with the organization of the committee "to study and make recommendations for the best possible program to promote a high energy physics program in the Midwest." There were to be three representatives from MURA, two from AMU, and one each from ANL and the University of Chicago. The Board offered to activate the committee and to finance its operating expenses.

On the sixteenth of January, it was the Policy Advisory Board's turn. Though several of its members saw the real issue as being larger than high-energy physics, it approved the proposed committee with the following charge:

> The Committee is charged with the responsibility of immediately studying procedures for advancing the high energy physics program in the nation and in particular in the Midwest area. The Committee's attention is especially directed to the near term problem of increasing the capabilities of the ZGS and its availability to users, and to the long range problem of assuring the continued growth and development of high energy physics in the Midwest area.[11]

That same day the proposed committee was being made part of the administration's apology for turning down MURA. President Johnson wrote his well distributed "Dear Hubert" letter explaining that he had killed MURA strictly on competitive economic considerations. Given its cost—now estimated at $170 million to build and $30 million a year to operate—balanced against the brand new $75 million ZGS and, as a bonus prize, a new $25 million research reactor for Argonne (A²R²) that was going into the 1965 budget, he just "found it impossible to justify starting another national laboratory close by." And then he wrote:

> I have . . . asked [Seaborg] to take all possible steps to make possible an increase in the participation of the academic institutions of the Midwest in the work of the Argonne Laboratory. He has outlined for me a concrete proposal to accomplish this. I share fully your strong desire to support the development of centers of scientific strength in the Midwest and I feel certain that with the right cooperation between the Government and the universities we can do a great deal to build at Argonne the nucleus of one of the finest research centers in the world.[12]

The President's letter, together with an AEC press release announcing support for the MURA group while it was moving to Argonne, was to be the formal reply to the numerous complaints being received in Washington.

The understanding that Seaborg, Stahr, and Beadle were going to work out an arrangement for university participation in managing ZGS was given wide distribution. Beyond this, there was also awareness, both at the Policy Advisory Board and in the Bureau of the Budget, that universities needed "a greater voice in the program for management" at Argonne.

The AEC press release (January 20) was headlined "Plans for Continued Support of Accelerator Design Announced." It was all about how the MURA group was going to receive continued support for new studies of a 1,000 Bev accelerator. "MURA scientists will be joined by scientists at the Argonne National Laboratory," the report said, where the work would be "centered." There was also mention that MURA, AMU, ANL, and the University of Chicago were "exploring ways whereby Midwestern universities would be able to participate more directly in the use and management of the ZGS." The last sentence, as an incidental aside, noted that "The reorientation follows a decision not to construct a 10-12.5 Bev high intensity accelerator which had been proposed by the MURA group."[13]

The new committee's membership was formally announced on January 21. Representing AMU were Goldwasser and Williams. Representing MURA were Bernard Waldman (Notre Dame), A. W. Peterson (Vice President at Wisconsin), and F. L. Hovde (President of Purdue). Crewe represented Argonne and Warren Johnson, the University of Chicago. F. Seitz was asked to serve as a part-time consultant. Of the eight people working on the committee, three had been members of the Ramsey Panel whose recommendation to build the MURA machine had not only been rejected but also, in the process, had tested Laboratory-university cooperation and found it wanting.

The first meeting of the committee was held in New York City on January 24. Williams was elected Chairman and what was initially called the Ad Hoc Committee on High Energy Physics set about to transform the relationship between the universities of the Midwest and Argonne National Laboratory.

CHAPTER 15

The Williams Committee

At its first meeting on January 24, the Williams Committee, as it was quickly called, discharged that part of its responsibilities that dealt with "the near term problem of increasing the capabilities of the ZGS. . . ." It decided to request the Users' Advisory Committee to review and update the list of desirable new support facilities for the ZGS and to assign priorities. It also decided to ask the MURA group to accept responsibility for preparing a proposal for a 200 Mev linear injector that could be used to boost the energy of the ZGS.

MURA responded quickly, expressing its willingness to cooperate with the Williams Committee and to undertake the injector proposal. The Users' Advisory Committee, in turn, assigned highest priority to the $17.5 million injector. Thus, on the surface at least, there was general agreement on a project that would increase the capabilities of the ZGS and, not incidentally, keep the MURA group intact and in the Midwest. In the meantime, the Williams Committee could go on to "the long-range problem of assuring continued growth and development of high-energy physics in the Midwest area."[1]

A clue to the variety of long range solutions available was contained in a letter that Frederick Seitz wrote to MURA President Elvis Stahr. He revealed that in 1956, after the Rettaliata Committee had reported and, presumably, before AMU had been founded, he, together with Chicago's Chancellor Kimpton and Business Manager Harrell, had gone to the AEC and proposed "that the Argonne contract be placed under a new organization of Midwestern universities, somewhat analogous to Associated Universities, Incorporated," which operated Brookhaven. The AEC rejected the proposal, Seitz felt, because it "was anxious to exert the maximum direct control feasible on the reactor program at Argonne. . . ."*

"I do not believe," he wrote Stahr, "that the present Commission would reject this proposal now. However, this solution is a relatively radical one and should be considered only as a last resort." The reason Seitz believed as he did was that Seaborg had told him the AEC would accept the concept of shared responsibility between the MURA universities and Chicago, at least for the high energy facilities at ANL.[2]

Other people, outside the Williams Committee, had similar ideas. A professor at Wisconsin, Ralph Huitt, proposed to President Fred Harrington a meeting of people "who are united on the proposition that we ought to hold the MURA physicists together at any cost and that we should secure an acceptable multi-university control over the facilities at the Argonne." Huitt did not believe that such a proposal would be drafted within the Williams Committee, that it had to be drafted by an outside group and "pushed through the Committee of Seven—with a four to three vote if necessary."[3]

Almost simultaneously, John Roberson, AMU's Executive Director, was asked by AMU's President, W. R. Marshall (Wisconsin), to circulate to the Executive Committee of the AMU Board a statement that juxtaposed two "disruptive occurrences" during the past two years—the graduate center proposal and the Laboratory opposition to FFAG—with the opinion that "a multi-university management of Argonne is necessary to achieve harmony." Possible candidates for the management job were "AMU, MURA, or an entirely new university association formed specifically for the purpose."

The Executive Committee, in turn, asked each Board member plus several Council members from schools not represented on the Board to put to his president, "in an informal and confidential manner," the question: "Will the presidents of the individual institutions give strong support, including their personal participation, in order to achieve the goal of a multi-university management of Argonne?"

Roberson sent the results to Williams. Seven answered yes, "with no or very little reservation." Five answered yes, "with an important reservation," e.g., if agreeable to the AEC, or to the University of Chicago, if invited to do so, and "if no new unpleasantness can be assured so there is no possibility of a public squabble. . . ." One president declined to respond and two were not avail-

---

*It has been reported that the request to change the contract was made because Chicago wanted Seitz to be the Laboratory Director, and this was his condition for accepting.

able. President George Beadle, though not polled, had been sent
a copy of both the statement and the question. With the results,
Roberson sent an invitation to Williams and E. L. Goldwasser, the
two AMU representatives, to attend the next Board meeting, on
March 11, and "give a progress report."[4]

Both men came and reported in general terms. Williams objected to the survey and asked to have any mention of it withdrawn
from the record of the meeting. Otherwise, he stated, it would
make the job of the ad hoc committee more difficult. His request
was honored, and the Board gave the Williams Committee a vote
of confidence, even though it was not certain what the committee
had been doing.[5]

Actually, the committee had been quite busy with a frequent
schedule of meetings at which it interviewed the people most directly concerned, the MURA physicists and the ANL high-energy
physics staff. The MURA people expressed little desire to move to
Argonne, which had failed to support them and where they would
feel like "prisoners of war." Argonne, they contended, would represent Midwest high energy physics only when the universities were
in a position of authority. Partly because of this lack of university
responsibility, they said, the Argonne group was only second rate.
If the MURA people were to end up at Argonne, they wanted a
separate division for themselves.

The Argonne staff had a more diverse point of view. Not unex-
pectedly, they felt that the ZGS scheduling policy, which was yet
to go into effect but which had rejected two of their proposals, was
unfair to them. Some of the ANL physicists, however, shared the
university view that the best talent in the field was out on the
campuses. They saw the unique management role of Chicago as
inconsistent with this distribution. Though they thought that Chicago's management, described as a "hands off" policy, was good,
they agreed that a more active management role for universities
would mean a broader and more salutary participation in decisions.[6]

The Williams Committee quickly came to a majority conclusion.
At the February 27 meeting, it was suggested that "an ideal atmosphere" would exist if Chicago would invite a dozen or more universities in as partners in the management of the Laboratory. AMU
was excluded for being too large and too broad. What people had
in mind was a replica of the Brookhaven arrangement. A straw vote
was taken on the question "Do you favor the transfer of the prime
contract for management of the Argonne National Laboratory to
some corporation formed of a group of Midwestern universities?"
Williams as chairman, Seitz as observer, and Stahr as alternate did

not vote. The others voted four to two in favor; Albert Crewe and Warren Johnson were the minority.

Before setting this in writing, the committee invited Beadle and his staff to meet with them to discuss the possibility of changing the contract. Instead, Beadle sent a proposal to the General Advisory Committee of the AEC, entitled "Memorandum Setting Forth Suggestions by the University of Chicago to Increase Participation by Midwestern Academic Institutions in the Over-All Work and Programs of the Argonne National Laboratory." This document was divided into two parts. The first reviewed the history of the Williams Committee and cited its charge as being narrow in scope, restricted to high energy physics—which covered approximately ten per cent of the Laboratory staff and 18 per cent of its budget. The University of Chicago, it went on, had taken on a broader scope—"improving the usefulness of the Laboratory as a total unit," guided by the "underlying objectives and principles" of its contract with the AEC. These were identified as follows:

1. ANL is a national laboratory;

2. the University of Chicago must have clear responsibility;

3. the University of Chicago "shall administer in a spirit of cooperation" with the government and the university community;

4. the University of Chicago must attract and keep a good staff;

5. the Laboratory must have an atmosphere of scholarly free inquiry "subject, of course, to security requirements and contractual responsibilities;"

6. the University of Chicago must minimize conflicts to maximize fulfillment of its responsibilities.

Part two of the memorandum carried the specific recommendation—the creation of an Argonne-universities board in place of the Policy Advisory Board. The new board, whose chairman would be the President of the University of Chicago, would be composed of representatives from nine to twenty schools. The board would:

—advise on and consent to the appointment of the director and the deputy director;

—be informed in advance of appointments of associate directors and division directors;

—be consulted on all committee appointments;

—approve rules and regulations governing the use of facilities;

—approve the rules for program committees that would schedule experiments on major facilities "subject to the overriding requirements of the AEC;"

—appoint a special complaint committee to adjudicate and make recommendations;

—review general policy;

—review educational use.

The General Advisory Committee,* instead of acting on Chicago's proposal, referred it to the Williams Committee. On March 9, 1964, Beadle, Harrell, and Julian Levi, a University of Chicago professor, met with the committee. Beadle questioned the appropriateness of the committee's concern on grounds that it was exceeding its charge. Williams defended the action of the committee by asserting that it had been charged by several groups, not just the University of Chicago. It was understandable that two days later, when Williams and Goldwasser met with the AMU Board, they were rankled by the implications that they were not cognizant of their obligation to AMU.

Since the majority of the Williams Committee rejected Chicago's proposal, the next suggestion came from minority member Warren Johnson, namely that the majority state its opinion in writing and submit it to the University of Chicago for reaction. One member of the Williams Committee, Vice President A. W. Peterson of Wisconsin, objected. "I do not believe we should be 'bargaining' with the University of Chicago," he wrote Williams. "We should not submit a proposal for the *approval* of the University of Chicago." Instead, Peterson wanted the committee to prepare its final report and submit it to all the parent organizations, which would include AMU and MURA. Peterson outlined his ideas on form and content. Specifically, he wanted to explain how they had moved from high-energy physics to recommending a change in the basic contract for the entire Argonne operation. He proposed that they recommend that the contract between the AEC and the University of Chicago be continued until June 30, 1965, subject to negotiations between the

*The General Advisory Committee, in 1964, had a composition that was unusually pertinent to the problem under discussion. Its nine members included Norman Ramsey; Stephen Lawroski, an Associate Director of Argonne who had been a member of the Rettaliata Committee; and Williams himself. The chairman was Lawrence R. Hafstad.

AEC and the officers of AMU and MURA for establishing a corporation of universities that would operate Argonne, effective July 1,
1965. Peterson said he would be willing to let the AEC-University of
Chicago contract run its course till June 1966 if that would help get
what they wanted.[7]

The committee did not follow Peterson's advice on procedure.
Instead, on April 3, it sent to the University of Chicago an interim
report of the "tentative opinions of a majority of the Committee."
These included establishing a corporation of representatives of approximately fifteen universities that would hold the prime contract
for the Laboratory and giving the board of the corporation the
authority to determine "major items of policy governing the operation of the total activities" of Argonne. The majority also recommended that "in establishing the new organization consideration be
given to the possibility of subcontracting, to the University of Chicago, the detailed management of the Laboratory." And, finally, they
recommended that "the past contributions and present unique
competence of the University of Chicago . . . warrant the appointment of President Beadle . . . as President of the new board. . . ."

The purpose of the interim report was "to serve as a focus for
further discussion in hope that it can be made acceptable to all
parties concerned" and that a unanimous report would be possible.
It was presented to the Chicago administration April 6 and ignored.

Chicago's response, through Johnson and Crewe, was to ask for
a committee meeting at which the Chicago proposal would be discussed. The committee met with Harrell and Julian Levi, and voted
on whether it favored its own proposal or the Chicago proposal. The
vote was six to two, with Williams and Seitz participating. The committee then asked Warren Johnson to submit the majority proposal
to the appropriate authorities at the University of Chicago. In the
meantime, the majority members would meet with the Commissioners of the AEC and tell them their conclusions.[8]

Chicago immediately tried to seek support for its own proposal.
Vice President Harrell and Julian Levi began to visit the executive officers of the larger universities. Their message was twofold:
1) that the question of the management of Argonne should be resolved by the presidents of the universities of the Midwest; and 2)
that the recommendations of the Williams Committee, characterized
as beyond the competence of the committee, were a major disservice
to higher education. To Levi, at issue were questions even broader
than those raised previously, such as cooperation between public
and private universities. At the Wisconsin meeting with President
Harrington and Vice President Peterson, who was a member of the

Williams Committee, Levi and Harrell were told that the Williams Committee was obligated to report to its parent groups, and that the final decision would be made elsewhere.[9]

Beadle then presented both the Chicago memorandum and the Williams Committee report to an executive session of the Policy Advisory Board. "The discussion," the minutes report, "led to general agreement that more intimate involvement on the part of the Midwestern universities in the activities and management operations of the Argonne National Laboratory is both desirable and necessary. Most of the members of the Board expressed the opinion that to achieve this objective a multi-university type of organization should be established."[10]

Despite its vagueness, the motion supported the majority proposal of the Williams Committee. The University of Chicago was unwilling to accept the inevitable. Four days after the Policy Advisory Board meeting, Beadle replied formally to Williams on the reactions of Chicago's Board of Trustees, "principal administrators," "interested faculty," and "key" members of Argonne. The issue, he said, needed further discussion and proceeded, amidst some flowery and obtuse language that was not his usual style, to delineate the "issues," "principles," and "fundamental points" involved. These included "the informal comity which must exist, if we are to be successful in our high missions, among the universities of the Midwest," and "the response of educational institutions of higher learning to the responsibilities imposed upon them by our Federal Government, and the requirement that our response to these responsibilities take into account that measure of independence and cooperation which must be preserved if the freedom which has made possible our strong systems of state supported and private education is to be preserved." These "considerations," he wrote, were "uppermost in our minds" and, therefore, prior to making a definitive response, Chicago was going to consult with the presidents of its "sister institutions."

The letter then went on to list several problems that multi-university management appeared to raise—that it was not clear "where ultimate responsibility and liability would rest;" that to keep the corporation size within "reasonable bounds" many schools had to be omitted and it was not clear how their interests would be preserved; and that Laboratory management should not "reflect the interests of high energy physics alone."

Beadle then restated the idea of a new policy board that had been proposed in the earlier memorandum. Chicago's hopes were clear.

Surely, through discussion with our sister institutions, we should be able to devise a system of shared policy responsibility which yet reserves for a single institution, as trustee for the others, the successful management of the enterprise so important for us all, and which does not place the trustee in the position of a mere caretaker and an ineffective policy voice for the Laboratory.

"In the last analysis," Beadle added, "it is not up to the University of Chicago, but rather to the Atomic Energy Commission. . . ."[11]

Beadle was correct, and the Commission made the decision two days later. On April 22, the majority members of the Williams Committee met with AEC Commissioners Glenn Seaborg, John Palfrey, Gerald Tape, and James Ramey. They brought three documents with them, the Chicago proposal, their own majority proposal, and Beadle's letter of the 20th. Seaborg decided to negotiate an agreement then and there. Palfrey suggested a tripartite contractual arrangement in which Chicago's role as manager would be part of the prime contract.* Seaborg phoned Beadle in Chicago and got his agreement "in principle" to a four-part proposal.

1. A new corporation will be formed, in essence an Association of Midwestern Universities.

2. This corporation will hold the prime contract for the operation of Argonne National Laboratory and the responsibility appertaining thereto. It will be responsible for the formulation of major policy and program orientation for the Laboratory.

2. The management of the Laboratory will be handled by the University of Chicago.

4. The enabling document that will spell out this management responsibility and the concomitant authority will be written into the prime contract for operation of the Laboratory, thus involving the AEC in the negotiations along with the new corporation as prime contractor and the University of Chicago as manager.

The minutes of the meeting report that "President Beadle concurred in this summary."[12]

---

*At the University of Chicago, Edward Levi, the current president, is credited with originating the tripartite compromise. (G. Beadle to F. Rossini, September 23, 1970.)

On May 7, Beadle defined his understanding of the agreement in a report of a meeting of university presidents at which they had "expressed their approval of a plan to change the prime contract into a tri-partite arrangement."

"Such an arrangement," Beadle wrote, "will have to carry out the principle of shared policy responsibility . . . of management by a single institution as trustee for the others [and] . . . spell out also the essential authority which must be given to the University of Chicago so that it may be an effective manager of the Laboratory."[13]

On May 11, the Williams Committee approved a more precise motion recommending a new multi-university corporation whose purpose would be "to hold and supervise the contract" for Argonne. It also recommended that the contract "specifically provide for the management of the ANL to be vested in the University of Chicago, who shall be a primary party to the contract." The details for "sharing policy and managerial responsibilities between the new Corporation and the University of Chicago are to be worked out by the parties to the contract." It then requested the Presidents of MURA, AMU, and Chicago to take the necessary steps to establish the new corporation as soon as possible.

These statements were not without their ambiguities. The difference in reading can be illustrated by two diagrams included in the minutes of the meeting. The first

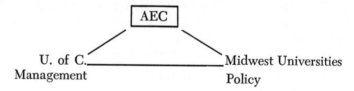

represented the Chicago interpretation. The second diagram

represented the majority interpretation.[14]

Goldwasser suggested changing the wording of the committee's motion to clarify the difference, "hold and supervise the contract" was to read "hold the contract and be responsible for Laboratory policy and program direction." More important was the statement, "The detailed delineation of the management responsibilities which are to be *delegated* to the University of Chicago as trustee for the new corporation . . . is to be reserved for negotiation. . . ." (Italics added.)

Chicago objected strongly and personally, so much so that Goldwasser offered to resign from the committee if it were felt his continued membership would prevent an agreement with Chicago.[15]

Both the progress and the disagreements were kept secret from the broader membership of the parent organizations. The Executive Committee of the Board of Directors of AMU was aware of some of the developments but decided not to report on the negotiations at the Annual Council Meeting in June. AMU President J. Russell Bright (Wayne State University) told the Council only that a report was expected in the fall. In acting in this close manner, the Executive Committee was being responsive to Williams' earlier view that his committee needed *carte blanche* in order to work out a solution with Chicago. As a result, there were frustrating moments within the AMU organization. Executive Director Roberson, at the end of May, had recommended severing relations with the Williams Committee, in a "nondestructive fashion," on the grounds that the AMU representatives were "not responsive to AMU in the sense of reporting or accepting instructions, and therefore have not been representative in any accountable way." The Board of Directors was divided on having more direct participation in the Williams Committee's deliberations. The view of the Executive Committee held. There were some informal discussions with Williams on keeping AMU, as an institution, formally aware of what was happening, but the results were to leave matters as they were, with private negotiations going on between the executives of the University of Chicago and the Williams Committee. A pattern of secrecy was also adopted by the Policy Advisory Board. On July 16, it unanimously endorsed the principles of the May 11 statement. However, the official minutes do not mention the action, nor, for that matter, even that the subject had been discussed. The Policy Advisory Board's endorsement was possible because Chicago had agreed by then to the general proposal and had even written its version of how the prime contract for Argonne between the AEC and the University might be changed to a tripartite agreement between the AEC, the University, and the new corporation.[16]

The Chicago version did not resolve the impasse between the

Williams Committee and the Chicago administration. Harrell produced a new revision by the end of July which essentially made the Executive Committee of the new corporation an advisory board on Argonne National Laboratory. The majority members rejected this in a telephone conference on July 29 and agreed to make their own public statement along lines suggested by Peterson which clearly distinguished between the duties of the "Board of Directors" and those of the "Business Manager."[17]

Though the final report of the Williams Committee was still not scheduled to be ready until the fall, there was general discussion of its ramifications. The new President of AMU, Bryce Crawford (Minnesota), outlined three possibilities for his own organization. It could take on the new and larger assignment, i.e., be the corporation that was a party to the contract; it would continue as a parallel organization; or it could simply disappear. The latter would be acceptable, Crawford felt, if the various AMU programs were taken over by the new corporation.[18]

The final report of what was now officially called the AMU-Argonne-Chicago-MURA Ad Hoc Committee was agreed upon unanimously on September 23, 1964. It was a straightforward report that reviewed the history of the committee, its charge, its method of operating, and the conclusions it had reached on both improving the ZGS facilities and on reorganizing the management of Argonne. It then made six recommendations, stressing the unanimity of the committee in presenting them. Since Crewe, the Laboratory Director, and Johnson, Chicago's Vice President for Special Projects, were members, their agreement was an important factor in assuring that the report could be implemented.

The six recommendations were:

1. The committee recommends that the prime contract for the operation and management of the Argonne National Laboratory for the Atomic Energy Commission be changed to a tripartite agreement, the parties to be the AEC, a not-for-profit corporation to be organized by a group of Midwestern universities, and the University of Chicago. The activities of the parties pursuant to this plan shall at all times be subject to the provisions of the tripartite contract.

2. The function of the new not-for-profit corporation of Midwestern universities shall be to formulate, approve and review Laboratory policies and programs.

3. The function of the University of Chicago shall be to operate

the Argonne National Laboratory in a manner responsive to the policies established and approved by the new corporation.

4. The terms and conditions of the new tripartite contract shall be such as to assure the new not-for-profit corporation of Midwestern universities that their decisions shall be carried out, and that policies approved by the corporation shall be put into effect.

5. The terms and conditions of the new tripartite contract shall be such as to assure the University of Chicago that it will be able effectively to operate the Laboratory in a manner responsive to the policies established by the new corporation.

6. The committee recommends further that the parties recognize (a) that they share a mutual responsibility for promoting the maximum scientific progress and engineering development made possible by the funds and facilities provided by the Government, (b) that they must cooperate in order to stimulate scientific and technological advancement in the Midwest community and the nation, and (c) that these purposes can be attained only by continued emphasis on recruiting and retaining on the staff of the Laboratory the most competent and creative scientists and engineers available and by affording them full support.

What remained was formal approval by the parent organizations and the creation of a committee to implement the recommendations to bring a new tripartite arrangement into being.

CHAPTER 16

Defining Tripartite

The final concept of a tripartite contract represented an improvement in the University of Chicago's position. The majority of the Williams Committee had originally proposed to give the prime contract to the new corporation with the possibility that it would subcontract "detailed management" to the University of Chicago. Under the new proposal, to gain unanimity, Chicago, as operator, was placed on a par with the new corporation, to which it would belong in its role of Chicago, as a university. The general distinction between establishing policy and programs (the corporation's responsibility) and operation of the Laboratory (Chicago's responsibility) appeared to be clear. Still to be spelled out were the mechanisms for establishing policy, the roles of the various parties, present and future, and the means for assuring that operation was responsive to policy.

These questions, to which there could be no definitive answer until actual documents had been written, colored the fall of 1964 when the AMU Board and Council were asked to approve the agreement. Inbred skepticism about the future, a distrust of Chicago, a sense of inability to achieve change began to emerge. President Beadle suggested that Bryce Crawford of AMU and Elvis Stahr of MURA meet with him during October to make certain they all understood the recommendations and to discuss the process of writing a Founders Agreement. The executive officers of Chicago were confident that the Williams Report could form the basis of "a viable tripartite agreement." Their optimism was not shared. John Roberson, AMU's Executive Director, expressed doubt that the three could write an interpretation that would be acceptable to all four parent organizations. His appraisal was reinforced when the Board of Directors of AMU met on October 14. It unanimously passed a motion accepting the Williams Committee Report, but not before covering several critical areas:

—the optimum number of schools that should be in the new organization and the criteria for membership;

—the possible demise of AMU because of the new arrangement;

—the possibility of excluding Chicago from the new organization on the grounds that a dual role raised the possibility of a conflict of interests, e.g., that Chicago would vote itself a higher fee than the estimated $1.2 million it currently received for operating the Laboratory.

At one point during the meeting Crawford told the Board that it could instruct him to implement the report or to have no part of it. If they told him the latter, he would stay home. E. L. Goldwasser, who had just become a Board member, joined Crawford in trying to have the Board accept on faith what the Williams Committee had in mind for the contractual realities. He urged them to believe that the major gain—that the policies of Argonne were to be set by the new corporation composed of many schools and not by one school—overrode any negative aspects. The Board approved, but not without reflecting over past failures.[1]

The Policy Advisory Board met the next day and adopted the Williams Committee Report unanimously "without changes or reservations." MURA had acted similarly. On October 21, 1964, the AEC announced its approval "in principle." The news release spelled out the varied roles—"the new corporation will formulate the Laboratory's policies and programs;" the University of Chicago "will continue to operate the Laboratory responsive to the policies of the corporation within the terms of the contract;" "the Argonne National Laboratory will continue to be operated in accordance with the policies and requirements of the Atomic Energy Commission."

Science, in reporting the tripartite concord, announced, "The Midwest: New Arrangement for Argonne Holds Promise of Greater Financial Aid for the Region." D. S. Greenberg wrote that when one of Argonne's administrators was asked what the Laboratory and the University of Chicago would gain from the new agreement, he replied, "Peace and quiet."[2]

The suspicion that this possibility might be more serious than facetious was making the rounds. Lacking precise details on the organization of the new corporation, people feared that it might result in a concentration on high-energy physics and a loss of the established programs of AMU. The President of the AMU Council, Philip Powers (Purdue), appointed a Special Task Force to report on the relationship between the proposed corporation and AMU.

Without any details about the new organization to work with, the
Task Force could only turn introspective. It came to three
conclusions:

—"that at least during some interim period, AMU continue to
operate with substantially the same relationship it now has
to ANL and the AEC." When it became clear what was going
to happen, AMU should be reexamined;

—that the new corporation be either large or small but not
"middle size";

—that the new corporation should have a full-time president
and enough staff so as not to diminish into an advisory
board.[3]

This report was presented to a special meeting of the AMU
Council on December 20, 1964. For most of the delegates, this meeting was their first detailed exposure to the interpretation of the Williams Committee. AEC Commissioner Gerald Tape, who had been
working with Crawford, Stahr, and Beadle, began the session with
a clear statement of the AEC's position. "There is no intention," he
said, "of giving Argonne National Laboratory to universities to
run. We are thinking about participation on a broader base." He
went on to talk about the management of big business, the need to
have people "who are responsible as operators of a big business."
He meant Chicago and expressed the Commission's satisfaction with
past arrangements. "We look upon the new arrangement as trying
to get the best of all possible worlds. . . . [to] let us maintain those
things in the management . . . which have been successful, and at
the same time . . . bring in broader participation."

Tape was followed by Crawford, who explained some of the
preliminary structural thoughts of the Special Committee of Beadle,
Stahr, and himself. He was followed by W. R. Marshall (Wisconsin),
who presented the Task Force report. Then it was open season. The
main concern was why AMU was not to be the proposed corporation. Lesser issues were: How were the AMU programs going to be
continued? Who would present the budget to the AEC? Why hadn't
the Williams Committee reported while it worked and allowed AMU
to debate the issues? The discussion was diffuse and inconclusive.
At best, it was informational along particular lines of interest. At
worst, and some Council members came away with this impression,
it did not make clear that there would be any substantive difference
in the way Argonne was managed.

Goldwasser later wrote a response to critics of the Williams Committee that was appended to the official record of the Council meeting. Goldwasser maintained that the sensitivity of the matter, the necessity of persuading Chicago to relinquish some of its authority and responsibility, demanded privacy in negotiation. At all times, he maintained, they had kept the chief executives of all the organizations informed.

To the touchy issue—why not AMU?—he said that the proposed corporation had different functions and responsibilities. Should it be an exact copy of AMU, "a certain amount of effort would have been wasted." AMU, he predicted, would last as long as it had a purpose. "It should be the objective of the organization, and not the organization itself," he wrote, "which holds the interest and dedication of its members."[4]

The Special Committee of Beadle, Crawford, and Stahr hired a law firm, the same one that had drawn up the legal papers incorporating MURA, and scheduled a Founders Meeting for February 25, 1965. Because of the weather, representatives from seven schools were unable to attend. Still it went reasonably well. The committee proposed a name for the new corporation, Argonne Universities Association, and six initial members of the Board of Directors:

F. Harrington—President of the University of Wisconsin
W. K. Pierpont—Vice President of the University of Michigan
George Pake—Provost of Washington University
J. C. Warner—President Emeritus of Carnegie Institute of Technology
E. L. Goldwasser—Professor of Physics, University of Illinois
Philip Powers—Chairman of Nuclear Engineering, Purdue University

The principal opposition at the meeting came from Director-designate Harrington. He reported that at Wisconsin the proposed arrangement was seen "as not much more than an advisory agreement." At issue were the methods for choosing the Board of Directors, the responsibilities of the Directors to their home schools, and the extent to which the Board would have budgetary control over Argonne. The group agreed that the Special Committee should rewrite the Founders Agreement in light of the discussion, have it approved by the proposed Directors, and then send it out for approval by the schools. If 15 schools agreed, the Argonne Universities Association would be incorporated.[5]

The AMU Task Force met for a second time in April to react to the Founders Agreement and draft some guidelines for AMU.

This it did, the most important of which was to recommend "an ultimate merging" of AMU with the new corporation. Its report was adopted by the Council at its annual meeting.

A new Founders Agreement circulated in May. There were some objections, principally to the question of Chicago representation on both the Board of Directors, which would range in size from 16 to 20, and on a more select group—an Executive Committee that was to be elected by the Directors and specifically charged with the responsibility for "Argonne affairs."

As written, the Agreement provided that one Board member would be named by Chicago and that he would also be a member of the Executive Committee for Argonne. There were objections to this, the sense of the group being that a Chicago representative on the Board should be elected in a normal way on a par with other schools, i.e., Chicago should not automatically have a representative. However, it could, primarily for communication purposes, have a non-voting ex officio Board member. The lawyer who was assisting the Committee saw no difficulty in arranging this and gave the opinion that ex officio members generally did not have a vote. It was proposed, therefore, that the Agreement be rewritten to provide that "in addition to any elected directors from Chicago, there shall also be designated by Chicago a representative who shall serve as a non-voting ex-officio member of the Board." In addition, the ex officio Chicago Director would be on the Executive Committee for Argonne. Beadle said he could not agree to the change without consulting with his staff.[6]

The Founders Agreement was redrafted the next day—the term Director was changed to Trustee—with the ex officio terminology being used but without specifically indicating that the Chicago ex officio Trustee had no vote. It was assumed that the intent would be clear; but when Chicago refused to agree to the compromise, wanting its Trustee to vote on both the Board and the Executive Committee, the precise legal interpretation of ex officio was to Chicago's advantage. President Harrington of Wisconsin said he would support the May 31 agreement only and wished to be recorded as dissenting if the rest of the Committee agreed to Chicago's position. Stahr was "dismayed" by the Chicago refusal and wrote Beadle a strong personal plea to reconsider in the interests of "a total Midwest effort." Chicago held out for a compromise of the compromise. They would have an ex officio member on the Board of Trustees with a vote, who would serve on the Executive Committee for Argonne without a vote. They got what they wanted, though, as Crawford wrote, "some of us reached this agreement somewhat reluctantly."[7]

The Founders Agreement, as unanimously agreed upon by the Special Committee and by the Directors-designate, was sent out for approval by the schools on June 29, 1965. It gave the Argonne Universities Association seven policy-making functions:

—the formulation, approval and review of Laboratory policies and programs;

—the review and approval of all budget proposals and modifications, plans for modifying existing facilities and programs and plans for establishing new facilities and programs;

—the full participation, through the duly authorized agents of the Corporation, with the University of Chicago (which is to operate the Laboratory in accordance with Section 5 and the Tripartite Agreement) in the negotiation of all matters affecting policy, including the Tripartite Agreement, with the Atomic Energy Commission;

—the initial and continuing approval of appointments to the positions of Laboratory Director and Deputy and Associate Laboratory Directors . . .;

—the establishment of the general goals for cooperative research and educational programs between the academic community and the Laboratory;

—the establishment of criteria and means for deciding priorities among the users of Laboratory scientific facilities, provided that the Signatory Universities agree not to cause the Corporation to adopt any criteria based upon whether such user of, or the person applying for use of, the Laboratory facilities is on the staff of a Signatory University, since the principal purpose of the Corporation is to promote scientific excellence throughout the Midwest region; and

—the right to recruit and maintain sufficient staff of the Corporation to effectuate the purposes and policies of the Corporation.

It gave Chicago the duty to operate Argonne, to:

—recruit and employ the Laboratory staff, subject, in the case of the Laboratory Director and all Deputy and Associate

Laboratory Directors, to the initial and continuing approval
by the Board of Trustees of the Corporation of the appointment of all such Directors;

—maintain and operate the facilities of the Laboratory; and

—maintain contact with the Atomic Energy Commission on all
operating matters. The University of Chicago shall also have
fiscal responsibility for the activities and operations of the
Laboratory, subject to the provisions of Section 6(b) of this
Agreement and to the indemnity and reimbursement provisions of the Tripartite Agreement.

To the AEC, as the press release of the previous October had said it
would, it gave the assurance that Argonne would function within
the Commission's "overall policy and requirements."

By July 20, fifteen schools had indicated their readiness to
sign, to pay the $10,000 membership fee (and up to $15,000 more if
needed). On July 22, 1965, Argonne Universities Association was
incorporated. The first meeting of the Board of Trustees was held
on September 15, 1965, by which time twenty-six schools had joined.
The Board elected temporary officers and adopted temporary by-
laws, pending the expansion to a full Board by the next meeting.
Argonne now had its fourth university structure in twenty years.
As soon as the actual tripartite contract was signed between the
AEC, the University of Chicago, and AUA, the new corporation
would legally have more authority than had been vested in any of its
predecessors. In the meantime, AMU still existed, looking at its
potential successor with a wary eye.

CHAPTER 17

"That It May Prove Better"

The Board of Directors of AMU endorsed the Founders Agreement by quoting at length from Benjamin Franklin's qualified approval of the document produced by the Constitutional Convention of 1787. In similar spirit, the members accepted the tripartite plan "not because it provides an ideal solution but because it seems the best presently practicable step forward, believing that it may prove better in operation than it appears in design. . . ." However, in case it didn't, AMU continued to operate, even to expand, always with a frame of reference that included an awareness of AUA. To its existing activities—the support of the Accelerator Users' Group, the High Voltage Electron Microscope Project, a fellowship program, the Nuclear Engineering Education Committee with its Summer Practice School and its periodic conferences—AMU added a Committee on Graduate Education, a Committee on Biology, and an Ad Hoc Committee on Ecology. Each was intended to improve the interaction between the Laboratory and the universities.

The Board also continued to fill a watchdog function. In the summer and fall of 1965, there was a growing dissatisfaction with the operation of the ZGS. It was not functioning at as high an intensity as the older Brookhaven AGS. There were complaints about errors in choosing experiments, in building equipment, and, worse, in predicting the availability of experimental beams. The thrust of the criticism was that the errors resulted in extensive down time for the machine, the expenditure of time and money on equipment that could not be used, and the preparation of experiments that could not be run. When the negatives were balanced against the successful experiments at ZGS, one member of the Users' Group concluded that it was "a very small output for a major accelerator."

Solutions could include, at one end, restructuring the administration of the High Energy Physics and the Particle Accelerator Divisions, or, more simply, to increase the input of the university physicists. When it was also reported to the Board of Directors that the role of the Users' Advisory Committee had diminished during the past year, that the High Energy Physics Division was not relying on it, the Board's response was to urge that the Users' Advisory Committee be "reestablished," that it meet regularly, and that it both give advice and "make decisions on behalf of the physics community." The letter to Beadle conveying these ideas and a presentation to the Policy Advisory Board created a small irritation. A second letter had to be sent substituting "reassumed" for "reestablished" and disavowing any intent that the Users' Advisory Committee make management decisions. At the same time, the Laboratory, through Crewe and Sachs, agreed to increase the role of the Users' Advisory Committee and to make the selection of its members more independent of the Laboratory management.[1]

Simultaneously, there was a move to initiate a users' group for the new high flux research reactor, A^2R^2 (Argonne Advanced Research Reactor), that had been authorized for construction in fiscal 1965, partly as a consolation prize to the Midwest for not getting the MURA accelerator. Argonne's reactors were still not available to university people, except under special circumstances. The reasons were several. The reactors had been built for the Laboratory and were saturated with experiments. The type of policy used on the accelerator—that experiments be scheduled according to scientific merit and not proprietary rights—had never been considered for the reactors. In addition, there was a price tag, and a high one, on neutrons from the reactor, though protons from the ZGS were free. In the fall of 1965, the Nuclear Engineering Education Committee posed three questions to Crewe:

1) Would university people have access to A^2R^2?

2) Would they be able to participate in planning of both the reactor and supporting facilities?

3) What do you suggest as a mechanism?

The answers came in a meeting with Winston Manning, formerly head of the Chemistry Division and the new Associate Director for Basic Research. Yes, they would have access. No, they would not be able to participate in design of the reactor, but were, through an ANL Neutron Diffraction Committee, participating in the decisions on facilities. No mechanism was suggested.[2]

A formal proposal to set up a users' group was made by AMU in February of 1966. Crewe responded by suggesting an organizational meeting in April that would also consider the use of the

other Argonne reactors, CP-5, EBWR, and Juggernaut, and offered
to organize the group. By mid-May there had been no meeting, but
familiar conversations had been initiated in Washington. The A^2R^2
was being reviewed by the Bureau of the Budget and the AEC.
The possibility existed that A^2R^2 would never exist. Suddenly, university participation meant political support, and university use
of A^2R^2's high flux began to be cited by the Laboratory as a justifi-
cation for the reactor. The needs of the university community could
make a case for A^2R^2. Nine AMU schools had their own reactors,
but the highest available power was two megawatts, with a five
megawatt reactor soon to begin operation. The 100 megawatt A^2R^2
represented a substantial increase in flux (one hundred-fold), which
extended the types of possible experiments, provided it was made
available. AUA entered into the discussion, writing to the Commission to urge the construction of the reactor. By late 1966, the
Bureau of the Budget agreed to allow the planning to continue
and construction to be initiated. Argonne went ahead, and in March
1967, the AMU Board decided once again to push for a users'
group. An *ad hoc* committee actually met once—in December of
1967. The atmosphere of the meeting was negative. There was little
confidence that A^2R^2 would be built. There was no strong interest by
the Laboratory people to organize the users' group at that time.
Some university people felt strongly that the idea was premature,
that they should wait until the reactor was finished. Still others
simply did not have the acquisitiveness of the high-energy physicists.
Either they didn't want to or didn't believe they could control this
source of neutrons. The group dissolved. So did A^2R^2. It was pro-
nounced absolutely dead on April 3, 1968, a victim of Vietnam,
inflation, and a general lack of enthusiasm.[3]

Among the mementos of A^2R^2 was a unique ground-breaking
ceremony that was held in 1967 on a June day when the budget
appeared firm. Participating in turning the first shovelful were
Winston Manning, Acting Director of ANL; the A^2R^2 Project Director; Vice President Harrell of Chicago; the Manager of the
AEC's Chicago Operations Office; and the President of AUA. They
used one shovel, but it had five handles.

At the same time that AMU expanded its own activities, it
sought to fill a service role for AUA. Recognizing that the main
business of AUA during the first year would be the negotiation of
the tripartite contract, AMU proposed to take the responsibility for
those aspects of AUA that were concerned with education and
university relations. A formal proposal was sent to AUA, in which
it was made clear that AMU would be acting as the agent of AUA,

with full disclosure to both AUA and the University of Chicago, and in accordance with policy decisions made by either AUA or the University of Chicago. The proposal was accepted with some language changes that left no uncertainty that AMU was operating within AUA territory and that the arrangement could be cancelled at any time by either party. This agreement was not difficult to reach as the two principal officers of AMU, under the terms of the Founders Agreement, had been elected Trustees of AUA.[4]

Negotiations between the AEC, the University of Chicago, and AUA took up most of 1966. The tripartite contract was signed on November 1 and the responsibilities of the new organization legitimatized. As the contract clearly stated, it had among its purposes:

> *a.* To add the Association as a party to the prime contract with the primary role of formulating, approving and reviewing policies and programs of the research and development laboratory known as Argonne National Laboratory, which is one of the Commission's multiprogram laboratories;
>
> *b.* To acknowledge the revision in the role of the University to that of operator of the Laboratory in accordance with policies established by the Association, and subject to the provisions of this contract. . . .

It further stated: "It is the intent of the Commission, the Association and the University that this contract shall be administered in a spirit of friendly cooperation with a maximum effort in achieving common objectives."[5]

In anticipation that each party would put its signature to paper, the Policy Advisory Board held its last meeting on October 20, 1966. The mood was nostalgic but anticipatory. Everyone felt they were moving in the right direction and that a challenging period lay in front of them.

To round out the tableau, there remained only the necessity of phasing AMU out of existence. On July 12, 1967, William Kerr (Michigan), the President of AMU, proposed that AMU was ready to merge with AUA and needed only a positive response. He suggested a target date of September 30, 1968, when the AMU contract with the AEC was to expire. Plans for the transfer of AMU activities were drawn up, with programs, i.e., fellowships, conferences, research cooperation, going to Argonne and a proposed Center for Education, and with committees going to AUA. The AUA Trustees approved the merger in early October and were followed by the

AMU Board of Directors that same month. The AMU Council met for the last time on March 27, 1968, and similarly approved.[6]

The final meeting of the Board of Directors of AMU was held on June 12, 1968. The Articles of Merger were signed immediately after the meeting by Frederick Rossini on behalf of AMU and Philip Powers on behalf of AUA. AMU had lasted ten years and two days. AUA was already two and one-half years old. Under the terms of the tripartite contract, it would come up for review in 1971.

Epilogue

The remaining question is—Has the tripartite arrangement worked better than its predecessors?

The answer can be approached through parochial perspectives. Does Argonne Universities Association set Argonne's policies and determine its programs? Does the University of Chicago operate the Laboratory? Does the Laboratory staff work on research of its own choosing? Is the government's programmatic research being pursued by the best scientists? The answer can also be approached through a broader perspective that depends on an elusive qualitative value. Does Argonne National Laboratory serve the "national interest?"

Even with the best intentions, the answers are not likely to be clean, an unequivocal yes or no. The lines of authority at Argonne no longer run vertically, but diagonally and often horizontally. The people directly involved in the four groups would probably give contradictory answers that differed in public from what they would in private. More significantly, the answers will have a relativity that needs to be measured from an awareness of what the past relationships were intended to be like and what they were like. The heritage of cooperation at Argonne is weak, and the answers may have to be, "Compared to 1949, the universities determine Argonne's program," or "Compared to 1952, the University of Chicago has less operating responsibility," or. . . .

A major problem in evaluating the tripartite arrangement is that the parameters are not static. Since the prime contract was signed, since AMU merged with and disappeared into AUA, the logic of the compromise has been weakened by new developments. MURA is dead but URA (University Research Association) is very much alive. The 12.5 Bev FFAG accelerator never got built. A 500 Bev machine is under construction within a half-hour's drive of Argonne, at the new National Accelerator Laboratory. NAL is fifteen miles by crow, twenty-two miles by car, from ANL. The two laboratories are even in the same county. Experiments are expected to begin at NAL in late 1971, with full start-up scheduled for 1972.

Without too much publicity, there have been small moments of irritation and continuing moments of cooperation between the two laboratories. People have left ANL for NAL. The National Accelerator Laboratory is using the Argonne computer. There was some brief talk of merger; there is talk of sharing a new computer facility. But, more importantly, as the time for start-up approaches, the relative value of Argonne's ZGS, the threat to its life span, should recreate the problems and anxieties that marked Argonne's entrance into the accelerator field.

High-energy physics was the catalyst by which AUA came into existence and the tripartite relationship created. If and when high-energy physicists depart from Argonne, and this may be as soon as five years after NAL begins operating, an important component of AUA's own membership will depart with them. In their place could come faculty from the small colleges that are now transmuting into large universities. They are already organized into regional groups—Associated Colleges of the Midwest, Central States Universities Incorporated, Associated Colleges of the Chicago area—organizations that have had their own special relationships with Argonne independent of AMU and AUA. In past years, the small schools were the second-class citizens of academia and could be ignored in the distribution of authority. Today many of them, certainly in size and often in excellence in specific disciplines, are where the larger, more prestigious universities were fifteen and twenty years ago when their needs were considered in devising a management system for Argonne. Conversely, Argonne may need them.

A third external parameter is the Atomic Energy Commission itself. There are science-critics who believe that not just the laboratories have lost their missions, but the AEC as well. These critics argue that the pursuit of nuclear technology within separate laboratories is not as sensible as the pursuit of objectives, or fields, within which nuclear technology is one of several tools. They envision the national laboratories under a new agency, a Department of Science, for example, and assigned not to means but to ends—such as biological research, or fusion power sources, or pollution control, the best possible parallels to the pointed missions of the World War II period.

Within the tripartite structure, internal changes have created new balances. In December 1967, the senior scientific staff formed itself into the Argonne Senate, borrowing the name of the traditional faculty organization on campuses. The parallel to universities is meant seriously—to create a sense of staff independent of administration. In addition to improving self-identity, the Senate is intended to influence Laboratory policy, and to influence that policy in apposition with the input from AUA. The first document published by the Argonne Senate was a response to the initial policy statement by the President of AUA. The Senate's second major document is on Laboratory-university relations.

In 1967, Argonne National Laboratory got its fourth director, Robert Duffield, a former member of the Illinois faculty who came to the Laboratory from the nuclear power industry.* Not much has been said in the literature of science about the role of the directors of large laboratories. Walter Zinn, Norman Hilberry, and Albert Crewe had distinctive personalities and imparted them to the Laboratory.** Duffield's term coincides with AUA's tenure. An evaluation of the efficacy of the tripartite arrangement has to consider the particular contribution of his style and concerns. Given a different director, what proves workable could become intolerable.

Finally, it is reasonable to expect that individuals from the universities are playing determining roles, as John Williams and Frederick Seitz did in a multiplicity of overlapping positions, or as William Harrell did, whose administrative presence from 1945 past his retirement into the 1970's provided valuable continuity to the University of Chicago, or John Roberson, who did the same for AMU from 1959 till its merger with AUA. The prime candidates are those whose participation goes back to AMU, to the Users' Group, to the Nuclear Engineering Education Committee.

The new university association, headed by Philip Powers, is a large structure. It has delegates, trustees, officers, an administrative staff of full- and part-time employees. It has an executive committee for Argonne affairs, board committees, special committees, and divisional review committees. Though there is some repetition, with the same person filling several slots, over two hundred faculty are involved in what is officially described as "an orderly flow of information and ideas."

This history is part of that flow. It is intended to bring readers with a particular concern for Argonne up to a base line, to impart to those faculty working in AUA, to the University of Chicago

---

*For a brief period in 1967, Winston Manning was Acting Director.
**In 1969, Zinn received the Enrico Fermi Award, and Hilberry received a special citation from the AEC for outstanding service to the nation's atomic energy program.

administration, to the Laboratory staff, to the Atomic Energy Commission, a perspective from which they might answer the important question that remains for them—Has the tripartite arrangement worked? Hopefully, this book will enable them to recognize the past as it comes toward them for yet one more time.

Beyond the concern this history has for Argonne as a specific institution, it also has a larger intention, to reflect outward from the particular to the general, from Argonne and the Midwest to federal laboratories and universities. Pseudo-aphorisms suggest themselves. The scientific process does not occur in purely scientific environments. The scientific process does not respond solely to rational arguments. The scientific process does not implicitly ensure cooperation between its practitioners.

Identifiable groups come into conflict—university professors, government administrators, laboratory scientists, and then the innumerable disciplinary subdivisions, physicists, high-energy physicists, nuclear engineers, proponents of fast breeder reactors, advocates of fusion power—and each with its special interest, and all capable of believing that their interest is the nation's interest. People who are not immersed in the scientific and administrative practices of large schools and large laboratories need to recognize these special interests at work, to balance them and to identify a personal concept of the ideal relationship between regional universities and national laboratories. The conception is difficult. The achievement is even more difficult.

Appendix

The Ohio State University
Oklahoma State University
The Pennsylvania State
University
Purdue University
Saint Louis University
Washington University
Wayne State University
Western Reserve University
The University of Wisconsin

MIDWESTERN UNIVERSITIES
RESEARCH ASSOCIATION

The University of Chicago
*University of Illinois
*Iowa State University
*State University of Iowa
*Indiana University
University of Kansas
*The University of Michigan
Michigan State University
*University of Minnesota
Northwestern University
University of Notre Dame
Ohio State University
Purdue University
Washington University
*University of Wisconsin

ARGONNE UNIVERSITIES
ASSOCIATION

The University of Arizona

Carnegie-Mellon University
Case-Western Reserve
University
The University of Chicago
University of Cincinnati
Illinois Institute of Technology
University of Illinois
Indiana University
Iowa State University
The University of Iowa
Kansas State University
The University of Kansas
Loyola University
Marquette University
Michigan State University
The University of Michigan
University of Minnesota
University of Missouri
Northwestern University
University of Notre Dame
The Ohio State University
Ohio University
The Pennsylvania State
University
Purdue University
Saint Louis University
Southern Illinois University
The University of Texas
at Austin
Washington University
Wayne State University
The University of Wisconsin

Argonne National Laboratory Administration

	Dates Served	
Directors	Beginning	Ending
Walter H. Zinn	1946	1956
Norman Hilberry	1957	1961
Albert V. Crewe	1961	1967
Robert B. Duffield	1967	....
Deputy Directors		
Norman Hilberry	1949	1956
Louis A. Turner	1959	1964
Michael V. Nevitt	1969	....

*Founding schools

Associate Director

Norman Hilberry	1946	1949

Associate Directors for Education and University Relations

Joseph C. Boyce	1950	1955
Stuart McLain	1956	1957
Frank E. Myers	1958	1966
Shelby A. Miller	1969	....

Associate Directors for High Energy Physics

Roger H. Hildebrand	1958	1964
Robert G. Sachs	1964	1968
Bruce Cork	1968	....

Associate Directors for Basic Research (Physical and Biological Sciences)

Morton Hamermesh	1963	1965
Winston M. Manning	1965	....

Associate Directors for Reactor Development

Stephen Lawroski	1963	1969
Robert V. Laney	1970	....

Chief Administrative Officers of the University of Chicago
Directly Associated with Argonne National Laboratory

	Dates Served	
Presidents/Chancellors	*Beginning*	*Ending*
Robert M. Hutchins		
President	1929	1945
Chancellor	1945	1951
Lawrence R. Kimpton		
Chancellor	1951	1960
George W. Beadle		
Chancellor & President	1961	1968
Edward H. Levi		
President	1968	....

Vice Presidents

William B. Harrell	1953	1968
Warren C. Johnson	1958	1967
William B. Cannon	1968	....

Bibliography

Manuscript Collections:

Associated Midwest Universities Files, located at Argonne National Laboratory.

Argonne National Laboratory Files, located at Argonne National Laboratory (ANL).

Arthur Holly Compton Papers, located at University Archives and Research Collection, Olin Library, Washington University (Washington).

Harlan Hatcher Papers, located at Michigan Historical Collections, The University of Michigan.

Policy Advisory Board Files of the University of Chicago, located at Argonne National Laboratory (Chicago).

University of Chicago Administrative Files, located at the University of Chicago (Chicago).

Unless noted otherwise, manuscripts are from the files of the Associated Midwest Universities.

Publications of the Atomic Energy Commission:

1st Semi-annual AEC Report. *Letter from the Members of the United States Atomic Energy Commission Transmitting the Initial Report of the Commission,* 1947.

2nd Semi-annual AEC Report. *Letter from the Chairman and Members of the United States Atomic Energy Commission Transmitting Pursuant to Law the Second Semi-annual Report of the United States Atomic Energy Commission,* 1947.

Atomic Power and Private Enterprise. The Joint Committee on Atomic Energy (82d Congress, 2d Session), May 28, 1947.

Letter from the Chairman and Members of the United States Atomic Energy Commission transmitting Pursuant to Law the Third Semiannual Report of the United States Atomic Energy Commission (80th Congress, 2d Session), 1948.

Fourth Semiannual Report of the United States Atomic Energy Commission, 1948.

Seventh Semiannual Report of the Atomic Energy Commission, 1950.

Major Developments January-June 1950, Eighth Semiannual Report of the Atomic Energy Commission, 1950.

Atomic Energy Commission Contract Policy and Operations. United States Atomic Energy Commission, 1951.

Major Activities in the Atomic Energy Programs, January-June 1951. United States Atomic Energy Commission, 1951.

Some Applications of Atomic Energy in Plant Science. United States Atomic Energy Commission, 1952.

Major Activities in the Atomic Energy Programs, January-June 1952. United States Atomic Energy Commission, 1952.

Assuring Public Safety in Continental Weapons Tests. United States Atomic Energy Commission, 1953.

Major Activities in the Atomic Energy Programs, January-June 1953. United States Atomic Energy Commission, 1953.

Fifteenth Semiannual Report of the Atomic Energy Commission, 1954.

Major Activities in the Atomic Energy Programs, July-December 1954. United States Atomic Energy Commission, 1955.

Major Activities in the Atomic Energy Programs. United States Atomic Energy Commission, 1955.

Twentieth Semiannual Report of the Atomic Energy Commission, 1956.

Progress in the Peaceful Uses of Atomic Energy, July-December 1957. United States Atomic Energy Commission, 1958.

Norman F. Ramsey, et. al. *Report of the Panel on High Energy Accelerator Physics of the General Advisory Committee to the Atomic Energy Commission and the President's Science Advisory Committee.* United States Atomic Energy Commission, 1963.

Major Activities in the Atomic Energy Programs, January-December 1964. United States Atomic Energy Commission, 1965.

United States Atomic Energy Commission 1969 Financial Report.

Argonne National Laboratory Publications:

The Argonne News, A Retrospective Issue. Argonne National Laboratory, 1966.

Argonne National Laboratory: Long-Range Program, Vol. I (March 1959) and Vol. II (February 1959).

A Statement by the Argonne National Laboratory Senate, 1968.

Norman Hilberry. *Elements of Basic Management Philosophy at Argonne National Laboratory, with Applications to Personnel Management and Salary Administration.* Argonne National Laboratory, 1953.

"Proposal for an Advanced Research Reactor for the Argonne National Laboratory. *The AARR*" (July 15, 1961). Argonne National Laboratory.

Publications of Congressional hearings and legislation:

Atomic Energy Act of 1946 and Amendments, compiled by Gilman G. Udell, 1966.

Hearings before the Joint Committee on Atomic Energy, Congress of the United States, Parts 1-21 (May 26, 1949 to July 8, 1949), (81st Congress, 1st Session), 1949.

Hearings before the Subcommittee on Legislation of the Joint Committee on Atomic Energy, Congress of the United States (85th Congress, 1st Session), on authorizing legislation for the Atomic Energy Commission's Fiscal Year 1958 Construction Budget.

Hearings before the Subcommittee on Legislation of the Joint Committee on Atomic Energy, Congress of the United States (85th Congress, 2nd Session), 1958.

Hearings before the Subcommittee on Research and Development and the Subcommittee on Legislation of the Joint Committee on Atomic Energy, Congress of the United States (86th Congress, 1st Session), 1959.

The Future Role of the Atomic Energy Commission Laboratories. The Joint Committee on Atomic Energy, Congress of the United States, 1960.

The Future Role of the Atomic Energy Commission Laboratories, Supplementary Materials, Vol. II (January 1960).

Atomic Energy Commission Authorizing Legislation, Fiscal Year 1963. Hearings before the Subcommittee on Legislation of the Joint Committee on Atomic Energy (87th Congress, 2d Session), 1962.

Atomic Energy Commission Authorizing Legislation, Fiscal Year 1964. Hearings before the Subcommittee on Legislation of the Joint Committee on Atomic Energy, Congress of the United States, 1963.

Atomic Energy Legislation through 90th Congress, 1st Session, December 1967, Joint Committee on Atomic Energy, Congress of the United States, 1968.

Atomic Energy Commission Authorizing Legislation, Fiscal Year 1965. Hearings before the Joint Committee on Atomic Energy, Congress of the United States (88th Congress), Part 3, 1964.

High Energy Physics Program: Report on National Policy and Background Information. Joint Committee on Atomic Energy, Congress of the United States, 1965.

High Energy Physics Research. Hearings before the Subcommittee on Research, Development and Radiation of the Joint Committee on Atomic Energy (89th Congress, 1st Session), March 2-5, 1965.

Hearings before the Subcommittee on Science, Research, and Development of the Committee on Science and Astronautics. U. S. House of Representatives, 90th Congress, 2d Session, 1968.

Other publications:

A Challenge to Midwestern Universities, A Report by the President of Argonne Universities Association. Argonne Universities Association, October 1967.

Associated Midwest Universities Board of Directors, John Roberson, ed. *Special Meeting*, Allerton Estate, University of Illinois, 1962.

Associated Universities, Inc., a Review of the Organization and Objectives, 1965 Supplement. Brookhaven National Laboratory and National Radio Astronomy Observatory.

Philip M. Boffey. "Progress Report on the Big Accelerators, Batavia," *Science*, Vol. 168, no. 3935 (May 29, 1970).

Sir John Cockcroft, ed. *The Organization of Research Establishments*. Cambridge, 1965.

Arthur Holly Compton. *Atomic Quest, A Personal Narrative*. New York, 1956.

Albert V. Crewe. "Science on a Regional Scale," in Keenan, *Science and the University*.

Farrington Daniels. "The Argonne National Laboratory," *Bulletin of the Atomic Scientists*, Vol. 4, no. 6 (June 1948).

Federal Funds for Research, Development, and Other Scientific Activities, Fiscal Year 1968, 1969, 1970, Vol. XVIII. Surveys of Science Research Series. National Science Foundation, NSF 69-31.

Enrico Fermi. *Collected Papers (Note E Memorie)*, Vol. II, United States 1939–1954. Chicago, 1965.

Laura Fermi. *Atoms in the Family: My Life with Enrico Fermi.* Chicago, 1954.

Fourth Inter-American Symposium on the Peaceful Application of Nuclear Energy. A Symposium sponsored by the Inter-American Nuclear Energy Commission and the National Nuclear Energy Commission of Mexico, with the cooperation of the U. S. Atomic Energy Commission. At Mexico City, April 9–13. In two volumes.

Harold P. Green and Alan Rosenthal. *Government of the Atom: The Integration of Powers.* New York, 1963.

Daniel S. Greenberg. *The Politics of Pure Science.* New York, 1967.

————. "High-Energy Physics: Major Fight Brewing as Midwestern Legislators Take Stand on MURA Accelerator," *Science,* Vol. 142 (October 11, 1963).

————. "The Midwest: New Arrangement for Argonne Holds Promise of Greater Federal Financial Aid for Region," *Science,* Vol. 146 (November 6, 1964).

————. "The MURA Accelerator: Compromise for the Mid-West," *Science,* Vol. 142 (January 31, 1964).

Leslie R. Groves. *Now It Can Be Told.* New York, 1962.

Richard G. Hewlett and Oscar E. Anderson, Jr. *The New World, 1939/1946. Vol. I, A History of the United States Atomic Energy Commission.* University Park, 1969.

Richard G. Hewlett and Francis Duncan. *Atomic Shield, 1947/1952. Vol. II, A History of the United States Atomic Energy Commission.* University Park, 1969.

Boyd R. Keenan, ed. *Science and the University.* New York, 1966.

David E. Lilienthal. *The Journals of David E. Lilienthal. Volume II, The Atomic Energy Years, 1945–1950.* New York, 1964.

"Mura Organized," *Physics Today,* Vol. VIII, no. 2 (February 1955).

National Science Foundation. *Government-University Relationships in Federally Sponsored Scientific Research and Development.* 1958, NSF 58–10.

Harold Orlans. *Contracting for Atoms.* Washington, D. C., 1967.

Philip N. Powers. "The History of Nuclear Engineering Education," *Journal of Engineering Education,* Vol. 54, no. 10 (June 1964).

"Scientific Progress, The Universities and the Federal Government." Statement by the President's Science Advisory Committee. Washington, D. C., U. S. Government Printing Office, November 15, 1960.

Don K. Price. *The Scientific Estate.* Cambridge, Mass., 1965.

Norman F. Ramsey. *Early History of Associated Universities and Brookhaven National Laboratory,* from the Brookhaven Lecture

Series No. 55 (March 30, 1966). Brookhaven National Laboratory.

Frederick Seitz, ed. *Science, Government and the Universities.* Seattle, 1966.

Alice Kimball Smith. *A Peril and a Hope: The Scientists' Movement in America, 1945–1947.* Chicago, 1965.

————. "Behind the Decision to Use the Atomic Bomb: Chicago 1944–45," *Bulletin of the Atomic Scientists,* Vol. XIV, no. 8 (October 1958).

H. D. Smyth. *A General Account of the Development of Methods of Using Atomic Energy for Military Purposes Under the Auspices of the United States Government, 1940–1945.* Washington, D. C., 1945.

Irvin Stewart. *Organizing Scientific Research for War: The Administrative History of the Office of Scientific Research and Development.* Boston, 1948.

K. R. Symon, D. W. Kerst, L. W. Jones, L. J. Laslett, and K. M. Terwilliger. "Fixed-Field Alternating-Gradient Particle Accelerators," reprinted from *The Physical Review,* Vol. 103, no. 6 (September 15, 1956).

Alvin Weinberg. *Reflections on Big Science.* Cambridge, Mass., 1967.

————. "The Federal Laboratories and Science Education," *Science,* Vol. 136, April 6, 1962.

Notes

PROLOGUE

1. *The Future Role of the Atomic Energy Commission Laboratories* (Joint Committee Print, 1960), p. 9.
2. Brief accounts of Brookhaven's history and administrative structure are in Norman F. Ramsey, "Early History of Associated Universities and Brookhaven National Laboratory," Brookhaven Lecture Series, No. 55, March 30, 1966, and in "Associated Universities, Inc. A Review of the Organization and Objectives."
3. Self-reported figures for FY 1966 and in "1967 IR Survey of University Research," *Industrial Research*, April, 1967. Government support of university research in FY 1968 is listed in *Federal Support of Research and Development at Universities and Colleges and Selected Nonprofit Institutions, Fiscal Year 1968. National Science Foundation*, NSF 69–33.
4. *Federal Funds for Research, Development, and other Scientific Activities, Fiscal Year 1968, 1969, 1970*, XVIII, Surveys of Science Resources Series, National Science Foundation, NSF 69–31.

CHAPTER 1

1. The terminology for basic research and war research was abundantly used in the correspondence between General Groves and A. H. Compton during 1943 through 1945. The attitude of Groves and the Military Policy Committee toward winning the war and their judgment that post-war plans were not in their jurisdiction is first reported in Compton to S. K. Allison, June 6, 1944. An official statement to this effect (Groves to Compton, February 27, 1945) is quoted in Compton's budget for 1945–46 in Compton to Area Engineer, April 10, 1945 (ANL).
2. Compton to Groves, July 10, 1945, and July 17, 1945 (ANL).
3. Compton's early ideas on post-war needs are in his letter to J. C. Marshall, March 6, 1943. Compton's "State of the Nation" report is dated October 1943. Groves's limit on basic research is quoted in Compton to Allison, July 10, 1944 (ANL).

4. Compton's version of the offer to Fermi is in his report, "Mr. Fermi, the Argonne Laboratory and the University of Chicago," July 28, 1944 (ANL).

5. H. D. Smyth's proposal is in Appendix 2, "Preliminary Report on Peacetime Plans for the DSM Projects," in the Metallurgical Project program proposed for 1944–1945. It was submitted by Compton to Groves, March 30, 1944 (ANL).

6. The pertinent section of the Jeffries Report, "Prospectus on Nucleonics" (November 18, 1944), is published in A. K. Smith, *A Peril and a Hope*, Appendix A, pp. 539–559. The conclusions of the Tolman Committee, December 28, 1944, are reported in R. G. Hewlett and O. E. Anderson, *The New World, 1939–1946*, p. 325.

7. Compton's attempts to increase the basic research at the Met Lab are detailed in numerous letters: Compton to Area Engineer, August 10, 1944 (ANL); Compton to James B. Conant, August 15, 1944 (ANL); Compton to Groves, October 6, 1944, (ANL). The effect of personnel shifts are in Compton to Groves, December 7, 1944 (ANL). Staff size at the Metallurgical Project is in Compton to K. D. Nichols, January 25, 1945 (ANL). As of January 1, Clinton had 334 employees; Ames, 45; Berkeley, 51; and MIT, 56. The March 1945 reduction is in Compton to Directors, March 20, 1945. His request to close the Project is a teletype message to Nichols, April 12, 1945 (ANL).

8. Compton's conditions are in Compton to Nichols, July 7, 1945 (ANL). His regional interests were expressed in letters to his brother Karl, President of MIT, and to W. W. Watson, both July 5, 1945 (ANL).

9. Compton's request and Groves's refusal (Groves to Hutchins, August 12, 1945) are reported in D. S. Greenberg, *The Politics of Pure Science*, p. 102f. The report of the Met Lab staff to the Interim Committee is in two forms; a preliminary report dated June 15, 1945, which contains individual staff views conveyed to Walter Bartky, and in a longer, comprehensive report, "Suggestions to the Interim Committee on the Subject of Post War Organization," dated July 17, 1945. The homely details of how the University of Chicago organized the Institute for Nuclear Studies are related in Laura Fermi's *Atoms in the Family*, pp. 247–248. The administrative details are in Allison to Bartky, July 27, 1945 (ANL).

10. R. Hutchins to L. Groves, October 7, 1945 (Washington University).

CHAPTER 2

1. Nichols to Compton, November 19, 1945 (ANL).

2. Reported in William B. Harrell to Colonel Arthur H. Frye, Jr., March 9, 1946.

3. "Plan for Continued Operation of Argonne Laboratory," Committee Memo to K. D. Nichols, December 5, 1945. Norman Hilberry is listed as Secretary.

4. Harrell to Frye, March 9, 1946.
5. The report of the Advisory Committee on Research and Development is Attachment No. 1 to the notes of the Advisory Council Meeting of April 5, 1946. It was written on March 8 and 9, 1946.
6. Hewlett and Anderson, p. 635.
7. A. V. Peterson to Nichols, March 28, 1946.
8. Minutes of the Board of Governors meeting, April 6, 1946.
9. Letter Contract No. W-31-109-eng-38 was addressed to Harrell and signed by Colonel E. E. Kirkpatrick, Corps of Engineers, Contracting Office (University of Chicago). The changes are in Harrell to Kirkpatrick, April 19, 1946, and Kirkpatrick to Harrell, May 16, 1946 (Chicago).
10. Minutes, Board of Governors, May 6, 1946; June 5, 1946.
11. The original draft of the By-Laws had been written by Norman Hilberry, May 7, 1946. Harrell's staff rewrote it and provided the name change. Hilberry to Board of Governors, May 16, 1946. Groves's approval is a memo to "The Director, Argonne National Laboratory" (Chicago).
12. Contract No. W-31-109-eng-38 was signed by Harrell and Kirkpatrick on November 29, 1946 (Chicago).
13. The full title of the press release was "Statement of Headquarters, Manhattan Project, and Chicago Area Office on Establishment of Argonne National Laboratory and on Activities of the Metallurgical Laboratory, Operated under the Manhattan Project at the University of Chicago."

CHAPTER 3

1. The Appropriations Committee's preference for federal land was reported by Nichols at the June 6, 1946, meeting of the Board of Governors. The method by which Camp Upton was selected as the site for Brookhaven National Laboratory is related in N. F. Ramsey, "Early History of Associated Universities and Brookhaven National Laboratory," Brookhaven Lecture No. 55 (March 30, 1966), BNL. W. Zinn's preference for the Argonne site is indicated in his memo to the Board of Governors, July 26, 1946. The Board of Governor's reasons for preferring the Du Page site are in F. Daniels to L. R. Groves, October 18, 1946. A history of the Du Page site is in "Historical Background of the Laboratory Area" in *The Argonne News*, June 6, 1951, p. 6. The attitude of Lilienthal and the Commission is reported in his journals, *The Journals of David E. Lilienthal, Vol. II, The Atomic Energy Years*, p. 114, and in Hewlett and Anderson, pp. 642–645. Groves's shift is reported in Daniels to Loomis, November 8, 1946. Daniels informed the Board of Governors that the Du Page site had been selected on January 29, 1947, though he did not receive official notice until February 13, 1947, Lilienthal to Daniels.

2. "Plans for Nuclear Research in U. S." *Bulletin of the Atomic Scientists,* II, No. 5, p. 20. *First Semiannual AEC Report,* January 31, 1947. *Letter from the Members of the United States Atomic Energy Commission Transmitting the Initial Report of the Commission,* 1947, p. 3. *Second Semiannual Report of the United States Atomic Energy Commission,* 1947, p. 3.
3. Minutes of the Board of Governors, December 2, 1946, and Daniels to Lilienthal, December 3, 1946.
4. Minutes of the Board of Governors, December 1, 1947.
5. "The Argonne National Laboratory," *Bulletin of the Atomic Scientists,* Vol. 4, no. 6, June 1948, p. 180.
6. The difficulties in formulating research policies that the Commission found during 1947, and its decision to centralize reactor work at Argonne are extensively covered in R. G. Hewlett and F. Duncan, *Atomic Shield,* Chapter IV, pp. 96–126. The Lilienthal Journals cover the specific relationship with the University of Chicago on pp. 245, 268, 272, and 280–281.

CHAPTER 4

1. Minutes of the Board of Governors, January 4, 1948.
2. Letter from the Chairman and Members of the United States Atomic Energy Commission, February 2, 1948, p. 23. The effects on laboratory size and budget are in Hilberry to Daniels, February 5, 1948. Zinn to Harrell, February 4, 1948. T. S. Chapman to Daniels, March 30, 1948, and the Minutes of the Board of Governors, March 13, 1948.
3. Daniels, "Argonne National Laboratory," *Bulletin of the Atomic Scientists,* Vol. 4, no. 6, June 1948, pp. 178, 179.
4. Minutes of the Board of Governors, January 4, 1948.
5. Minutes of the meeting of the Council of Representatives of Participating Institutions, Argonne National Laboratories, May 3, 1948.
6. H. K. Stephenson to A. Tammaro, October 8, 1948.
7. The background to Hafstad's appointment is in Hewlett and Duncan, Chapter 7, particularly pp. 209–210.
8. The Laboratory's position vis à vis the AEC is in Lilienthal, pp. 415 and 439–440. The Laboratory staff's attitude to the universities is reflected in Zinn's presentations to the Board of Governors on March 7, 1949 and March 13, 1949.
9. Board of Governors, March 7, 1949. The Board's statement of support is in Zinn to Tammaro, April 27, 1949.
10. J. T. Tate to Zinn, April 21, 1949; Minutes of the Board of Governors, May 2, 1949; Minutes of the Council, May 3, 1949.

CHAPTER 5

1. J. Boyce to Zinn, August 29, 1949. The "Proposed Draft of Revised By-Laws" is dated August 26, 1949.

2. Minutes of the Board of Governors, October 2, 1949.

3. Minutes of "A Special Meeting of the Board of Governors," November 7, 1949.

4. The only record of the December 5, 1949, meeting of the Board of Governors is in Hilberry to Hafstad, March 10, 1950.

5. Transcript of the Board of Governors meeting, March 6, 1950. The history of the numerous drafts of the By-Laws is long. It is possible that they began in a memo from Tammaro to Hafstad, October 3, 1949. Hafstad's first draft was dated October 21. Two subsequent drafts were November 4, and November 14. Tammaro commented on November 21, Hilberry revised it on November 28, J. T. Bobbitt of the Laboratory staff commented on November 28. Zinn's and Hilberry's revision was dated December 15, 1949; Hafstad's final version, dated January 9, 1950, was approved by Harrell and Zinn on February 27, 1950, and transmitted to the Board of Governors on February 28, 1950.

6. Hilberry to Hafstad, March 10, 1950.

7. The Turner Committee Report is in the Minutes of the Board of Governors, March 30, 1950.

8. Hilberry to Council Representatives, April 14, 1950.

9. Board of Governors, May 1, 1950. Council of Participating Institutions, May 2, 1950.

10. J. J. Flaherty to Warren C. Johnson, June 9, 1950.

11. Seventh Semi-Annual Report, January, 1950, p. 184.

12. H. D. Smyth's address was published as "The Role of the National Laboratories in Atomic Energy Development," *Bulletin of the Atomic Scientists*, Vol. III, No. 1, January 1950, pp. 6, 7.

13. The complete record of the Hickenlooper Hearings are in *Hearings before the Joint Committee on Atomic Energy*, Congress of the United States. Part 1–21 (May 26, 1949 to July 8, 1949). The attitude of Carroll Wilson toward Gordon Dean is reported in Hewlett and Duncan, pp. 466–467.

CHAPTER 6

1. Boyce's report is titled "Participating Institutions Program." A pencil notation says "for GAC meeting." The story about the faculty member refused permission to attend a lecture was in a letter from the Dean of Illinois Institute of Technology that was read into the minutes of the Board of Governors meeting, May 2, 1950.

2. Minutes of the Council Executive Board, October 2, 1950.

3. The Council Executive Board approved the By-Laws on January 8, 1951. The Council approved on March 6, 1951. Hilberry's comment is in his 1951 Summary Report (ANL).

4. The Memorandum of Agreement was drafted in June 1951. Council Minutes, March 6, 1951. Minutes of the Council Executive Board Meeting, June 4, 1951.

5. Gordon Dean's criticism of Argonne is the subject of Zinn to Dean, August, 13, 1951 (ANL). Zinn's letter was based on the two memos from Boyce to Zinn on August 1, 1951.
6. Minutes of Council Executive Board, March 3, 1952. Minutes of Council of Participating Institutions, March 4, 1952.
7. Minutes of Council Executive Board, October 6, 1952.

CHAPTER 7

1. The accelerator at the National Accelerator Laboratory was originally to have an energy of 200 billion electron volts. Design improvements during construction boosted estimates on the initial power expected to 500 Bev. See "Progress Report on the Big Accelerators," *Science*, Vol. 168, May 29, 1970, pp. 1071–1073. Projections on staff size are as of April 1969, and are quoted from AEC Press release No. M-104.
2. D. S. Greenberg, *The Politics of Pure Science*, 1967, pp. 209–270.
3. Zinn's position as originator of the accelerator idea is explained in his letter to T. H. Johnson, January 27, 1954 (ANL), and in a memo "Notes on the Midwest Cosmotron Project," J. C. Boyce to Zinn, April 29, 1953. Kruger and Fermi's roles are referred to in various CEB minutes during the fall of 1952 and winter of 1953.
4. The attitude of the AEC officials is in three documents: Saxe to T. H. Johnson, February 3, 1953; Tammaro to Hafstad, February 26, 1953, and Johnson to Zinn, February 16, 1953 (ANL).
5. Kruger's and Mitchell's doubts were recorded in the minutes of the Council Executive Board, March 2, 1953. Loomis's opposition is in Loomis to Boyce, February 23, 1953. The various statements at official meetings are in Minutes of the Council Executive Board, March 2, April 18, and June 1, 1953, and in the minutes of the Council of Participating Institutions, March 3, 1953. The results of the meeting with Commissioner Smyth were reported at the June 1 meeting.
6. The research plans and financial problems of the Midwest Group are detailed in two memos from Boyce to Zinn, July 30, 1953, and September 16, 1953 (ANL). They are also reported in more general ways, in minutes of the Council Executive Board and in a document prepared by the Midwest Universities Research Association in late 1954 (undated) that explained MURA's origin and purpose. A general history is in "News and Views," *Physics Today*, 8, 2, February 1955, pp. 6–8.
7. Boyce's letter to chairmen of Physics Departments was dated July 30, 1953. His opinions were expressed to Zinn in the memos of July 30 and September 16. Libby's advice was in his letter to Zinn on September 23, 1953 (ANL). The CEB meeting was on October 5, 1953.
8. Attempts to lift security restrictions are noted in Boyce to Division Directors, September 30, 1953 and Boyce to Zinn, November 20,

1953 (ANL). The action of the Argonne Advisory Committee on December 17, 1953, is not from official minutes but as reported in the letter from Zinn to T. H. Johnson, January 27, 1954 (ANL).

9. These memos and letters are all from ANL files.

10. CEB minutes, March 1, 1954, Council minutes, March 2, 1954. The NSF Panel Report is "Report of the National Science Foundation Advisory Panel, on Ultrahigh Energy Nuclear Accelerators, May 2, 1954." It is published in Joint Committee on Atomic Energy Print, *High Energy Physics Program: Report on National Policy and Background Information*, Feb. 1965, 89th Congress, 1st Session, as Appendix 6, pp. 165–169. The quote is from p. 166.

11. The events of May are reported in AEC document 603/17, "Argonne Accelerator Project," dated June 3, 1954 (ANL).

12. K. D. Nichols to the Atomic Energy Commission, June 11, 1954 (ANL).

CHAPTER 8

1. Critchfield to Zinn, June 22, 1954; Warner to Zinn, June 27, 1954 (ANL); Kruger to Zinn, June 19, 1954; Minutes of a Special Meeting, CEB, July 8, 1954.

2. Harrell of Chicago (July 16), Boyce of Argonne (July 16), A. L. Hughes of Washington University and a member of the CEB (July 20), David Saxe of the AEC's Chicago Operations Office (July 30), and Kruger for MURA (August 25) wrote reports on this meeting. All are in ANL files.

3. Chicago's statement (undated) is in ANL files. Zinn to Kruger, August 4. The action of the MURA Board is in Kruger to Zinn, October 11, 1954. Strauss to Hughes, October 21, 1954; CEB Minutes, October 25, 1954. The Chicago physicists who tried to bridge the gap were S. C. Wright, R. Hildebrand, M. Gell-Mann, V. L. Telegdi, D. E. Nagle, M. L. Goldberger. (ANL, undated, received Nov. 20, 1954.)

4. "The Desirable Conditions for a Midwest Laboratory" was written in late 1954 or early 1955. Some copies are hand-dated January 17, 1955, when it was discussed at the CEB. Minutes, January 17, 1955. The conclusions of the executive session of the CEB are in Hymer Friedell to Zinn, January 24, 1955. Zinn to Friedell, April 8, 1955; the meeting of four university presidents on April 13 was reported in the CEB Minutes of May 16, 1955.

5. Kruger to T. H. Johnson, May 6, 1955. Johnson to Kruger, May 18, 1955 (ANL).
CEB Minutes, May 16, 1955. Shankland to Friedell, May 18, 1955. Friedell to Hughes, May 31, 1955.
Zinn's proposal was on July 28, 1955.

6. Hatcher to Strauss, June 9, 1955. Strauss to Hatcher *et al*, July 20, 1955. The August 3 meeting between the presidents of the 12 universities and the AEC commissioners is taken from two sources: a

set of notes in the AMU files and the personal notes of President Hatcher of Michigan in the Michigan Historical Collection. Hatcher to Libby, August 4, states the formal results.

7. Zinn to Strauss, October 14, 1955, Strauss to Zinn, October 18, 1955; Zinn to File, October 21, 1955 (ANL).

8. The account of the November 8 meeting with Strauss, Von Neumann and Libby is taken from Hatcher's notes (Michigan Historical Collection). The November 13 meeting is from notes and minutes in the AMU files.

9. Strauss to Hovde, December 1, 1955. The trip to Washington by Zinn *et al* is reported in minutes of a Special Meeting of the Council Executive Board on December 7, 1955.

10. The public announcement of the two-accelerator compromise was not made until February 17, 1956, under the title "AEC Authorizes Two Accelerator Projects." (AEC press release #785.)

CHAPTER 9

1. Minutes, CEB, March 16, 1956. The charge and Kimpton's promise are quoted in Minutes, Council Meeting of May 8, 1956.

2. The representative quotations are from responses in the files of the Rettaliata Committee. Jensen to Rettaliata, July 17, 1956; Shankland to Rettaliata, October 29, 1956.

3. The final version of the six page report was transmitted on February 8, 1957.

4. Kimpton to Shankland, February 19, 1957; Tammaro to Kimpton, March 26, 1957; Minutes, CEB, March 27, 1957; Flaherty to Kimpton, March 28, 1957; Harrell to Jensen, April 4, 1957. The approval of Hilberry and his staff is reported in Kimpton to Rettaliata, April 22, 1957. Morrill's objections were in his letter to Kimpton of May 16, 1957.

5. Minutes, Council Meeting, May 20, 1957. Argonne Laboratory Press Release ANL-P10-8, May 20, 1957.

6. Minutes, CEB, July 31, 1957, September 6, 1957. Minutes, Council Meeting, October 15, 1957. CEB, May 8, 1958.
The remarks of Strauss, J. R. Killian, Jr., Carl T. Durham and Melvin Price were reported in *The Argonne News* for June, 1958, p. 7.

CHAPTER 10

1. Minutes, Policy Advisory Board, July 17, 1957 (University of Chicago).

2. *Authorizing Legislation*. Hearings before the Subcommittee on Legislation of the Joint Committee on Atomic Energy, 84th Congress, 2d Session, February 17 and March 27, 1956, pp. 26–28. Final approval by Congress was in Public Law 506, 84th Congress, Chapter 233, 2nd Session. Published in G. Udell, *Atomic Energy Act of 1946 and Amendments*, p. 98, 1966.

3. "Report of the Advisory Panel on High-Energy Accelerators to the

National Science Foundation—October 25, 1956," published in *High Energy Physics Program: Report on National Policy and Background Information* as Appendix 5, pp. 151–164. P. 154 and p. 161 contain the quoted remarks.

4. *Authorizing Legislation.* 85th Congress, 1st Session. April 10 . . . June 27, 1957, pp. 62–64. Udell, *Atomic Energy Act of 1946 and Amendments,* p. 114.
5. Hesburgh's statement is in the files of the Policy Advisory Board (Chicago) with a covering letter from Morrill to Kimpton, dated July 10, 1957. Kimpton to Morrill, July 12, 1957. Cooper to Kimpton, July 11, 1957 (Chicago).
6. PAB Minutes, January 15, 1958.
7. Symon's testimony is in *Physical Research Program,* Hearings before the Subcommittee on Research and Development, Joint Committee on Atomic Energy, 85th Congress, February 3–14, 1958, pp. 679–710. The quotations are from p. 697.
8. *AEC Authorizing Legislation.* Hearings before the Subcommittee on Legislation of the Joint Committee on Atomic Energy, 85th Congress, May 14–June 11, 1958, pp. 159–203. Senator Wiley's remarks are on p. 162. The summary of the technical review is on pp. 197–198.

CHAPTER 11

1. A history of the origin of nuclear engineering as an academic discipline is in P. N. Powers "The History of Nuclear Engineering Education," *Journal of Engineering Education, 54,* No. 10 June 1964. pp. 364–370.
   The review of federal funding of university research is in *Government-University Relationships in Federally Sponsored Scientific Research and Development,* National Science Foundation, 1958.
2. *The Argonne News,* 8, June 1958, p. 3.
3. "Supplement to the Report of the Advisory Panel on High-Energy Accelerators to the National Science Foundation—August 7–8, 1958," dated, September 11, 1958.—published as Appendix 4 in *High Energy Physics Program: Report on National Policy and Background Information,* pp. 143–150.
4. "Piore Panel Report—1958," published as Appendix 3, in *High Energy Physics Program,* pp. 135–142.
5. Telegram, A. L. Hughes to J. H. Jensen, April 26, 1957.
6. Goldwasser to physicists, December 11, 1958. The initial activities of the Users' Group are reported by Goldwasser in "Introduction and Report on Work to be Done" (undated).
7. Goldwasser's appraisal is from his remarks to the AMU Council Meeting, May 8, 1962, Appendix E, Minutes of the meeting.

CHAPTER 12

1. N. Hilberry in remarks to the Policy Advisory Board, January 21, 1959.

2. *Long Range Program, Vol. II*, Appendices, February 1959. pp. 347–359. The Brookhaven figures are from *The Future Role of the Atomic Energy Commission Laboratories*, p. 42. Joint Committee Print.

3. *The Future Role of the Atomic Energy Commission Laboratories*, January 1969, Vol. II, p. 10.

4. *The Future Role of the Atomic Energy Commission Laboratories*, Vol. I, pp. 75–84. The quotation is from p. 78, the remarks about ZGS are on p. 79.

5. The responses to the AEC report were published in the Joint Committee Print dated October 1960. Roberson's letter is on p. 199, Kimpton's on pp. 200–201, Hillberry's on pp. 216–219.

6. PAB Minutes, October 15, 1958. A. G. Norman to Kimpton, October 27, 1958. Kimpton to Norman, October 31, 1958 (Chicago).

7. PAB Minutes, November 9, 1959 (Chicago).

8. PAB Minutes, April 15, 1959, and October 18, 1961 (Chicago).

9. PAB Minutes, September 23, 1961 (Chicago).

10. R. Hildebrand's policy statements are in a paper titled "Experimental Facilities, Use of the ZGS," January 15, 1960.

11. The letter submitting the MURA Bubble Chamber proposal was R. O. Rollefson to Paul McDaniel, January 11, 1960. The AEC approval is in S. V. White to M. Keith, March 23, 1960. The final modification is in White to Rollefson, as reported in a memo from White to McDaniel, April 27, 1960.

12. Symon to Roberts, November 1, 1960.

13. Symon *et al* to Hildebrand, January 4, 1961. Symon's notes of the meetings of December 15, 1960, February 25, 1961.

14. Hildebrand to Symon, June 27, 1961, "Policy for Operation of Detection Equipment for General Use."

15. The schematic is from Hildebrand's presentation to the Users Group on June 21, 1961.

16. "Summary of Budget Problems for ANL High Energy Physics," A. V. Crewe and R. Hildebrand, September 27, 1961. Goldwasser to L. J. Laslett of the AEC, September 21, 1961.

17. Hildebrand to Symon, January 2, 1962.

18. Minutes, AMU Council, May 12, 1959. Board of Directors, October 15, 1959; Council, May 9, 1960; Board of Directors, July 19, 1960, October 18, 1960.

19. R. S. Shankland to Warren Johnson, January 18, 1961. This letter was approved by the Board of Directors at its January 12, 1961, meeting.

20. Minutes of the Council Meeting of May 8–9, 1961.

21. "Special Meeting, Allerton Estate, Uni. of Ill.," January 5–6, 1962, published February 2, 1962, by AMU.

22. PAB Minutes, January 17, 1962 (Chicago).

23. Everitt to Beadle, April 25, 1962; Beadle to Everitt, May 3, 1962; Harrell to Beadle, May 3, 1962 (Chicago).

24. Council Minutes, May 8, 1962. Board of Directors, July 17, 1962.

CHAPTER 13

1. A. Weinberg, "The Federal Laboratories and Science Education," *Science, 136,* April 6, 1962, pp. 27–30. He recanted in his essay "The Federal Grant University and the Federal Laboratory," in *Reflections on Big Science,* 167, p. 171.
2. "Conference with Dr. A. V. Crewe," Marshall to AMU Board of Directors, undated.
3. J. Roberson to J. C. Warner, July 26, 1962.
4. "Some Notes on an Informal Presentation to be given to the General Advisory Committee on October 4, 1962." Crewe to Marshall, September 26, 1962.
5. Minutes, Board of Directors, October 16, 1962.
6. PAB Minutes, October 17, 1962, and transcript of the meeting (Chicago).
7. J. Roberson, November 6, 1962.
8. "AMU Notes on the meeting with the AEC on November 13, 1962" dated November 16, 1962. Marshall to Beadle, January 11, 1963.
9. Notes on the meeting of Deans of the Graduate Schools of AMU. January 14–15, 1963.
10. PAB Minutes, January 16, 1963 (Chicago).
11. Minutes, Review Committee for Educational Affairs, April 16, 1963.
12. Minutes, AMU Council, May 14, 1963.
13. The Review Committee's conclusions about the graduate center at Argonne are in a series of reports dated January 9, 1964, March 24, 1964, and July 7, 1964.

CHAPTER 14

1. "Report of the Panel on High Energy Accelerator Physics of the General Advisory Committee to the Atomic Energy Commission and the President's Science Advisory Committee, April 26, 1963," TID-18636, Published as Appendix 1 in *High Energy Physics Programs,* February 1965, pp. 85–121.
   Greenberg's interpretation is in *The Politics of Pure Science,* pp. 241–244.
2. PAB Minutes, April 17, 1963 (Chicago).
3. PAB Minutes, July 17, 1963, and transcripts of the meeting (Chicago).
4. Beadle to Seaborg, July 22, 1963 (Chicago).
5. R. Hildebrand to K. Terwilliger, July 23, 1963; Terwilliger to User's Advisory Committee, July 31, 1963; Terwilliger to Hildebrand, User's Advisory Committee to P. McDaniel, and Terwilliger to Beadle, August 16, 1963.
6. A. Roberts to P. McDaniel, September 6, 1963, and to members of the User's Group, September 11, 1963. The negative comments by Seitz and Beadle were made at the PAB meeting of October 16, 1963 (Chicago).
   Goldwasser's letter was sent to members of the User's Group, September 27, 1963.

7. PAB Minutes and transcript, October 16, 1963 (Chicago).

8. Board of Directors Minutes, October 17, 1963.

9. A. G. Norman to Crewe, October 21, 1963; Seitz to Crewe, October 24, 1963; Crewe to Norman, December 11, 1963 (Chicago).

10. The reports of these two review committees are published in Annex B, pp. 119–212, in *High Energy Physics Program*, 1965. The Ramsey Panel's second attempt is Annex A, p. 119. Greenberg's comments are in *Politics of Pure Science*, pp. 262–268. Two interesting articles by him, which differ slightly from the book, are in "News and Comments," *Science, 142*, October 11, 1963, pp. 208–210, and *143*, January 31, 1964, pp. 450–452.

11. The synopsis of the meetings of January 1964 is from notes and transcripts in the files of the PAB (Chicago) and AMU, from Minutes of meetings of the PAB and Board of Directors, from a Memorandum to President Johnson from Elmer B. Staats, the Deputy Director of the Bureau of the Budget, January 18, 1964, and from a memorandum by F. Seitz, January 17, 1964.

12. Lyndon Johnson to Hubert Humphrey, January 16, 1964.

13. AEC Press Release No. G-14. January 20, 1964.

CHAPTER 15

1. Williams Committee Minutes, January 24, February 1, 1964.

2. F. Seitz to E. Stahr, January 21, 1964, Seitz to file, January 17, 1964, on his meeting on that day with Seaborg, Staats, Wiesmer, and Humphrey's assistant, Connell.

3. R. Huitt to F. Harrington, February 6, 1964.

4. J. Roberson to Board of Directors, February 10, 1964; Roberson to J. Williams, February 17, 1964.

5. Board of Directors Minutes, March 11, 1964.

6. Williams Committee Minutes, February 8, February 18, 1964.

7. Williams Committee Minutes, March 3, March 9, 1964. Williams to Committee, March 19, 1964. A. W. Peterson to Williams, March 25, 1964.

8. Williams Committee Minutes, April 6, 1964.

9. Memorandum. A. W. Peterson on April 13, 1964, meeting with Julian Levi and William Harrell.

10. PAB Minutes (Chicago).

11. G. Beadle to Williams, April 20, 1964.

12. Williams Committee Minutes, April 22, 1964.

13. Beadle to Williams, May 7, 1964.

14. Williams Committee Minutes, May 11, 1964.

15. Goldwasser to Williams Committee, May 15, 1964. Beadle to Williams, May 27, 1964, Johnson to Goldwasser, May 28, 1964, Crewe to Goldwasser, June 2, 1964, Goldwasser to Williams, June 9, 1964.

16. "Outline of Plan of Operation for Argonne National Laboratory Under Tripartite Agreement," July 13, 1964.

17. Williams Committee Minutes, August 11, 1964.
18. B. Crawford to J. Roberson, July 23, 1964.

CHAPTER 16

1. G. Beadle to B. Crawford, September 25, 1964; J. Roberson to Crawford, October 2, 1964; Board of Directors Minutes, October 14, 1964.
2. Executive Session, PAB Minutes, October 15, 1964 (Chicago); MURA approved the Williams Committee report on October 19, 1964; AEC press release, October 21, 1964 "News and Comment," *Science, 146,* November 6, 1964, pp. 749–751.
3. The full Report of the Special Task Force (dated May 4, 1965) appears in the AMU Council Meeting of May 10, 1965. They initially reported at a special meeting of the Council on December 20, 1964.
4. Minutes, Special Council Meeting, December 20, 1964; Goldwasser to Powers, January 5, 1965.
5. "Notes from the AUA Founders Meeting held February 25, 1965, Argonne National Laboratory," prepared by John Roberson.
6. "Meeting of the Special Committee with the Directors-designate regarding the Argonne Universities Association," May 31, 1965, prepared by Bryce Crawford.
7. F. Harrington to B. Crawford, June 8, 1965; E. Stahr to G. Beadle, June 7, 1965. The matter was reviewed in Crawford to the Special Committee, June 21, 1965.

CHAPTER 17

1. Board of Directors Minutes, July 14, 1965, October 20, 1965.
2. W. Kerr to A. Crewe, October 14, 1965, meeting of the Nuclear Engineering Education Committee, November 23, 1965.
3. Board of Directors Minutes, February 16, 1966; J. Cooper to Crewe, February 21, 1966; Crewe to Cooper, March 3, 1966; S. Lawroski to P. McDaniel, August 19, 1966; P. Powers to G. Tape, August 31, 1966; R. Duffield to staff, April 3, 1968.
4. Board of Directors Minutes, February 16, 1966, May 9, 1966.
5. Contract W-31-109-Eng-38, Supplement No. 16, November 1, 1966. (Fourth rewrite) The contract number has not changed since the first contract between the Manhattan Engineer District and the University of Chicago.
6. PAB Minutes, October 20, 1966; W. Kerr to P. Powers, July 12, 1967. Board of Directors Minutes, October 25, 1967. Council Minutes, March 27, 1968.

Index

Abelson, P., 143n, 150n

Accelerator Users' Group, 119–21, 126–31, 133, 154–55, 159, 181, 189; *see also* Users' Advisory Committee

Adams, R., 112

Ad Hoc Committee on High Energy Physics, 161; *see also* Williams Committee

Advisory Committee on Research and Development, 16, 18

Advisory Council, 18–19; *see also* Council of Participating Institutions

Advisory Panel on High Energy Accelerators (1956), 94–95

Advisory Panel on Ultrahigh Energy Nuclear Accelerators (1954), 68–69

Allerton Conference, 135–37

Allison, Samuel K., 6, 59, 63, 75, 81, 118n

Alternating Gradient Synchrotron (AGS), 65, 81, 127, 151, 181

Alvarez, Luis, 46n

Ambrose, Fred W., 63n

American Academy of Sciences, 158

American Federation of Labor, 28

Ames Laboratory, xvii, 13–14

AMU-Argonne-Chicago-MURA Ad Hoc Committee, 172; *see* Williams Committee

Anderson, H. L., 118n

Appropriations Committee, 94

Argonne Advanced Research Reactor (AARR, A²R²), 134, 160, 182–83

Argonne Advisory Committee, 41–42, 52, 56, 61, 66

Argonne Forest, 7–8, 14, 18, 22–23, 25, 35

Argonne Graduate Center 138–49

Argonne Laboratory (1945–1946), 7, 9, 11, 12

Argonne National Laboratory Plan of Organization and Statement of Operating Policy, 19–20, 36–37, 42

Argonne Regional Committee, 18

Argonne Senate, 188–89

Argonne Universities Association (AUA), xv, xvii, xix, 177–81, 183–89; Board of Directors, 177–78; Board of Trustees, 180, 184

Armstrong, W. D., 107

Articles of Merger (AUA-AMU), 185

Associate Director for Education, Argonne National Laboratory, 116, 119, 141; *see also* Myers, Frank

Associate Director in Charge of Educational Programs and University Relations, ANL, 42, 51; *see also,* Boyce, Joseph C.

Associated Colleges of the Chicago Area, 188

Associated Colleges of the Midwest, 188

Associated Midwest Universities (AMU), xix, 58, 91–93, 101, 104–13, 116–17, 119–25, 130–38, 141–50, 154–56, 158–61, 163–64, 166, 170–72, 174–87; Board of Directors, xix, 92, 119–21, 125, 131–33, 136–38, 141, 144–45, 147–50, 156, 159, 163–64, 166, 171–72, 174, 181–83, 185;

215